ERP Information at the Speed of Reality

Wayne L. Staley

Cover designed by: Phase Four Graphics LL

Copyright © 2012 by Affinity Systems LLC

All rights reserved. No part of this book may be reproduced or transmitted in any form or by any means, electronic or mechanical, including photocopying, recording, or by any information storage and retrieval systems, without permission in writing from the copyright owner.

ISBN-13: 978-1479133697

ISBN-10: 1479133698

Dedications

It was a joy participating in new technology, computers, and the passion and hard work to write and build effective software systems. It has been great working and traveling down this awesome path with knowledgeable and caring people.

William Karas
Roger Angst
Gary Mueller
Bob Switowski
James Kornowski
Chuck Straub
Patrick Kelly

Enlightened Executive Management

Chris McCain
Clive Bailey
John Slayton
Fred Darling
Tom Poberezny
Bill Jordan

Table of Contents

DEDICATIONS	IV
TABLE OF CONTENTS	V
FOREWORD	VI
ACKNOWLEDGEMENTS	VIII
1 ERP REALITIES	2
2 LESSONS LEARNED	12
3 MODULAR SYSTEMS	17
4 ON PREMISE VS. CLOUD	23
5 ENGINEERING	29
6 ERP CONCEPTS	42
7 CLOSED LOOP ERP	56
8 ENTERPRISE SHAPES AND COMPLEXITY PROFILE	67
9 JUST-IN-TIME (JIT)	83
10 THIRD PARTY SOFTWARE	88
11 SUPPLY CHAIN MANAGEMENT	95
12 PARKING LOT LISTS, MODIFICATIONS AND MIDDLEWARE	106
13 SOFTWARE SUCCESS FACTORS	112
14 LESSONS LEARNED – STORIES FROM THE DARK SIDE	121
15 FAILURE TO LOOK BEYOND THE STATUS QUO	135
16 SECURITY	139
17 PROCESS IMPROVEMENT -VALUE MANAGEMENT PROGRAMS	141
18 METRICS	149
19 STRUCTURED PROCESS	152
STEP 1 CURRENT / FUTURE BUSINESS STATE (STRATEGIC DIRECTION)	157
STEP 2 CURRENT OPERATIONAL STATE-BUSINESS SYSTEMS ASSESSMENT	166
STEP 3 PLANNED FUTURE STATE - CONCEPTUAL PLAN	181
STEP 4 DECISION TO ACHIEVE THE FUTURE STATE	202
STEP 5 ORGANIZE FOR THE PROJECT	206
STEP 6 ERP SELECTION	220
STEP 7 IMPLEMENTATION	249
STEP 8 MEASURE POST OPERATIONAL STATE	260
STEP 9 CONTINUOUS IMPROVEMENTS - PERFECT THE SYSTEM	264
ABOUT THE AUTHOR	266
PATHWAY TO ADAPTABILITY	267
CRUNCH TIME FOR HEALTH CARE	268
BIBLIOGRAPHY	269

Foreword

Competition is about speed, quality, adaptability, and productivity. This includes customer service, production, supply chains, and decision-making. The faster industry moves the more information sensitive it becomes. As velocity increases, the information stream must retain high levels of integrity and provide actionable data in real time.

Enterprise Resource Planning (ERP) is a competitive management tool. These systems are expensive to justify, prepare for, install, and use. They are the information super highways for adaptive and agile processes.

Lean Six Sigma improves processes in the physical world, where people, energy, time, and material come together. Ideally, processes travel within the formal constraints on the information super highway instead of unstructured informal processes and work-a-rounds.

Business has fifty years of history with ERP systems and process improvement methodology. When companies invest capital to improve competitive capability, they need positive return on investment (ROI), but many programs fall to meet this objective. Why, and what are the lessons learned?

No one is surprised that poor due diligence is a significant source for failure, but other contributing factors are fuzzy. This book reveals harsh examples and realities. Remember, in each case, a business paid for the failure.

Due diligence bridges the gap between old and new capabilities. Technologies always expand options, and ERP systems are perpetually transitioning through technology and application sophistication.

The mountains of monolithic software packages are eroding as technologies like SaaS refine both product and delivery. Business intelligence (BI) and related decision support systems such as analytics are providing positive results. Regardless, without data accuracy, the increased speed and use of sophisticated software are useless.

Affinity Systems LLC is a consulting company with experience in designing, programming, and implementing information systems in addition to process improvement programs. We helped select and install numerous ERP systems in manufacturing, distribution, agribusiness, government, and convention management. Divergent business types share common characteristics of software selection and installation. A new way to look at your business information model has been developed and presented.

Businesses must compete within a circle of constraints such as capital formation, growth, automation, and global competition. The life cycles for many ERP and Lean Six Sigma programs are approaching final stages where they also become constraints. New and better approaches are available. To compete, companies must have contemporary systems facilitating perpetual time compression.

ERP and process improvement programs complement and support each other, but compete for resources. While ERP is dramatically changing, it remains the core planning and control system, overlaying the physical realities of the business systems. Process improvement is for the hard, practical world where work methods have to be improved. ERP and process improvement are both core business components. The physical and informational perspectives are important considerations when performing any need's assessment.

Acknowledgements

Affinity Systems LLC has a comprehensive portfolio of ERP and Process Improvement classes. Data mining the presentations resulted in a fund raising seminar for the Wisconsin Valley APICS Chapter. Jim Kornowski and Pat Kelly helped with the seminar. We lost Jim, an excellent person working for IBM, shortly after the presentation. This seminar, coupled with other materials, is the source for ERP Information at the Speed of Reality. The objective is to construct a solid information framework for the smart enterprise.

The inputs into the book are varied. A number of software suppliers filled out questionnaires on the selection process. Systems clients scored the software performance. They provided insights into suppliers, their software products, and performance levels. We appreciate their time, patience, and honesty.

The following persons provided support on selected topics:

Christine Koski, nMetric, Manufacturing Execution Systems
Angela Talano and Luke Russell, Resolv, Appleton, WI, CRM
Garry Gossard, IQR International, Inventory Management

This book deals with highly technical information for which accuracy is a prerequisite. To ensure quality, we thank the following persons: Natalie Staley, Lisa Guenther, Angela Berntsen, Scott Guenther, Jim Kornowski, Pat Kelly, Tania Behselich, and Jon Bingol.

We acknowledge the work of the founding fathers of ERP:

Oliver Wight
Joseph Orlicky
Walter E Goddard
George Plossl

Part 1
Due Diligence

*If you're trying to achieve, there will be roadblocks.
I've had them; everybody has had them.
But obstacles don't have to stop you.
If you run into a wall, don't turn around and give up.
Figure out how to climb it, go through it,
or work around it.
- Michael Jordan-*

1 ERP Realities

Enterprise Resource Planning (ERP) systems superimpose upon, and integrate the business systems as the information foundation for planning and execution. Business competes in an intelligence driven world, at both the logical and virtual level. ERP systems are tools that constantly need revision, as business races to stay parallel or ahead of the competition. Expensive systems, many installed in the last five years, are functional, yet unable to facilitate the smart enterprise.

Business must pursue the smart enterprise because without intelligence all the capability in the world is a waste. Success results from the ability to react at the speed of reality to advantages in the marketplace, regardless of how slender or temporary. To leverage any event requires knowledge and positive action. This means rapidly converting data into information, interpreted as decisions, then into agile, adaptive, and predictive responses by every user regardless of location. None of these is possible without an accurate and timely information backbone, in the majority of enterprises this will be the ERP system.

Information and intelligence are half of the equation. The other half is flexible and adaptive production processes that can swiftly respond to threats and/or opportunities. This requires automation, real-time proficiency, and active fast-paced process improvement programs, managed by information at the speed of reality.

This book is about selecting and installing modern ERP systems, forming the evidence-based foundation needed to achieve unrivaled success. To realize that purpose, the forces reshaping business and information integration need review. Every business is a system, functioning within extrinsic macro-systems, and composed of complex, integrated internal structures. The search for business solutions, be it software, process improvement, or some other approach, must address these total systems relationships.

Speed

Business activities are an effect of the marketplace and competitive pressures, changing the strategies and information requirements. As business velocity increases, the necessity for rapid information assimilation increases comparatively.

Software converts data into information. Information systems are strategic and therefore, software belongs to management. Fast, high-volume information flows fuel the smart enterprise.

Business is under extreme pressure to perform faster while supplying a rapid succession of personalized new products. This translates into smaller run quantities with shorter demand horizons and order to cash processes. Output continues towards the theoretical goal of one to one production. Customers' experiences need to be positive, whether it is buying home furnishings or a new car. In the new instant world, online reviews punish poor product or service performance.

Automation

Automation has dramatically collapsed production cycle times, altering the way information is captured and used. Contemporary systems drive manufacturing machines directly from designs. Automation, including event reporting and sensors, collect data from the shop floor, warehouse, transportation, and supply chain. Real-time data capture dramatically increases the volume of data to organize, store, and process. Database systems need to be integrated, powerful, scalable, and capable of converting large data volumes into usable information. Automation speeds up both the operational and information reality.

Computing Power and Data Transmission Speeds

In 1974, production and distribution functioned in monthly and weekly "buckets." The same year, Intel announced the 8080, 8-bit computer chip, credited with powering the world into the information age. Since its introduction, chips are many times more powerful and much faster.

A smart phone has computer technology greater than America used to put a man on the moon. Today, information travels in a near real-time reality, tied into the global nervous system. While technology continues to speed up the business cycle, there are other forces at work.

Businesses were once concerned with the high cost and availability of storage and processing. Computer programs and methods considered these factors. One example is batch processing. Computers were not fast or large enough to support real-time transaction processing at every level, much less the ability to provide users with a continuous stream of information.

These limitations have disappeared. Companies without storage capacity can purchase it at reasonable prices on the cloud. The rapid accumulation of relevant data, storage, and super-fast conversion into information is one of the keys to the smart enterprise.

E-Commerce

The second part of the computing power equation is bandwidth or internet speed. Businesses and individuals have the ability to transmit large volumes of data/information anywhere in the world, and/or interact with business and each other in real-time.

The consumer world has changed, with more of the action moving to the Internet. Business-to-customer (B2C) and business-to-business (B2B) applications are escalating. On-line sales of products on Black Monday, free of shipping costs, show annual growth greater than 15%.

The Internet provides alternatives to traditional on-premise information processing. The emerging trend is SaaS, where processing takes place at a remote server. Rented software, priced on usage, replaces software normally purchased and installed on-premise. Internet applications are propelling enterprises into ever-higher velocity opportunities with worldwide integration capabilities. This will enable transformation into virtual enterprises, with the option to bypass traditional plant integration.

Mobile Technology

Mobile technology has moved the information reality from the office to the world, from voice to image and text, from status to content rich streaming flows. Actionable information is real-time and social media such as Facebook or Linked-In enables global collaboration. The differences between hand-held devices and PCs are increasingly blurred, separated more by personal choice and ease of use than functionality. The technology as applied to business is equally pervasive. Orders are tracked from any location as the product moves through the factory, warehouse, and onto the truck. GPS follows the order location in transit, and notifies the customer the second it arrives.

The increased use of mobile devices for pricing, order inquiry, available to promise, placing orders, shop reporting, order picking, and customer specific information translates into real-time information processing. Mobile technology, consuming data in enormous volumes, is one force driving information at the speed of reality. ERP databases unable to support these devices are technically obsolete.

Integration

The ability to integrate systems seamlessly is partially dependent on the selected software approach.

An integrated system offers full functionality to a vertical industry, such as manufacturing, distribution, or construction. Decomposing the manufacturing vertical one layer results in the following business types: process, repetitive, or engineer to order. The type of processes they use, for example, metal casting, fabrication, machining, and/or assembly further defines the business activity and required functionality.

General-purpose software addresses the core needs of a vertical, providing broader but less detailed functionality. Conversely, best of breed or industry-specific software more precisely addresses narrower but deeper functionality requirements. Consequently, industry-specific software is normally less expensive and requires less modification during implementation.

The decomposition eventually stops at functionality, where there is a proliferation of software applications such as Customer Relationship Management (CRM), analytics, Manufacturing Execution Systems (MES), Point of Sales, literally every application imaginable. Like any software product, the quality varies from one end of the distribution curve to the other.

The downside is that functionality beyond the specialty, often purchased separately, requires integration. Later chapters will address software modules as conceptual "Lego" blocks. To achieve a Lego effect requires that modules be designed and programmed using the same master files, labels, and language. That is clearly not the reality.

Although the debate continues comparing best practices and integrated software, tools exist to integrate most systems. The issue is cost, time, and result. The problems are the differences in format, field sizes, formulas used, programing language and database technology. Each system is dissimilar in size and calculation, and conversion is required to move data back and forth from one system to the other. The reconciliation of these issues is basic to any form of automated integration, but the mashed result may prove that the sum total is worse than its parts.

Software code, defining how data will be processed and put into useful information, is relatively static. Modifications can be complicated and expensive. We devote one chapter to the topic. The term flexible information system is an oxymoron in some poorly structured software. ERP is a set of tightly designed and written procedures for executing repetitive formulas, requiring designed-in flexibility.

Flexibility comes in three forms. The first is architecture, where designed and coded functionality provide a number of solution pathways through seamless modules. The second level of flexibility is the ability to modify systems codes, features and functions, and upload or download data, sometimes into custom written subroutines. User fields add flexibility but lack the integrated functionality of standard system fields. The third flexibility is plug and play functionality for integrating third party or best of breed software. Adding significant ERP functionality such as CRM or Supply Chain Management (SCM) results in a system labeled "Extended ERP."

The decision to use industry specific or an integrated software package carries an implicit commitment to some level of integration, and for that reason, it is a critical selection criteria.

Big Data

Businesses are capturing large volumes of real-time data from multiple sources, including enterprise, vendors, and customers. This creates a condition labeled "big data." Where the prior evolutions of technology left business searching for viable analytical data, the problem today is how to manage and convert the data into useful information products. Most ERP suppliers provide data warehousing functionality. Find out if it is sophisticated enough to take advantage of the information opportunity.

In today's world, the resolution of big data is critical. If you are performing due diligence for a new system, there is a high probability your organization is not processing information at the speed of reality. If this becomes a critical selection criterion, then big data is in your future. Include the resolution in the future state and integration plans (Part Two, Structured Process).

Analytics

Enterprises have embraced the use of "business intelligence" tools. These come in a variety of sizes and shapes from simple drill down to complex analytics. The objective is to have functionality that builds information products-visualization, decision support, sales analysis, etc. in a timely and trustworthy fashion. Some programs require setting up reporting point codes within the software.

Include analytics in the future state and integration plans. Analytics may not be available in some standard packages, but provide useful functionality. Operational priority dictates rock solid ERP tools. The lack of the feature cannot override the core requirements if the balance of the package fills your needs.

A number of companies offer analytic software. Some are IBM, SAP, Oracle, Microsoft SharePoint, Epicor, SAP Crystal Reports, Alteryx, Pentaho, and GE Intelligent Platforms. Suppliers also offer analytics through the SaaS format. An excellent guide is available at http://www.pentaho.com/resources/pdf-stream/20/the-ultimate-guide-to-buying-business-analytics.

Process Improvement

ERP selection is normally divorced from Lean Six Sigma. In many important ways, the programs complement each other but compete for resources. Both improve the performance of the organization and require high corporate priorities, are team based, consume valuable resources during implementation and are expensive. Properly done both are cost effective. Poorly done, either can cripple the business.

Manufacturing and other types of businesses have embraced process improvement programs, resulting in shorter, faster action cycles. This translates into greater agility and higher success rates by optimizing the response to fast moving opportunities.

The classical definition of productivity is "output per hour worked." A more comprehensive definition will factor in effectiveness.

"Productivity is the use of time, technology, and resources, effectively adding value to goods and/or services."

The Just-in-Time (JIT), Lean Six Sigma attitude fixated on speed, efficiency and the elimination of non-value adding activities, labeled waste. Reducing time reduces inventory requirements, improves productivity, and drives up customer service. It increases the focus on operational priorities, doing the right thing, building the right product and doing it on time.

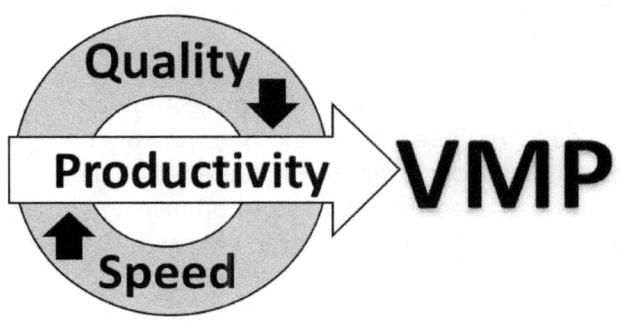

Value Management Program

Illustration: Cycle of Quality and Speed

Far too many process improvement initiatives are cost reduction efforts, sacrificing quality for short-term financial purposes. Any program to improve processes must include stringent quality standards, or it will devalue the product. This often occurs during recessionary periods. Returning products to acceptable standards has proven very expensive.

For readers interested in the quality approach to process improvement, we recommend the works of experts such as Shigeo Shingo, Edwards Deming, Joseph Juran, James P. Womack, Genichi Taguchi, George DeForest Edwards, and Philip B. Crosby. All Lean Six Sigma concepts contain high quality standards, but not all Lean programs are Lean Six Sigma. Process improvement must increase value.

Quality and speed must not become a paradox. Doing the wrong thing faster is not productive nor does poor quality add value. Process speed should never exceed the ability to produce quality results. The speed of reality includes information and process, both done with high quality.

The result of any process improvement program is to add value to the company, its products, and customer service. For those reasons, the term "value management programs" (VMP) more accurately defines the overall objective. For the balance of this book, the acronym VMP encompasses quality, process improvement, transformation process, and value added concepts. Lean, short for Lean Six Sigma, appears where appropriate.

VMP is an important part of any ERP project. Implementing Lean principles may delay the need for a new ERP system. Conversely, using Lean techniques may change the ERP requirement. Changing business processes always precedes getting a return on investment (ROI) and is part of any installation. The new infrastructure can facilitate the savings promised by Lean.

Any type of business may use visual or Lean techniques, and Lean companies frequently use ERP in innovative ways.

Any properly conducted search for the contemporary business reality will factor business transformation methodology into the equation. The study may indicate that culture change must precede a new ERP system. A changing business model may indicate a more complicated or time phased approach to several types of business solutions. It is becoming more obvious that companies applying VMP methodologies for software projects install systems faster and at lower cost.

Summary

Systems projects are complex and failure has consequences. Having an intimate knowledge of the playing field (business), the game (processes), the reward, and the consequences are vital. When it comes to ERP selection, the old adage of "what you don't know won't hurt you" is a recipe for disappointment. The firewall between the two is due diligence.

Short, rapid reaction capabilities are the key to building the smart enterprise, but it comes with a price. Real time systems may be more expensive but dramatically change business adaptability. For these reasons, VMP and information technology are partners in building competitive capability. They both compress time and speed up business.

Automation is the third component of speed, and needs to be part of the planned future state.

When selecting an ERP product, match your information and physical reality time. Make sure the future state system will be fast enough to support needed adaptability. Speed is an order winner and like chocolate and profits, everyone wants and covets more of it.

ERP projects require months or years, depending on the size and complexity of your business. An effective system does not require software on site. Computer technology and program functionality are changing rapidly, and technologies such as software as a service (SaaS) are expanding and maturing.

Due diligence is hard work, but imperative.

2 Lessons Learned

Companies of all sizes have invested in ERP systems with disappointing return on investment (ROI) and failed to gain competitive advantage. Worldwide, enterprises waste billions of dollars on failed or flawed systems. As many as 40-70% of ERP projects fail to meet expectations. Regardless of the reason, failure always involves financial loss, direct and collateral damage to participants, and unrealized opportunities.

The list of big companies with failed projects includes Gateway, Hershey Foods, K-Mart, Nike, Omni Hotels, Whirlpool, Dow Chemical, Boeing, Dell Computer, Apple Computer, HP, Waste Management, and the University of Minnesota. On November 14, 2012, Computerworld reported, "The U.S. Air Force has decided to scrap a major ERP (enterprise resource planning) software project after spending US$1 billion, concluding that finishing it would cost far too much more money for too little gain."

It is difficult to understand how large companies, with their high levels of expertise could be anything but successful. If large companies failed to get it right, what hope does a smaller company have? The answer: size is irrelevant. What matters are diligent front-end planning and high-quality execution.

Surveys isolate reasons for ERP project failure.

- Poor ERP selection because of incomplete due diligence
- Failure to manage project scope
- Inability to control costs
- Goals unclear because the future state is poorly defined
- Changing objectives because of poorly defined priorities
- Lack of accountability structure and enforcement
- Lack of management buy-in for the program
- Lack of role clarity in the project organization phase
- Ineffective leadership by executive staff, consultants and/or the project leader

- Low priority of the team
- Lack of team-based compensation

Any process step can contribute to failure since everyone participates in the game and introduces unneeded variables.

Not everyone understands the complexities of installing ERP systems. While executive management complains that, "systems do not work as advertised," they unknowingly make decisions that doom the project.

One case involved a company that allowed each of the internal silos to select ERP packages, than complained about integration incompatibility. Another company built a paperless warehouse management system based on verbal picking instructions, then misused the scanning technology. The employees understood how the system worked, but the heavy-handed methods used during implementation backfired. The employees laughed as management struggled, and the system failed.

These examples illustrate the importance of due diligence, team selection and involvement, and enabling a total system's perspective.

Following are statements received through our interview surveys. They add an important perspective.

"Our ERP system doesn't work very well. It lacks the functionality to meet our needs, but replacing it is expensive and time consuming."

"We drive our production by using Lean manufacturing techniques."

"I wish they would stop making changes to the (core functionality) software."

"We are not in the software business. We make our product. Anything distracting us is a liability."

"Software is a tool. We may not use it the way the book says, but we make it work for us."

"We drive our shop floor directly off of our engineering software."

"We face competition from the Asian rim, Mexico and South America every single day."

"Nothing is more irritating than being forced to serve the system instead of the system serving us."

"We didn't do a very good job of selecting our software because we were under the gun. It just isn't capable of doing what we need."

Clients, management, shop workers, consultants, IT personnel, and software representatives have made similar comments. The survey supports research by a number of reliable software organizations. It is a microcosm of the various stages of software utilization, introducing major issues affecting an assessment of software packages.

Our Survey and Interview Observations

Vendor surveys provided material on how to work with suppliers, and their major gripes. In response, we developed a two-step approach to the Request for Proposal (RFP) process dealing with business shape, features, and functions. This process more effectively translates strategy into software requirements. Failure often results by mismatching business strategy and the real capability to achieve it, reflecting a poorly designed future state or sloppy gap analysis.

Companies Not Using an ERP System

The number of small companies skews the percentage using ERP. These companies, like contract manufacturers, may use engineering systems to drive production. Nearly all larger companies use ERP systems, but the smaller ones are finding help on the cloud.

Companies with Obsolete Systems

Many companies are one or more software generations behind because they failed to apply upgrades. There are/were reasons for not updating on schedule. To avoid postponing the problem, resolve these issues before taking action. If the system is working correctly, logic dictates that upgrades would be a natural part of the process. If delays occurred because a major reimplementation is involved, weigh the value of staying with the current software and performing the upgrade, or buying and implementing a new ERP system.

Current systems may be working correctly, but lack the functionality to deal with the new rules of speed and technology, or the business has outgrown its capabilities. The solution is to acquire a system providing the required technology.

Homegrown Systems

Homegrown systems are at work in organizations of all sizes.

The owner of a Wisconsin company viewed his applications as unique and proprietary. For those reasons, his company maintains a homegrown system. Several years ago, his frustrated staff conducted a survey of ERP products meeting their specifications. The total cost of ownership was lower than the current system in every case. The owner was unimpressed. The staff continues to operate the system while struggling with the complex modifications needed to keep the business running. In this case, the product is both unique and highly profitable.

Manufacturing and Distribution

Those familiar with manufacturing often believe distribution, including warehouse management systems (WMS) and shipping functionality, are extensions of an ERP system. Many manufacturing consultants think distribution has fewer complexities. Both perspectives are incorrect. A distributor has intricate picking and fulfillment processes, including subassemblies, packaging, and conversion of product from one form to another. We recommend that companies with complex manufacturing and distribution requirements pay close attention to specific functionality.

Software Sophistication

Software suppliers service each market niche. Many of the features overlap, but the functionality varies widely in quality and scope. This diversity of both product and suppliers make software selection tedious and difficult. Companies must make the commitment to do the work or risk being stuck with mismatched or unsupported ERP systems.

Software suppliers buy other companies, who are than purchased by yet another company. Each acquisition potentially creates orphaned products. The best example of this process is Oracle, who purchased PeopleSoft after PeopleSoft acquired JD Edwards. Both enjoyed excellent reputations. Oracle repackaged PeopleSoft under the JD Edwards brand. Oracle withdrew JD Edwards Enterprise One Technology on September 16, 2010, which Oracle will continue to support through September 16, 2016, when it becomes an orphan. Oracle recently purchased two specialty software companies, Agile PLM and AutoVue.

Many software companies have rewritten their packages with all applications and functionality in the same language, on common databases. These systems are truly integrated with every module working in sync by design, instead of being mashed together using real or conceptual middleware. In the next chapter, we will discuss modular software in a different context.

Summary

While exploring solutions, some companies will discover that new ERP is not the answer. Re-implementing their system or applying all the updates offers potential solutions. Another option is to use the current system in more innovative ways. The key is to take a total systems approach to major projects.

3 Modular Systems

ERP systems are traditionally monolithic, with features and functions integrated into modules that are bundled into one package. The buyer gets full functionality in each module they purchase, regardless of need. Some packages offer scaled down versions, but embedded unused functionality is still part of the overhead. That has been the nature of the software business and for many reasons, it continues today.

For these reasons, you are "married" to the selected software system, but paying for unusable functionality, and dealing with greater implementation and operational complexity.

 An analogy is cars. If driving around town with one passenger, a small car will suffice. If fifty people are going across the country, take a bus. The point is not to pay for a bus when you need a small car.

The next illustration puts each ERP module into a discreet box and lists its functionality. The center block, "Requirements Planning – Foundations" is the core connector, the engine. The blocks without stars are modules included in virtually all manufacturing ERP packages. The five modules identified with a star are optional. Some, like MES, replace Shop Floor Control (SFC) and Production Activity Control (PAC) modules. Warehouse Management Systems (WMS), has greater application to distributors. CRM and Business Intelligence (BI) are expensive systems but are often platform independent. Content management supports internet business processes. Its cousin, Document Management (not listed) is associated with document storage and retrieval.

Engineering Data Control (CRP)	Sales Forecasting (SFC)	Inventory Control (IC)	Asset Management (EAM)	Shop Floor Control (SFC)
Basic records file organization Engineering drawings Engineering changes Product Structure Standard routing Shop floor integration	Model Selection Forecast Plans Evaluation and measurement	Stock Status Control ABC Inventory Analysis Order Policy Inventory maintenance Physical Inventory Cycle counting Statistics	Maintenance schedules Equipment performance Warranty management Hazardous material compliance Waste materials control Energy Management	Labor reporting Material movement Work-in-process feedback Creation of Factory Paper Machine Utilization

Capacity Planning (CRP)	Purchasing	Operation Scheduling Production Activity Control (PAC)	Financial (ACCT)	Human Relations-Human Capital Management (HCM)
Work center load report Planned order load Order start date calculations Load leveling	Requisition and P.O. Preparation Purchase Order follow-up Purchase evaluation Vendor evaluation and selection	Dispatching sequence Order estimator Load summary by work center Priority Rules Queue Time Analysis Tool Control	General Ledger Accounts Payable Accounts Receivable Project Accounting Budgeting Multi-operation	Payroll Time and attendance Training Compliance with regulations Federal State

Order Processing	Requirements Planning - Foundation		Customer Relationships (CRM)	Supply Chain Management (SCM)
Order management Available to promise Follow-up mechanisms Discounts Customer files	Finished production requirements – Gross to net Component requirements Gross to Net Special features Lot sizing Offset requirements Net Change	Pegged Requirements Full level Single level Multiple currencies Multiple plants / location Kitting	Relationship management Marketing analysis Inquiry by customer Order tracking Collaboration management Project management	Import/export management Product Visibility Customer information Product planning Logistics Track and Trace

Content Management	Warehouse Management (WMS)	Manufacturing Execution (MES)		Business Intelligence (BI)
Documents Images Web-sites	Labor scheduling & management Complex picking process Forward pick logic Location management Preplanned put-a-way	Product and process definitions (PPM) Lifecycle management (PLM) Shop floor management Data collection Track and trace Performance analysis		Analytics data warehousing data visualization (scorecards and dashboards)

Illustration- ERP System Modules

The following illustration shows each module broken into five segments of proportional size. Numbered from one to five, segment size equates to functionality - the larger the number, the greater the functionality. The use of five segments corresponds to the spider diagram used in the chapter titled "Enterprise Shapes," providing the opportunity to interrelate software and business complexity.

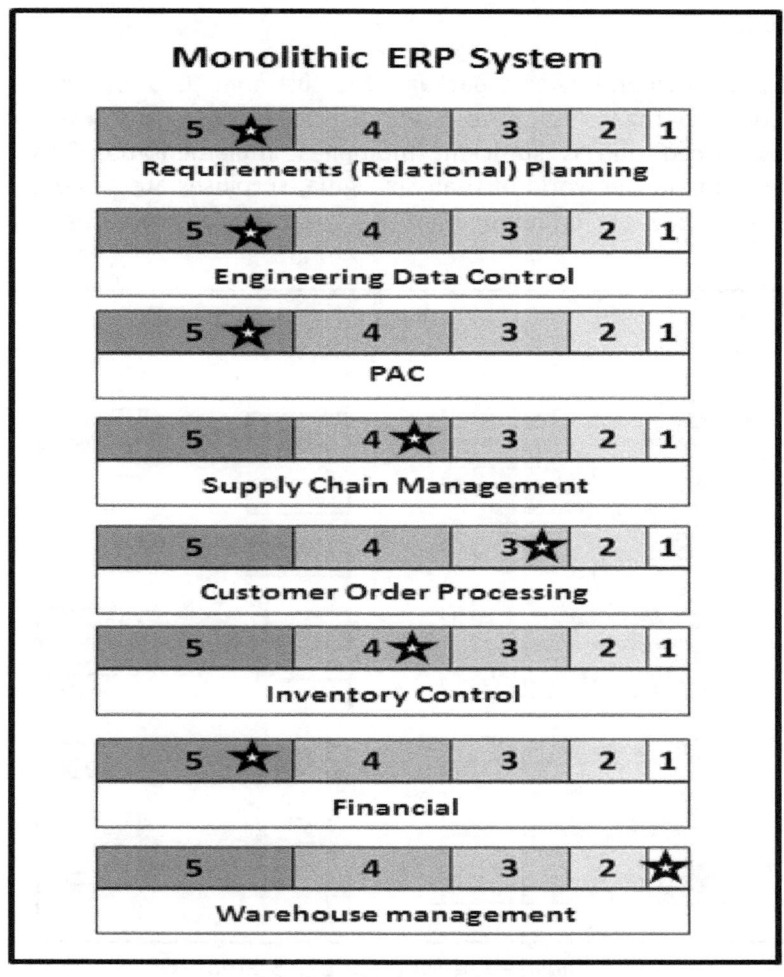

Illustration-Monolithic ERP System

The stars indicate the amount of functions needed by a complex, repetitive manufacturing company. This type of factory needs large segments for requirement's planning, engineering and PAC. In this example, the supply chain is a three, but most complex organizations have international supply chains. Order processing is straightforward, and a WMS is unnecessary. Inventory control rates a four, equaling the SCM requirement. Everyone seems to want a comprehensive financial system.

The point - when buying a package, the customer pays for "five" level functionality regardless of need. Purchasing expensive systems when a lower priced one is sufficient multiplies implementation cost and complexity. In the world of Lean Six Sigma, surpluses are a waste. One of the objectives is to find the right size system for your business.

Modular ERP System

	Repetitive Manufacturing	Distributor
5 4 3 2 1 Requirements (Relational) Planning	▓▓▓	☐
5 4 3 2 1 Engineering Data Control	▓▓▓	☐
5 4 3 2 1 PAC	▓▓▓	☐
5 4 3 2 1 Supply Chain Management	▓▓	▓▓▓
5 4 3 2 1 Customer Order Processing	▓	▓▓▓
5 4 3 2 1 Inventory Control	▓▓	▓▓▓
5 4 3 2 1 Financial	▓▓▓	▓▓▓
5 4 3 2 1 Warehouse management	☐	▓▓▓

Illustration-Modular ERP System

The concept illustrated by this chart is the equivalent of disassembling a vehicle back into components of different size. Customers purchase systems components of the right size and pay for the associated functionality, no more and no less. In the second column, the same selection process applies to a distributor.

The shift towards modular ERP is in process, but the majority of systems are monolithic. SaaS is evolving towards modular processing methodologies, but software design still lags manufacturing, where design is all about modularity and interchangeable parts.

Software Options

ERP companies are changing. Technology is not static and suppliers may be slow to adopt new languages and practices. Others may elect to integrate their current offering into a modular form to participate in SaaS. All suppliers are rapidly expanding or refining options, including, Warehouse Management, CRM, SCM, and Business Intelligence. The result is a variety of products with differing quality levels.

First-tier providers, Oracle, SAP, and Microsoft, serve the large, complex, multi-facility companies. They must also sell into the mid-market to survive. They offer scaled-down packages, with fewer features and functions to the small/medium sized (SMB) market. Functionality may be more than what tier two or three suppliers offer and make features and functions available in a competitive marketplace, but with a higher price tag.

Multiple features and functions are double-edged swords. With too many options, people attempt to use them all, and may not use any properly. The problem has a variation. Associates may not agree on which ones to use.

Tier two and three suppliers, Epicor, Sage, Intuit, Infor, Lawson, Syspro, and many others, have rich and varied software products.

Most ERP customers fall within the small/medium sized range. This market is the battleground for ERP suppliers.

With the expansion of software into Application Service Providers (ASP), Service Oriented Applications (SOA), and SaaS, it is possible to have all the software and processing at a solution provider. This increases selection options while adding complexity to selecting the right software solution.

Summary

Enterprise planning systems are evolving. Modular systems are slowly making inroads into markets once dominated by monolithic packages.

When evaluating software packages, it is useful to understand functionality requirements and matching available software. The unfortunate fact is that most ERP systems are not modular to the degree in this discussion, and the probability is high that companies will buy a monolithic package out of necessity. Understanding functionality size will help you to negotiate and to find the right size system for your company.

The functionality variations between ERP systems run from minor to extreme. Any function can be different. There are critical distinctions and the selection team must understand what they need, and look beyond simple definitions to find exactly what the software does.

ERP solutions will always be as complex as the problems they must solve. The solution may look elegantly simple. In the end, you get what you pay for. What you save on software, may be lost with deficient capability, limiting flexibility.

4 On Premise vs. Cloud

The "cloud" concept is gaining strength per the following:

"The SaaS-based delivery will experience healthy growth through 2015, when worldwide revenue is projected to reach $21.3 billion." Source: Gartner.com.

Although business has been dealing with cloud issues for a number of years, non-information ERP team members may be less familiar with the meaning. It is useful to review the concepts.

First, what is cloud computing?

Gartner defines cloud computing as "a style of computing in which scalable and elastic IT-enabled capabilities are delivered as a service using Internet technologies."

Affinity Systems loosely lumps all internet-processing activities under the cloud. The purists will take exception, but our interest is pragmatic. Some examples, all non-ERP, are Apple MobileMe, CreateSpace, Google+, WhiteSmoke, and social-networking services. We include multi-tenant service bureaus (by any name), SaaS, IaaS, and PaaS under the cloud umbrella, and all web based processing, such as Service Oriented Architecture (SOA) and Application Service Provider (ASP).

The Cloud

Cloud organizations rent storage and software services, paid for by subscription or amount of service used.

The following illustration provides visual definition.

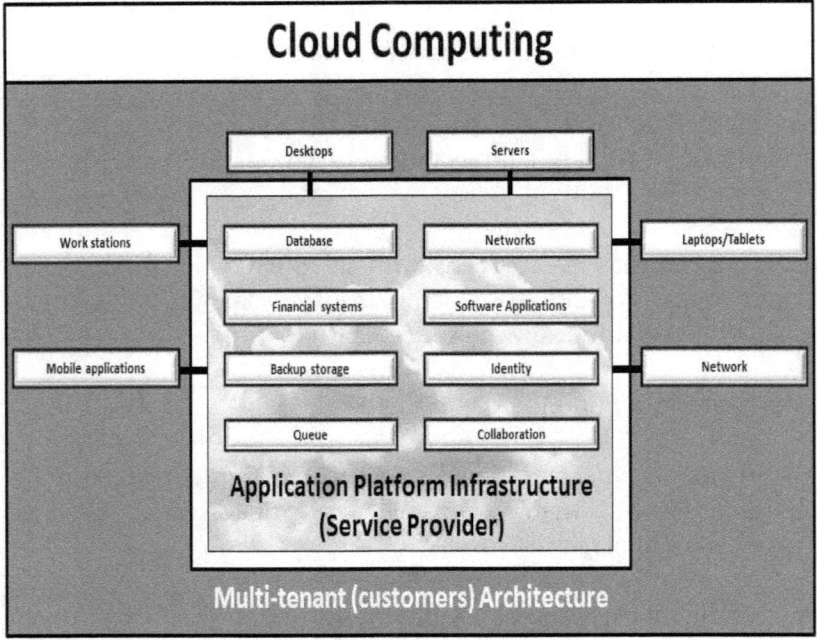

Illustration-Cloud

Service Bureaus

In the early years of ERP, giant corporations and entrepreneurs formed service bureaus, where the software lived on computers at the utility. Customers connected via an IBM developed process, "binary synchronous communications," commonly called "bisync" by the users.

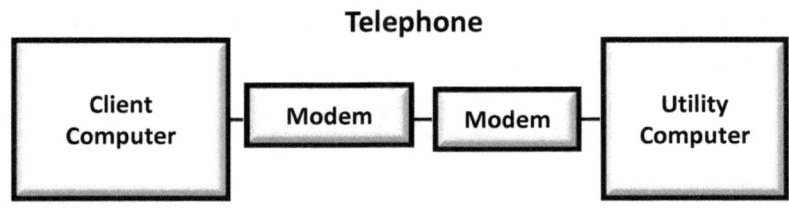

Transmission took place over a dial-up telephone line. Modulator/de-modular devices (modems) were required on each end, converting the digital signals into analog for transmission, and converting it back to digital while receiving.

Client and utility personnel synchronized the input-output devices before transferring the "binary" data. Data was not a continuous flow, but in packets, and synchronization problems often resulted in lost or garbled data. The major problem, however, was low transmission speeds and the high cost of the process. Most in-house ERP systems lacked sophistication, and the utilities appeared to be viable alternatives. As hardware prices dropped, and program sophistication increased, the service bureaus started to fade. The dependence on slow speed transmission extended the information time reality and hastened the end of the utilities.

Application Service Provider

Synonymous with the growth of the World Wide Web, software companies developed downloadable products, including software used "as is," like virus protection and operating systems. Program development followed specific principles, protocols, and procedures. As SOA evolved, Application Service Provider (ASP) replicated the old service bureaus, offering information services using proprietary software.

The cloud takes the utility concept to new levels. It involves processing multi-tenant customers on single or multiple offsite computers. Customer information may be stored anywhere in the cloud, without the customer knowing its specific location.

ASP is the new service bureau. The utility owns the software and has multiple customers using it. Computers transmit data from one digital device to another via high-speed networks. One or more devices reside in the on-premise system, and another is at the provider. Virtual systems allow nearly unlimited numbers of inquiries from computers or mobile devices.

Software as a Service (SaaS)

IT Staff
Development Staff

Operating System
E-Mail
Web presence
ERP System
Business Intelligences/ Analytics
Customer Relationship Management
Financial systems
HR
Data Collection
Backup

Web browsers
Work stations
Mainframe
Distributed
Networks

SaaS expands on all the above concepts, but is still one type of application among many referencing different applications "in the cloud."

Gartner defines SaaS as "software that is owned, delivered, and managed remotely by one or more providers. The provider delivers an application based on a single set of common code and data definitions, which is consumed in a one-to-many model by all contracted customers anytime on a pay-for-use basis, or as a subscription based on use metrics."

The software applications reside on a provider's computer, on their site or through a network. There are different levels of services, each with its specific label.

A traditional IT department, called "on premise" in SaaS, has staff, hardware, operating systems, and software applications.

The next illustration shows the hierarchy of the services and their relationship in the cloud.

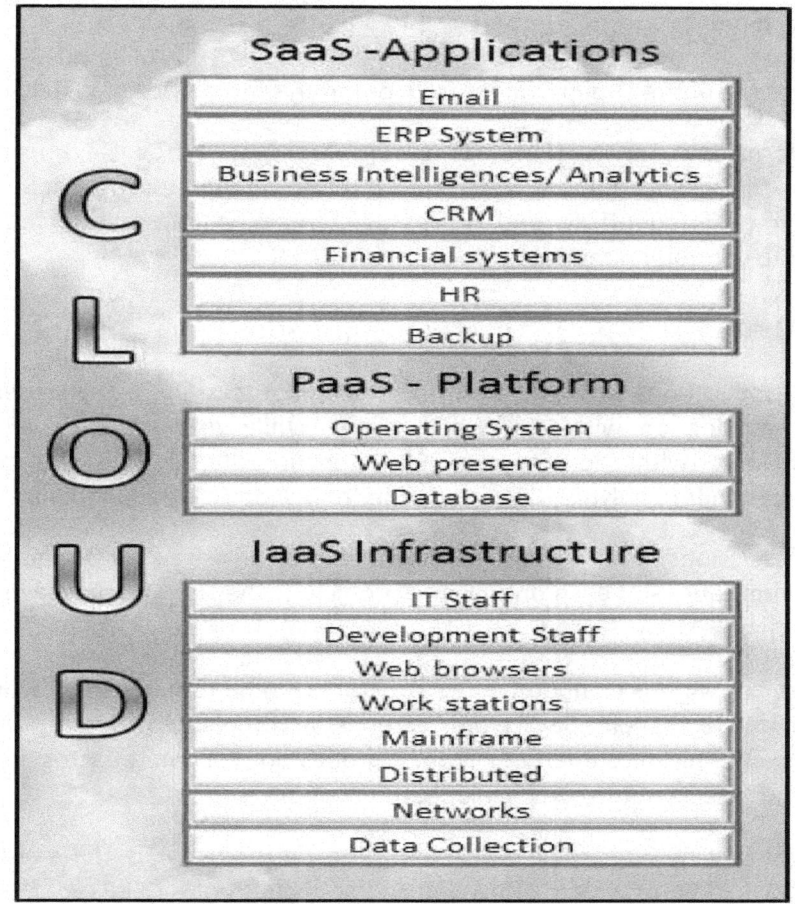

Illustration-SaaS Applications

For example, moving the analytics application blocks from on premise to software provided by the supplier, is SaaS if the service provider is multi-tenant.

A customer has the option of outsourcing all or part of their information needs, including ERP, with the exceptions of information needed to capture and process data on premise. Under the IaaS format, even these are candidates for outsourcing.

Infrastructure as a Service (IaaS) relates to the old facilities management concept. The service provider owns the equipment, and is responsible for running and managing the applications. In effect, it moves the entire IT department from on-premise to service provider.

Platform as a Service (PaaS) addresses IT issues. The SaaS Company owns the servers and software. Your internally generated transactions are transmitted offsite and processed. Streaming information flows back to your organization.

Summary

SaaS applications, with off-site programs and processing over the web, are catching on with on-premise users. While relevant to smaller companies with non-complex ERP functionality, it has greater application for analytics, CRM, and other non-shop related functions.

SaaS decisions require the IT hardware staff to advise management on the implications of each option. The problem is the IT staff jobs may be in jeopardy.

There are various competitive fee structures, and it requires homework to understand them. SaaS either extends or complicates the software decision process - sometimes both, but does not become a factor until future state solutions are developed.

As with all new technologies, finding the right partner is the key to success. Some providers of on-demand software, not all ERP, are PLEX Online, Sage Peachtree, Visibility, NetSuite, Epicor Express, Aplicor, Intacci, and Sales Force.

The selection process up to the ERP decision is the same for cloud applications as on-premise. The cloud carries the potential for significant savings in staff and equipment. Executive management and auditors must address the issues of security and business continuity, and implement control protocols.

5 Engineering

Engineering systems must receive a high priority. ERP starts with prints processes and bills of material, managed and maintained by engineering. ERP requires engineering to provide design and related specifications data to the Item Master and Bill of Material (Product Structure) files. To this list add shop information, routings and work center information, maintained by engineering or manufacturing.

The software addresses a complex set of program options and engineering requirements. Many engineering departments use third party systems such as Finite Element Analysis and Solid Modeling, which interface with the ERP system.

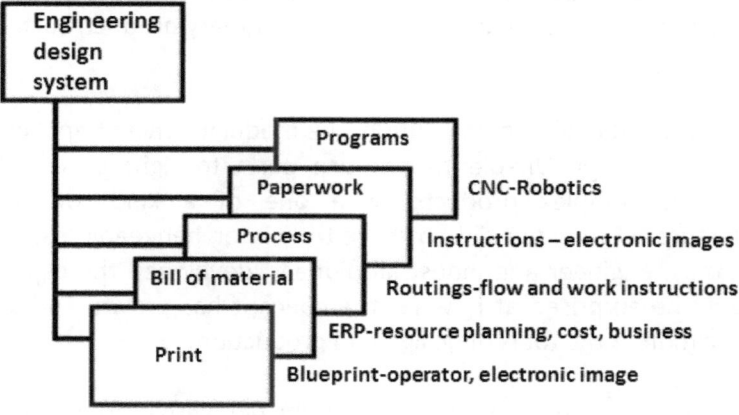

ERP systems must integrate design engineering and automated production systems. Modern production equipment blurs the dividing line between data needed for ERP, engineering and the shop. Production machines run directly from computer designs without the use of ERP and are computers themselves.

Companies with complex BOM must extend relational planning far into the engineering and manufacturing processes. Conversely, companies with fewer complexities, like distribution, may not need sophisticated engineering functionality.

Distribution ERP systems must contain kitting functionality.

Modular Designs

Modular design structurally breaks a product down into smaller parts or components. Each part is replicable, interchangeable, and scalable. The method supports mass production and mass customization, depending on the level of design granularity.

The concept of modular design has been around "forever." A spear has a shaft and blade, each available as an individual component. Nearly all products have a certain amount of modularity, with replacement components purchased and installed on the primary product, such as an engine in a car.

Until the second industrial revolution, the modular concept applied at a high product level. Unable to produce parts to tight specifications meant that complex products were one of a kind, or custom manufactured. Even guns did not have truly interchangeable parts until Eli Whitney, engineer and industrial pioneer, developed the capability. He would be surprised at how far the concept has grown, and at the sophistication of the tools of design and production.

Modular design capability is a core principle within repetitive ERP systems supporting manufacturing, and supply chain flexibility. The breakdown of bill of material (BOM) in Engineer to Order companies also follows the principle, with the majority of parts designed for interchangeability because of service requirements.

The following prints illustrate the modular concept.

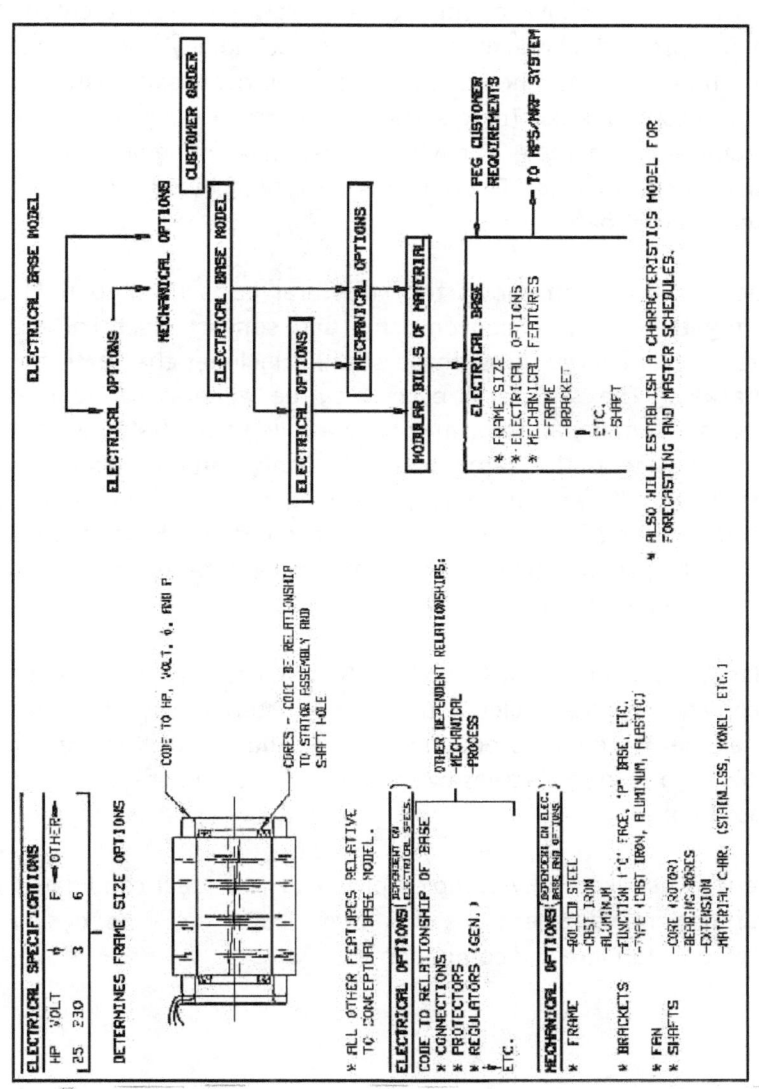

Modular Product Design 1

These two prints show a conceptual electric motor, created for developing product characteristics, group technology codes, and /or configuration elements. The first print is an electrical design without any mechanical components. The electrical data are on the print, and each is a parameter or characteristic when a customer or engineer is zeroing in on the specific product. The only modification allowed is for F1 or F2, the direction the shaft rotates.

The second illustration shows the structural parts used to hold the motor together, provide concentricity, and convert electrical energy into mechanical energy through the shaft. It includes the shaft, frame, and brackets. The structural parts may be general or application specific. For example, a motor may have a rolled steel frame instead of cast iron, but with the same electrical configuration. Some of the brackets have "C" face machining, meaning they can mount directly onto other pieces of equipment, and a machined bracket that mounts internal to the product. Belt driven motors use a different bracket and a shaft machined for a pulley.

Modular design provides flexibility. Summarized parts orders are produced and final assembled in the factory. Alternatively, standardized parts can be stored in production or distribution centers and final assembled to order, increasing flexibility and speeding up order response time.

Electric motors, like many complex products, are ideal candidates for configuration management systems that allow real time design of product from standardized components.

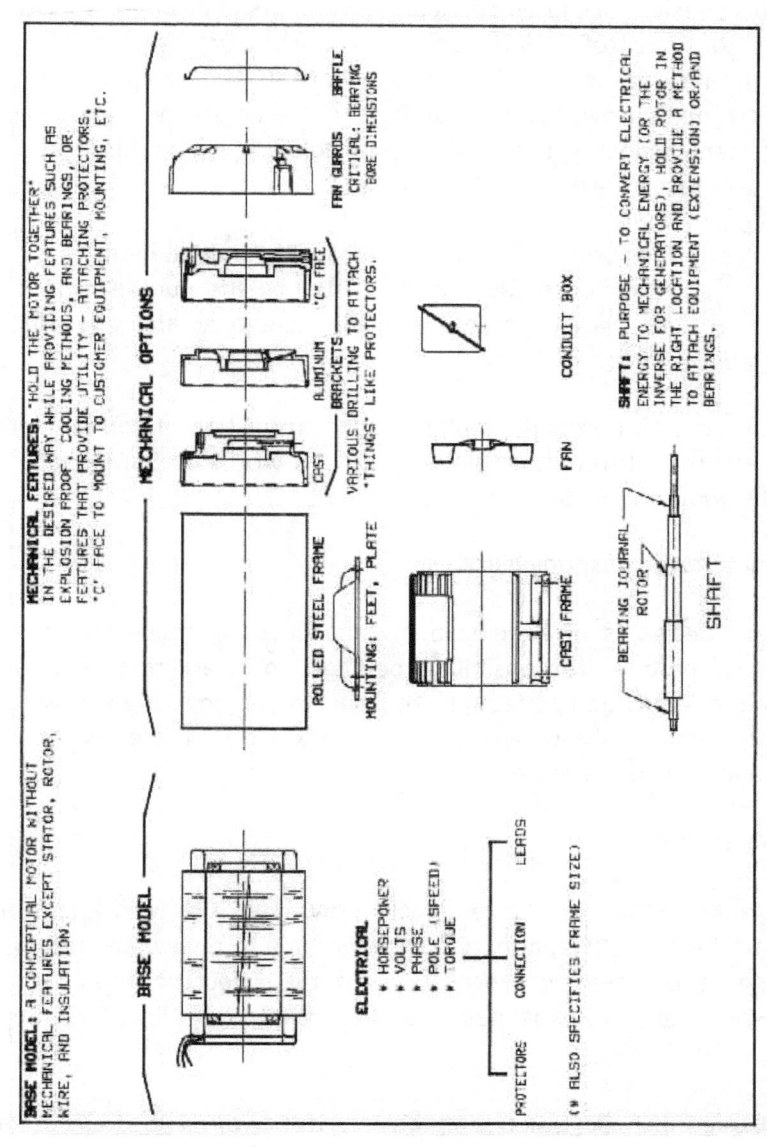

Modular Product Design 2

Modular design facilitates configuring products, allowing customers to select from a list of options. Anyone who has purchased merchandise over the Internet is familiar with the concept. An example is clothing. The first menu provides an option for style. Selecting the style brings up a size menu. Selecting the size brings up color. Selecting this last option, the buyer takes the order to the checkout.

Modular designs provide flexibility. Thoroughly understanding the bill of material and the processes enables flattening the number of tiers by adding routing data, thereby reducing inventory and speeding up production.

Modular design makes it simpler to split production of components or finished product from multiple producers. It works for SCM, supporting modifications in the distribution center.

Product Design Responsibility

Product design is not the sole providence of engineering. In some business models responsibility belongs to marketing and sales. Frequently, they do not require sophisticated engineering software but do require system's support of other types. Often, these involve color match and overseas communications.

Legacy Systems

Companies with legacy systems will know how to convert engineering data to the new ERP system, but take the time to review and rationalize the entire engineering process. Factor the effect of visual or Lean methodologies and expanded shop floor control applications into the review.

Companies installing their first ERP systems will struggle with BOM structuring. Numbering systems will be a specific problem. Be prepared to spend an inordinate amount of time on these activities but have patience. It is critical to get them right.

Rapid Sample Production

Rapid samples can be a game-changing application. The amount of time it takes to turn around a prototype or sample often determines who gets the business. This places extreme pressure on engineering and manufacturing. There is frequently little time to prepare a new BOM. The software must support "same as except" with the online ease of crossing off one part number and writing in another.

It must be easy to enter the design into the database. This is a complaint that ETO's and contractors have with iterative ERP systems. For them the bill is the equivalent of the gross level production schedule. For ETO, maintaining the BOM may be a redundant effort. With high levels of ECN (engineering change notices), it can be a non-value adding activity for engineering and production, but purchasing needs the requirements generated by the ERP system.

Rapid quote entry provides tracking and eases conversion into orders. One of our clients was stacking up paperwork while waiting for additional specifications. It required days to enter the quote, and it consumed time to find a specific one. Changing the process reduced the time to minutes, then real-time. The information allowed the shop to provide valuable inputs into the development process and effectively schedule production.

Lead-time Offsets

ERP manages time by using offsets provided through the engineering system. The three most-used factors are:

1. The bill of material planning horizon is the elapsed time starting with customer specifications (or order entry) and extending through the completion of an authorized bill of material in the ERP system. A specification stage frequently precedes order entry, and some enterprises may want to incorporate that component in the time chart. Design does not always result in an order and this step is part of the sales cycle.

2. Cycle time is comprised of queue, move, and run times, defining the length of time required, given the available resources, from the start to the completion of the product as planned. Machine, and process time all share the "cycle time" label.

3. From a customer's perspective, lead-time is the elapsed time from order entry until the customer receives the product on their dock.

Specifying the right offsets is important. Plans with too much offset time result in surplus work in process with capacity used out of phase. Specifying unrealistically short offsets result in planning production to be late because it understates the process time.

Calculated lead times separate tiers, reflecting the total queue, (run, and move sequence), used to time phase production.

Summing all lead-times from each level equals the theoretical product cycle time. The due dates for each part are calculated and used for the shop schedules.

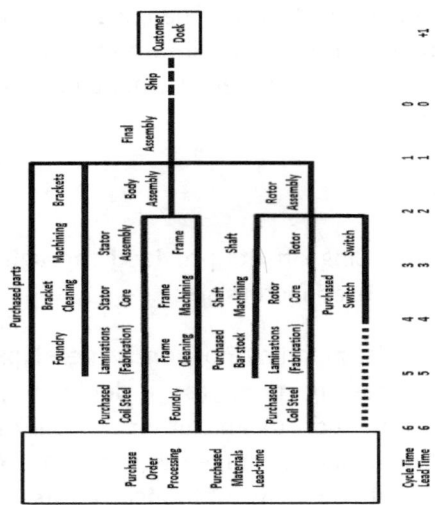

Illustration - Lead-time Offset

It is useful to have a current lead-time chart similar to this one of an electric motor. Turn the vertical structure to a horizontal view; fill in the lead-time offset between each tier. Adding the distribution, shipping and in transit time to the customer will yield the customer lead-time.

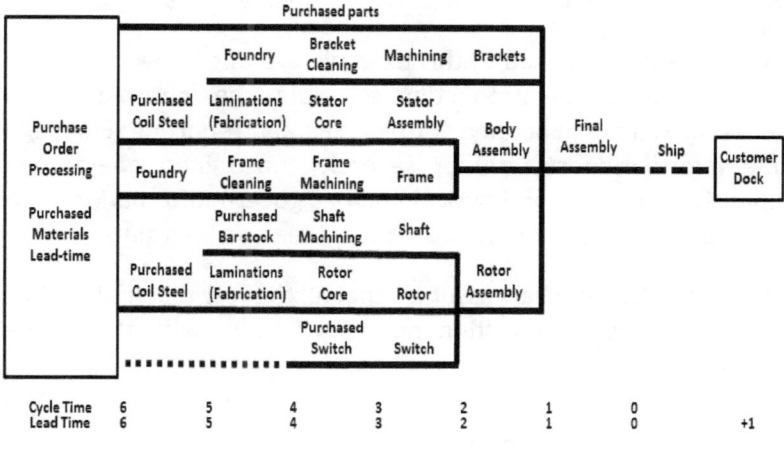

Illustration - Lead-Time Chart

In this example, all production activities, such as a body assembly, take one period. Six periods equal total cycle time - how long it takes, given the material, labor, machines and tooling, to make the product from start to finish.

Shipping from the plant to the customer dock is one period. Delivery time added to six periods cycle time equals a seven period customer lead-time.

To assemble a motor by the end of Period 0, the brackets, body assembly, rotor assembly, and final assembly purchased parts must be available at the end of Period 1.

A production schedule filled to absolute capacity has little flexibility to accommodate opportunities. Prioritizing orders is an option, but it creates winners and losers. If an emergency order from a priority customer needs rapid delivery, setups will be broken and other customer orders pushed back. A flexible shop with short setups will absorb the change with less schedule interruption.

Business needs to build shop flexibility to react to opportunities and risks. When the entire organization can respond quickly without high operational penalties, it is adaptive, and reality times are shorter.

If the time periods used in this example are one week, and it takes six weeks to affect the production schedule, the information reality is weeks for reaction and days for planning and reporting. Building a real-time information system for severely constrained operations is an expensive undertaking. Physical realities govern information speed, but information speed helps cut both cycle time and lead-time.

A derivation of this chart assumes that all the raw materials, fabrication, and subassembly production occurs off shore with three weeks in-transit.

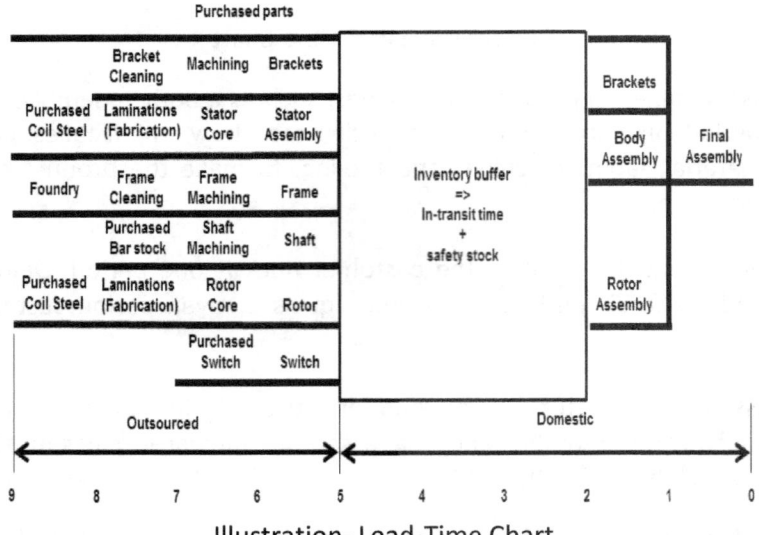

Illustration- Lead-Time Chart

Like the first example, eight weeks of physical reality does not justify a short information reality. Unlike the earlier example, this shop may be "Assemble to Order," where the final assembly schedule pulls components from inventory to feed assembly. If the inventory is interchangeable, the production cycle is two periods. If it is a "build to order" with components allocated to specific orders, the physical reality is nine periods. These longer cycle times are inherent in most companies with significant off shore purchased components.

Time offsets are required, even if minimal. They calculate product completion dates, the capacity plan and synchronize output. In a pull environment, or Kanban, where the using operation goes to the supplier, the supplier must still be able to replenish or fill demand in a timely fashion.

Nearly all ERP systems calculate and maintain the lead-time onsets. This does not mean abdication of responsibility to monitor and manage the system. The prudent act is to set up a periodic review schedule and audit the system.

Group Technology

There are additional options on the BOM. Group technology (GT) codes define product into finite, geometric shapes, functions, and characteristics. Group technology codes are descriptive, sortable, and highly significant. Engineering owns this field. It is a logical number for accessing a database in engineering terms and it maintains the significant data washed out of the item or part number. It is easier to group parts into families, control databases and to manage prints.

Features and Options

The features and option's functionality may be as useful for the ETO as for other business types. If required, make sure they are native to the package. Configuration management falls in this same category. Identify these types of requirements in the need's assessment. Configuration management, properly used is a powerful tool. This is one reason to get professional help in evaluating your system requirements.

Routing and Work Centers

Routings and work centers are also in ERP, but they belong here for technical discussion. The routings, or operation sequences, are determined by manufacturing engineering. They contain the cost and time elements from work centers used to plan capacity, labor, tooling, and crewing requirements. The standard cost system includes material, labor and burden or material, labor, burden and variable burden.

Companies using average cost systems need to guarantee that the ERP system supports the methodology. Some packages advertise average cost solutions but make sure the supplier demos this functionality to the complete satisfaction of your accountants and auditors.

Use routing records and bills of material to build up costs through the production chain, from raw materials through finished goods. Routing accuracy has financial implications.

Production and Engineering Systems

ERP requires multiple transaction reporting throughout the production and inventory chain, including production, receiving, and disbursal.

Manufacturing has developed a number of tools to help plan and manage production. These include visual methods, MES, APS (Advanced Planning and Scheduling), and finite planning techniques. Today, everyone is concerned about tracking parts, orders, and costs.

Engineering Change

The need for complex engineering change management varies by business. Some manufacturers need comprehensive ECN procedures. Drug companies are one example. They have to control the product from the cradle to grave. All companies need version control for maintenance, quality, and troubleshooting purposes. Product liability avoidance demands proper record keeping.

Summary

Abundant information on configuration management, features, and options is available, and companies need to do the research. With the widespread use of the web, these are valuable tools. The additional design and color match tools are generally not part of an ERP system. Many companies use Macs for design purposes. It is important to dig deeply and understand how all the options interact, and the software tools needed to get the job done right.

As stated, it is not our intent to make anyone an expert on engineering systems or ERP. Our experience has shown that many companies go into the selection process without a full understanding of what they are getting into. Companies with heavily engineered systems need to review the relationships and data accuracy of all the elements. The success of any ERP systems lies in the integrity of the engineering system, starting with accurate data base information.

6 ERP Concepts

An ERP system significantly aids asset management such as machine capacity and utilization, material's optimization, inventory management, and control of money through the financial system. Knowledge management is included in some human resources modules, and selective packages incorporate energy calculations.

Several important definitions are useful for understanding ERP.

Process

A process is a set of activities established for achieving a given purpose. A process includes resources (people, machines, materials, paperwork, and tooling).

A value-added steam is a chain of processes used to convert resources into goods or services. Many ERP practitioners extend the definition to include material's acquisition and order fulfillment.

Purpose of ERP in a Production Environment

The primary purpose of the ERP system in a production environment is to plan and control the processes through the value stream, then network the information throughout the enterprise.

Following is a summarized version of how ERP works. Reviewing the core concepts will help make effective use of this book.

Bill of Material

The Core ERP Document Is A Bill of Material.

Bill of Material

Level	Description	Make/Buy	Qty per Assmb	Material	Labor	Burden	Total
0	Finished product	M	1	$8.00	$1.60	$8.00	$17.60
1	Subassembly	M	1	$6.00	$1.20	$6.00	$13.20
2	Part 1 DP	M	1	$1.00	$0.20	$1.00	$2.20
2	Part 2 DP	M	1	$2.00	$0.40	$2.00	$4.40
2	Part 3 DP	B	1	$3.00	$0.60	$3.00	$6.60
1	Part X	M	1	$1.00	$0.20	$1.00	$2.20
1	Part Y	B	1	$1.00	$0.20	$1.00	$2.20

Illustration - Bill of Material

A bill of materials is a list of the parts needed to make a product and the core document behind ERP systems. The bill is a structured breakdown of the engineering design and product print. While all of these data are in the Master Item File, the bills are loaded into the computer as "product structure files," forming the structural data relationships for the ERP calculations.

Independent / Dependent Structure

The next illustration is a product structure. The product (item sold) is independent. The parts and subassemblies used to make it are dependent. The term relates to the relational calculations performed by ERP. Given the specific fields of information, any set of independent/dependent relationships can go through one or a sequence of calculations.

Independent factors include finished goods products and parts sold "independently."

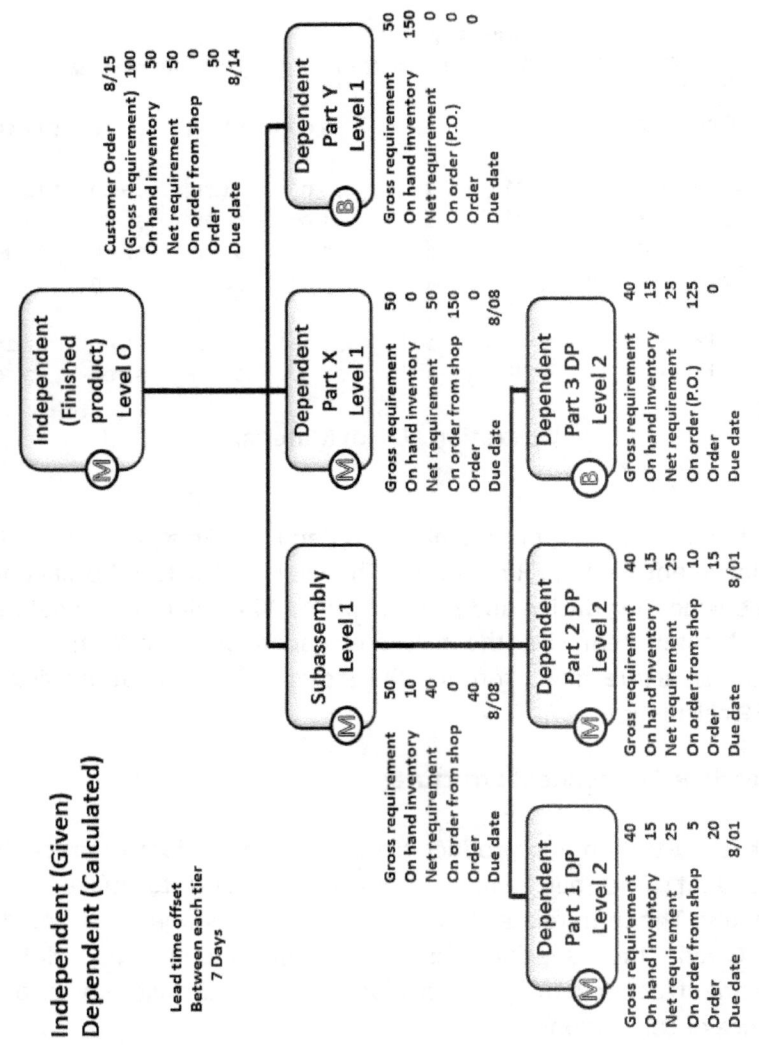

Illustration - Independent / Dependent

Dependent factors are the raw materials, parts, subassemblies, and components required to build or assemble the independent product. There are conditions where dependent parts become independent, such as service parts or planning production at the subassembly levels.

Make/Buy

Products and parts are broken into "make" or "buy" categories. Make/buy codes direct the requirements into either the production or purchase planning modules. The illustration uses an "M" for make and "B" for buy.

The problem is introduced when make parts are purchased or purchased parts are manufactured. In the horizontal system, with numerous outsourced parts mixed with internal production, the ability to manage this code is important. The system must provide user-friendly flexibility when switching back and forth.

The quantity per assembly is the amount or number of a specific part or material needed to make the higher part level.

Lead-time Offsets

The product structure is broken down by levels for calculation purposes. When a product structure is prepared, each level is a completed part. Each part or component has a master item record and a unique part number or SKU. We have numbered each level on the chart above.

Level Zero (0) products consume Level One (1) manufactured and purchased component, which consume Level Two 2 materials. The number of levels theoretically extends to infinity.

Buying, making, assembling and shipping product takes time. ERP systems use lead-time factors within each level to plan the time requirement in the calculations. In this example, each level takes one week to plan, produce, and make a product available to the next level.

Lead-time factors classically are longer than actual time, which does not consider the effect of mix or total load. Unlimited capacity is required to produce every order to actual time. This is economically impractical. Carefully work out formulas to balance actual to practical lead-times.

Requirements Planning Calculations

Gross requirements are the total dependent parts and quantities needed to produce the independent quantity. They are useful planning tools but difficult to use without net results. Nearly all systems are capable of a simple gross calculation.

Gross requirements are - independent demand times the bill of dependent parts. Per the illustration, independent (level 0) demand is 100. To make the product requires 100 subassemblies, and 100 each of Part X, Part Y, Part 1 DP, Part 2 DP, and Part 3 DP.

Subtracting, (netting) the materials on hand create a shortage or shopping list. This process applies to home projects, making oatmeal cookies and nearly any tasks with interwoven events and activities. Per the example, ERP calculations are performed one level at a time, although normally as a continuous gross to net chain. Referencing the illustration, if the finished product has 50 units on hand, production needs to make 50 more to fill the order. There are no open production orders, and the net converts to gross requirement for Level one.

The Level 1 gross of 50 minus the on-hand inventory for each part or component equals net requirements. For example, the gross requirement for the subassembly is 50, on-hand inventory is 10, and net requirement is 40. There are no open production orders, and the system recommends or places (based on rules and formulas) an order for 40 subassemblies. The net 40 becomes the gross for Level 2.

The calculation for Part 1D is gross 40, minus inventory on hand 15 results in 25 net. There is an open production order for 5 units, requiring an additional production order for 20 units.

Part 3 DP is coded buy, and netting the gross requirements for 40 against the 15 units on hand requires purchasing to acquire 15, but they have an outstanding purchase order for 150, so no action is required.

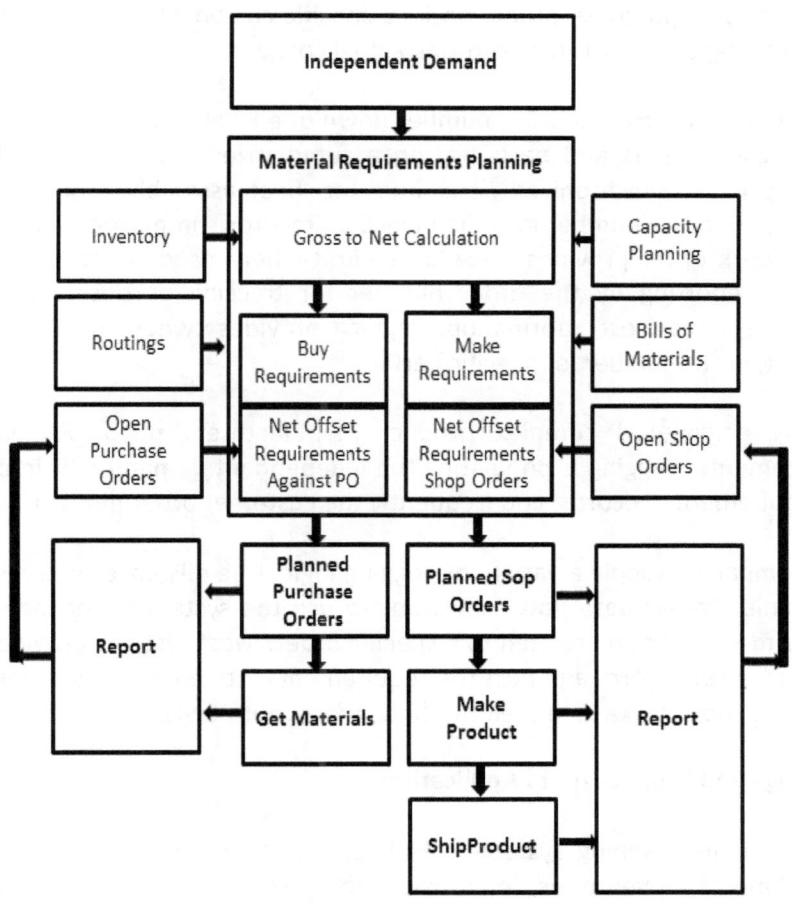

Illustration - Chart of Material Calculations

Pegged Requirements

Full level pegging is carrying the order number and/or SKU through every requirement and order record. This provides the ability to trace parts, shop or purchase orders back to specific customer orders. BTOs also use pegged records for capturing actual cost data.

Some systems carry the order number down one level. This is sufficient where components and parts are on a summarized work order and order pegging synchronizes parts into the final assembly schedule. Nesting the order number into the individual records summarized into a single work order provides a useful, limited where used capability. It enables reporting by the order number for tracking purposes, and capturing actual cost information. Pegging provides "where used" by product, order number, or specific parts.

Heavily engineered complex product manufacturers need pegged requirements. Pegging is populating the independent demand SKU into all requirements' records, and frequently the customer order number.

ERP companies supply a variety of pegging logic. Due diligence requires companies to evaluate how they want to use the system to manage, track orders and parts related to a specific order. Most systems provide pegging in some form and nest the requirements into a summary order for production. Make sure their method meets your needs.

Routings and Work Centers Application

Requirements planning systems calculates and time phases customer requirements, inventories, materials, labor, machines, tooling, and paperwork. Workflow and operational planning use routings attached to the part numbers. In the previous example, the materials were calculated. Routings and work centers plan asset utilization and manage cost information.

Routings are a list of actions and work center operations required to produce a part, component, sub-assembly, or final product.

Reverting to the structured example, the plan calls for 100 subassemblies in week 1. Each subassembly uses Part 1 DP, a machined component. Making it require a lathe, cutting tools, time, and material, labor and burden. In some systems, this is an average cost, a red flag for software selection. The operation contains information about time, including setup, run, labor, and move.

These factors are inputs to calculate labor requirements, inventory valuation, and financial effects. Simulation based on ERP outputs is a powerful planning tool for budgets and "what if" business planning.

Database

The database contains the master records and transactions. The original database (DB) concept is that all records of the business reside in one location. This prevented having to maintain the same data in multiple locations, a redundant and unnecessary requirement. Today, the database concept is more sophisticated and allows data to be broken into smaller chunks, and logical records may reside in many physical locations, or somewhere on the cloud.

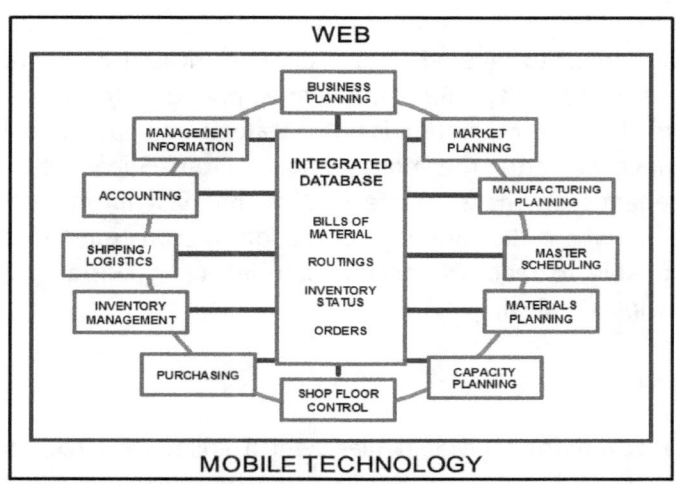

Illustration - Mobile technology

The purpose, however, is still to provide a common data source to the user community, made more urgent by the proliferation of mobile technology and its insatiable appetite for information. As shown below, everyone contributes to and enriches the data pool. Regardless of data standardization, the information obtained may be different when multiple programs use the same information but dissimilar calculations.

Most of the cloud-based technologies used by SaaS providers integrate mobile technologies. The issue is if and how they integrate with potential on premise databases.

Database Update Timing

Batch processing describes accumulating transactions throughout the day and processing the ERP calculations and updates on a predefined schedule, normally overnight. Batch processing includes master file changes and all operational transactions.

Real time means updating and processing transactions as they occur. Early computers did not have the power or speed to achieve real time processing. The restriction today is cost, not capability.

If companies want to take advantage of sophisticated BI or drastically speed up business agility, ERP systems must provide information at the speed of reality. This integration is both strategic and operational. Think about it now, not after the money is committed. Speed of decision-making depends on the software system, but fast information is of lessor value when the physical operation is constrained and the business unable to react. A specific plan, including ERP and Lean Six Sigma principles is ideal.

Master Files

There are dozens of individual files, which collectively comprise the database. The major files are the item master, customer master, and vendor master, bills of material (product structure), routings, and work centers.

The coding and classification structures behind these files are important and demand attention. These issues will come up throughout the book, but one code illustrates the effect on the selection process.

When every file contains plant codes, it is multi-plant or multi-company. This means that a number of plants with autonomous databases can use one system. Each can operate with its own chart of accounts, yet roll up all data for corporate financial planning purposes. All the information is selectively available for the facilities by design, instead of compiled from mixed files and reports.

If the system lacks multi-plant capability, it often uses different codes to split up information, making it appear like multi-plant. In these cases, there can normally be only one chart of accounts. The records for multiple locations are stored on one set of files, where anyone using the system has access to data from other facilities. Ask your software company for a detail breakdown of all files and fields.

The Master Item File contains specific information about product, components, parts, and materials. It states ordering and inventory rules for each item. The file, and how it is structured, will play a significant role in the success your installation.

The history of ERP implementations is replete with examples of the importance and complexity of dealing with the Master item file. It is one of the main sources for extending implementations. Everyone owns a portion, and it affects the entire organization. Marketing owns the finished product, manufacturing may own the components, and engineering own the number. It is not enough to tell the team to "get it done." Executive Management must delegate ownership of the master file conversion to a specific team of marketing/sales, engineering, and manufacturing personnel with direction from IT.

Part Number

The part, product, or model number is normally the stock keeping unit or SKU. The packaging demands of the mega-merchandisers can place extraordinary pressure on finding a way to call different packaging configurations the same number. An example is an eight pack for one customer and a six-pack for others. While there are schemes or work a round, they will cause confusion, excessive cost and lack of control. Bear in mind, there can be only one SKU per discrete part number.

There has been a long-running debate about part numbers. Should they be significant, carrying descriptive information or non-significant, that is, purely numeric. Internationalism supports this approach. So does internet processing with menus or configurations. This debate is not as simple as it appears although both often contain data, such as size. Engineering, production, inventory personnel, and sales all use short descriptive numbers. Computers can use either method. Current convention favors the non-significant part number or minimal alphanumeric data. In general, names are for people and numbers are for computers.

Each company must resolve the numbering system issue, but one word of caution. Trying to change numbering systems while selecting and installing an ERP system is dangerous. It introduces complex variables on top of other significant variables. Item numbers are meaningful, determined, and controlled by engineering. IT and engineering normally have the best perception of the usage and the price to change them. Changing SKU formats automatically requires changes to history, orders, inventory, locations, bar codes, and customer records. Think about how the number will affect forecasts, demand driven systems and your customer and vendor ERP systems.

Make sure the system can accommodate your number. Never modify a part number field on the software programs. It is the record key and permeates the entire system. A change to the field size is a major programming task. Either the field is big enough and usable, or it is not.

Descriptions

The description is an alphanumeric field used to put meaningful information into useful sequences. Any analysis of part numbers will include descriptions. If a non-significant part number is used, the description is more meaningful. Descriptions often have variable formats, making it difficult to sort them into useful sequences. Check how the system uses helper fields, such as commodity codes or user fields. They are set up like system's codes and established early in the implementation process.

Globalization and customer compliance has created a need for multiple descriptions. Customers may want different descriptions and have them in multiple languages.

Product Categories

Product codes and classifications differentiate product types. Product categories are summarized part numbers and descriptions. These occur within different parts of the system, primarily sales and purchasing. The sales department uses the code to differentiate types of sales and marketing activities. Purchasing summarizes materials by category to analyze cost, usage, and purchasing patterns.

Unit of Measure

The units of measure (U/M) modify the quantities per assembly. A quantity of one (1) may be a box, pound, inch, or any of a long list of definitions. The unit of measure is one of the rules established on the master SKU level. Per the chapter on supply chains, compliance issues dramatically affect units of measure by product within a customer. The unit of measure calculation methodology frequently delays distribution ERP projects. Clearly understand your needs before starting the ERP search.

Sales Commissions

ERP systems contain codes for sales territories and the salespeople. The method used for commission calculation generally falls short of need for distributors. Distributors must take an in-depth look at the functionality of the software since they often have more complex commission formulas.

Data, Files, Fields, and Codes

Files, fields, and system codes are mundane parts of the ERP selection process and seldom get attention until problems occur trying to implement the system. While not a leading cause for ERP failure, it is a contributor to delayed implementation. It is an obvious setback when discovering the system structure fails to support business needs.

Sales functionality for distribution companies is complicated. The customer order, not the item, connects the customer and the product. Each order contains all the nested item information. Distributors focus on completion of full orders instead of specific part numbers. A company needs to structure files and applications to manage by order and SKU. Complicating the issue, distribution companies on average have a greater number of SKUs packaged in multiple formats. A common practice is to break down a package with inventory and use the contents to complete an order.

Some data problems are:

- If the system is outdated, business requirements and software will be mismatched.

- If installing a new system, upgrade of current system or writing in house will consume significant time and resources.

- If installing a system for the first time, record preparation will be a major issue. All data and records require categorization, indexing, coding, cleansing, and data entry.

- If you are implementing a second or third-generation ERP, odds are high for data field sizes and calculation formula incompatibility. BOM offsets and ordering formulas are frequently out of date.

Summary

In spite of the complexity, fundamental everyday principles drive ERP systems. The formulas presented were simplified, but those with questions need to understand how they work before proceeding with the project. It is important to be diligent, thorough, and accurate when setting up files, codes, and data structures.

7 Closed Loop ERP

Following is a summarized closed-loop ERP process. It starts with business planning.

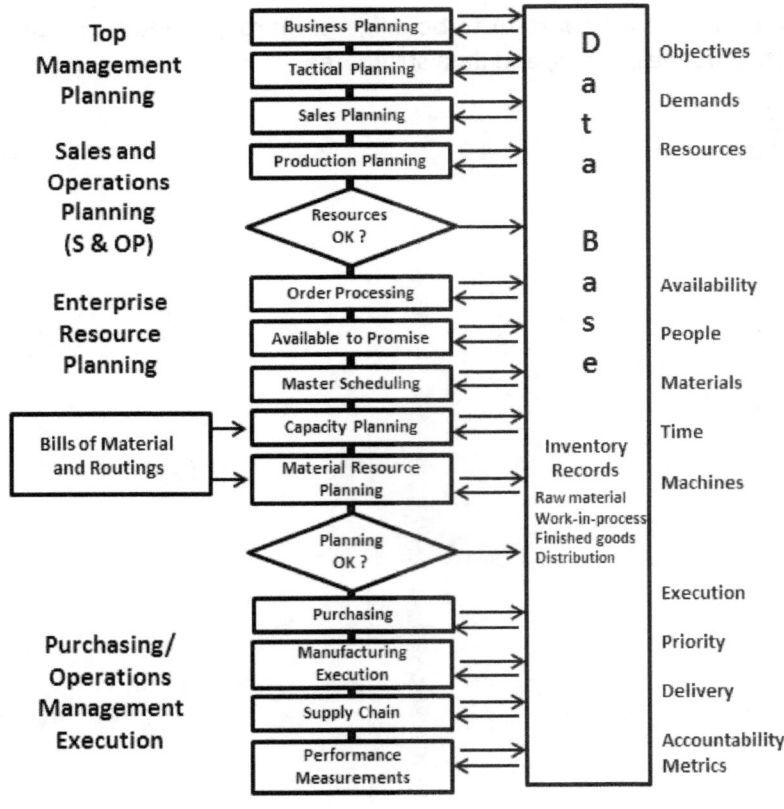

Illustration - Closed Loop ERP System

Top Management Planning

Strategic and tactical planning precedes closed loop operational planning, and establishes the business parameters for operational planning.

Distribution Requirements Planning

Distribution Requirements Planning (DRP) rolls up the inventory requirements from the various sales locations, either retail or distribution centers, into a requirement's plan. There are different methods to accomplish this process. One way is to establish a product structure functioning like a bill of material. Another is gross allocation of planned stock product. If you need distribution requirements planning, make sure the files and data operate exactly as needed. Keep the engineers involved.

Sales and Operations Planning (S&OP)

The APICS Dictionary defines S&OP as "The process brings together all the plans for the business (sales, marketing, and development, manufacturing, sourcing, and financial into one integrated set of plans)".

Planning is normally a weekly or monthly process, analyzing the sales forecast, budget, and performance measurements. The output from the meeting is sales planning, projected production rates, supply chain plans, inventory levels, and rough-cut capacity projections. In repetitive manufacturing companies, the adjusted production rates change the load points, resulting in re-balanced master schedules. S&OP is quickly gaining renewed focus as companies work to improve SCM programs.

Demand/Master Scheduling

Companies recognize demand in many ways, but their process labels may be different. Demand states what, when and how much product is required for customers and distribution. It is comprised of various combinations of the following:

- Customer orders
- Planned orders
- Firm planned orders
- Blanket orders
- Forecast
- Stock orders
- Distribution planning orders
- Demand pull

Forecasts and/or demand-pull orders are calculated using internal data or through collaboration with customers. Forecasted orders, in the APICS definition, equate to planned orders, which are "consumed" when firm planned orders are netted against them.

The Master Schedule of Production and Inventory Planning provides demand/supply reconciliation to stabilize schedules. The schedule is a time-phased matrix of capacity and production limits. Scheduled orders consume the plan. The master schedule, a mix of order types, feeds the ERP system. For companies using master scheduling, it is the independent demand input into the requirement's planning system. In some companies, master scheduling includes service parts.

The rough-cut capacity plan is at a relatively high level and used to determine overall capability requirements.

The system must also be able to perform capacity planning at the work center and department level, using production orders and unscheduled requirements. Resource capacity planning by distributors must include excellent worker assignment functionality.

Many business types do not use master scheduling. Shipment is based on actual orders, rules or available to promise position. Most distribution companies and many manufacturing types drive ERP directly from the order file.

For ETO or BTO, the demand plan is the estimate, design, and bill of material. While they must purchase materials, only part of it is repetitive.

Since the independent order file is in a constant state of change, the dependent requirements are also changing. To stabilize the shop, planning time fences containing freeze dates are sometimes used. This fence may be, for example, at the purchasing time horizon, where any new P.O. or due date change will cause expediting, or production changes result in breaking set-ups. The time fence freezes any changes to data inside the frozen period, preventing changes to due dates for raw materials, parts and components when they are due within this horizon.

Planning horizons are dangerous. They arbitrarily push out lead-times, affecting customer performance. Use automation, VMP, and information technology to maintain demand/supply timing relationships, and solve the schedule stabilization issue.

Order Processing

Order entry for both manufacturing and distribution companies are similar. Distributions tend to have larger volumes of line items on each order and a greater number of orders. The system requires built in editing routines to catch errors. Manually, error checking long complicated orders is at best an error-prone process but also one that delays fast order entry and visibility.

All ERP systems provide manual order entry, but some are more user-friendly than others are. Order entry involves looking up inventory position, credit information and a number of other activities. The order-entry person may have to view multiple screens to find all the information. Some systems provide hot keys, shortcuts, and/or special screens to help facilitate this movement. Other systems require laborious effort to move among a number of different screens or force the user through convoluted steps. This makes the process complicated, error prone and unfriendly.

Make sure the supplier demonstrates the entire order process. Invite all the order-processing associates to participate and try to enter orders. If the process is over complicated or cumbersome, it will affect both productivity and attitude. You are looking for simple, intuitive processing. Listen to the associates doing the work.

Mail, Fax, and Telephone

These are the traditional methods, requiring manual data entry. Telephone orders may require some type of transcription.

EDI

EDI, or electronic data interchange, is a widely accepted technology for transmitting orders directly from the customer into the ERP system. Nearly all the large companies use it in some form.

ERP systems use different formats and approaches to EDI, providing individual solutions. When evaluating ERP systems check out the EDI logic and edit formats required by your customers. Some EDI companies maintain it for a fee. Others allow third party suppliers or associates to update it. In this case, integration and maintenance are important issues. The key question is "Who will you call when there is a problem." If the answer is the ERP supplier, then proceed. If it is a combination of suppliers, think twice before proceeding. Arguments about responsibility can become expensive and add zero value.

Web Based Orders

Internet applications have exploded the use of order entry via the Web. Many companies provide shopping cart configuration capabilities where the order flows directly through the system without human intervention. Those using web-based order entry systems have carefully approached product configuration and set up menu-based selection processes. Other companies allow order entry through the Internet but print out those orders and reenter them. When the order volume is low, this is simple but wasteful. As on-line order volumes increase, it becomes both redundant and expensive.

Inventory Records

Inventory occurs at each level of production. Each level includes raw material, work in process, in transit and finished goods, often in multiple controlled and non-controlled locations. Multi-plant or multi-company functionality applies since it is necessary to know where assets are located.

This file is an area of intense and thorough review. Pay special attention to multi-plant processing, units of measure, classification, and location management. Where the need exists to switch product between dependent and independent status, make sure the fields and method are available to make the change fast and easy. Review the APICS Inventory module if you are uncertain how to evaluate the inventory component.

ABC inventory classification techniques help manage inventory. While falling into disfavor by academia, this is a valuable tool. Other required tools are cycle counting, inventory valuation and inventory classifications.

Requirements Planning

This is the calculation step of the ERP process. For the following walk-through of a closed-loop ERP system, the master files have been loaded with the relevant information - demand, the bills of material, (including the product structure), inventory balances and capacity factors are accurate and up to date.

Inputs into the ERP equation are demand quantities, inventory quantities, bills of material, routings, and work centers. The result is a gross to net calculation.

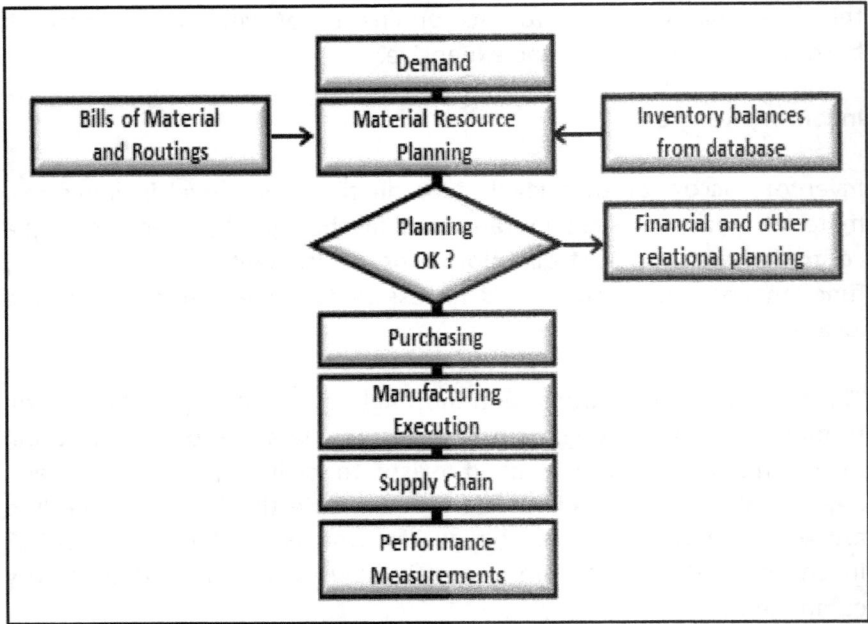

Illustration - ERP Inputs and Outputs

Net requirements are in two basic forms - purchased and manufactured. The requirements are offset using lead-time factors. Buy requirements precipitate purchasing actions, and make requirements drive shop schedules. Events are time phased. Transactions reporting production and receipts close the loop.

The core ERP calculates the following:

- Purchased and manufactured requirements and schedules
- Capacity planning (rough-cut, work center, machine)
- Direct labor requirements
- Shipping schedules

ERP extends the calculations into financial planning. Inclusion of Material, labor, and burden factors provide calculation for investment and timing for financial projections.

The transactions feed selected systems such as accounts payable, accounts receivable, inventory, and they update status fields. Mistakes in work centers, routings, and standard costs cause errors in all the associated systems.

Order pegging calculations tie requirements to a product, project, or order number.

Production Activity Control

In the classical ERP system, the PAC Module manages the order release (BOM, travelers, prints, etc.), work schedules, (priority plans) and capacity plans. Operations must produce the parts on time regardless of conditions at the next work center.

Travelers and shop schedules are queued in the shop office and released to the shop floor, just like fifty years ago. Nearly every system provides full electronic paperwork capability. The advantages are many, such as the elimination of paperwork creation, distribution, pick up and disposal. The major advantage is that engineering change is possible to the last moment before production. Releasing shop paperwork at the last minute, or using electronic images, keeps it in the office, simplifying the engineering change process.

Once produced, production pushes parts to the next operation without regard or knowledge of production status. The receiving operation may be ahead waiting for work or behind schedule. Their responsibility is to produce the new work along with the old, on schedule. This is the push system associated with ERP.

ERP is transaction intensive. The greater the number of levels, part numbers, work centers, employees, inventory locations, engineering changes and information needed by customers and management, the larger the volume of transactions. These transactions close the loop between plan and execution. Kanban ordering methods may require a third ordering type. The PAC Module is responsible for monitoring all shop floor activities and for all the transaction processing in the shop.

Reporting occurs upon completion of labor/operation, adding value and resulting in a new SKU. Labor reporting occurs at individual operations or by part completion. Parts flow to raw material/work-in-process areas or through reporting points on the shop floor. If the completed part is an inventory item, transactions report production, (which close the order), and entry into inventory. Final assembly post's production, validates quality, closes the order, and moves the stock into inventory. Subsequent receipts and disbursements may be required for locator systems.

Output Control

Output control is central to any ERP system. Many customers need product packaged into various configurations, each with different label demands. Compliance labeling may be required while the product is on the line. A manufacturing ERP system normally takes care of the reporting functions into and out of the warehouse and supports location control. It provides a picking list (or directed pick on mobile devices) for order fulfillment.

ERP systems offer varying levels of the sophisticated picking logic required by distribution companies. If bar code scanning is a business application, select an ERP system that supports it. Companies supplying the mega-merchandisers, Department of Defense (DOD), and the automotive industry must be aware of any requirement for radio frequency identification (RFID) processing and other scanning formats.

Output takes other forms such as wages and salaries, payment for goods, services, utilization, and other inputs.

All systems have waste components. They are time, materials, workers, money, opportunity, capacity, cash flow, talents, and production capability. Some software packages include energy calculations. These are opportunities for Lean programs.

Data Collection and Reporting

The system's assessment needs to evaluate, quantify, and decide how to do all the transactions in the business. Define your information needs and decide what is required real-time.

- ☐ Data entry
- ☐ Hand held devices including mobile technology
- ☐ Back flush production
- ☐ Bar codes and/or RFID
- ☐ Magnetic strips
- ☐ OCR
- ☐ Turnaround documents

Reporting Data Accuracy

Inaccurate data have always plagued ERP. The term GIGO (Garbage in Garbage Out) is an acronym for "lack of discipline." Only class "A" systems as defined by Oliver Wight ever achieved 98%, and few companies qualified. Most still suffer from excessive data error rates. Inaccurate records shutdown ERP systems and expand the chain of calculations, increasing the accumulated error per the following chart.

Accumulation of ERP Error Percentages	
Factor 1 BOM Accuracy	98%
Factor 2 Order Accuracy	98%
Error Factor for Gross Requirements	2-4%
Calculation for Net Requirements	
Factor 3 Inventory Accuracy	98%
Cum Error Factor for Net Requirements	2-6%
Calculation for Netting "On Order"	
Factor 3 Purchase Order Accuracy	98%
Factor 4 Production Order Accuracy	98%
Cum Error, Factor at PO & WO Level	2-10%

Illustration - Accumulation of Error Percentages

To do ERP requires accurate inputs

- Systems codes and usage rules
- BOM product structures
- BOM quantities per assembly
- Engineering change (ECN)
- Inventory balances
- Item master file
- Open purchase orders and production orders
- Order quantities (demand) - the order file of independent demand
- Lead-time offsets
- Routings
- Work centers
- Accurate costs including material, labor, burden and variable burden factors if available
- Units of measure and conversion tables
- Accurate customer and vendor files
- Formulas used for lot sizing, grouping and Kanban

Summary

ERP reduces to a chain of relational calculations performing all the core processes and acting as a transaction processor. Other systems bolt onto it, such as CRM and SCM. Understanding the core concepts helps to deal with the complexity. The loop starts with planning and ends with reporting that triggers the next planning cycle. Tight planning and execution must lock into an integrated, rigidly controlled, and predictable cycle.

8 Enterprise Shapes and Complexity Profile

This chapter explores conceptual metrics and elements that aid in defining business shape and complexity, two major considerations in software selection.

ERP functions on the premise that related causes/effects can be quantified and calculated. The more interrelationships and events there are, the greater the complexity, and the greater the integrated information opportunity.

Manufacturing is normally broken down by repetitive, job shop, process or assemble to order, and each needs a different mix of functionality. Distributors, hospitals, construction, agribusiness, government, and other business types need functionality that differ from manufacturing, but are equally complicated. For these reasons, complexity has very different meaning.

Affinity Systems LLC developed a new method to aid mapping business components to software functionality. It measures eight factors of complexity.

1. Product
2. Process
3. Multi-facility
4. Globalization
5. Spatial
6. Network
7. Transactional
8. Real time

A spider diagram labeled "complexity profile" represents the metrics for this chapter. The software selection chapter aligns business complexity to the software solution.

The following diagrams show the intent and importance of the exercise.

Large international companies like Boeing, Caterpillar, and General Motors, are complex in every metric. Filling out their spider diagram is uncomplicated because each metric is a five.

This diagram establishes the base for the evaluation.

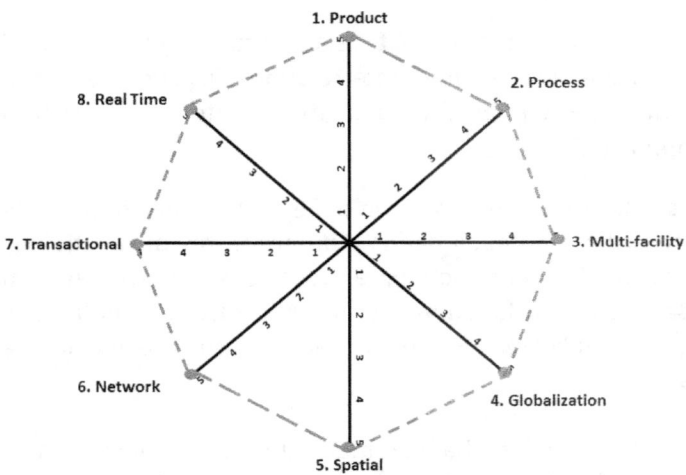

Complexity profile for a generic large manufacturing company

Greater complexity translates into requirements for a higher tier, more expensive, software solution such as SAP or Oracle. These software packages provide multiple layers of functionality.

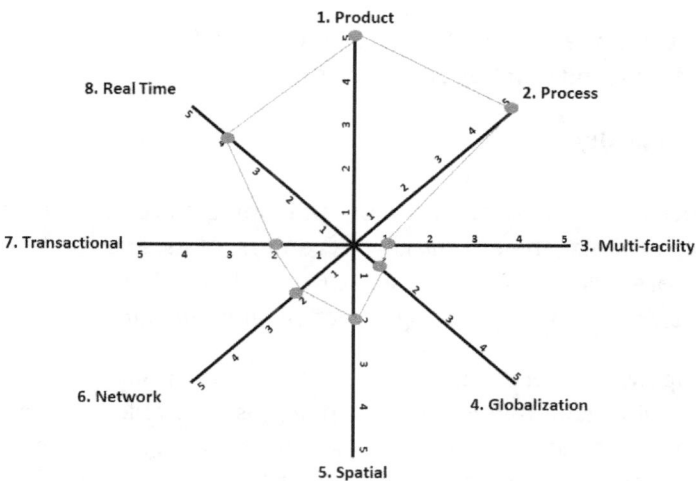

This diagram illustrates the software concept

For comparative purposes, the modular ERP example on page 20, illustrated above, is less complicated than the base example. A company with a similar profile would find the needed functionality in a tier two, three, or possibly a tier four solution.

When comparing these charts, any company with the second profile is wasting money if they purchase a tier one product. It is useful to define the implications.

- The cost of the system
- Greater implementation cost
- Additional time to install
- Greater maintenance costs

Products

Products are manufactured to BOM/blueprints specifications. The complexity of the product and bill of materials vary greatly between products and processes. The electric motors used as examples are complex, with five or more product structure levels. An automobile has greater complexity, while a packaged flashlight has less. Distribution companies have simpler, flatter bills of material. Product complexity includes the number of BOM levels, number of SKU's, complexity of design, diversity, and number of variables.

Process Complexity

All the processes, materials, machines, and workers are subordinate to the finished product. The routings, work centers, costs, and run times by operations are relational inputs tied to operations such as assembly, machining's, metal poring, forming, injection, and punching.

If the company is process oriented, such as wire rolling, then finite scheduling with continuous flow planning is a viable option. The majority of distribution companies kit or repackage the product. Capacity planning is an essential component, used for labor planning, sequencing production, and machine utilization.

Process complexity is defined by the degree of vertical integration, the type, number, and sophistication of operations, and the methods employed to perform work.

Multi-facility

Multi-facility is the number of facilities involved in the project. The project may be for one or many plants, with the complexity increasing by both the number of plants and the diversity of the products and processes.

The number of plants, what and how they produce, and where materials are purchased determines multi-facility complexity and product shipped.

Globalization

Globalization has created complex international supply chains with monetary, language, cultural and time differences. All complicate communications and control. When filling out the spider diagram for this leg consider:

- ☐ Where materials are sourced and product distributed
- ☐ How much of your product is outsourced
- ☐ What happens when supply chains are broken
- ☐ How complex is the chain - currency, language, cultural and time differences
- ☐ Do you have vertical backup on-site or from domestic suppliers

When performing the business evaluation, determine your contingency plans for supply chain interruption.

Demand-pull techniques introduce a real-time information-sharing element to the evaluation.

Spatial

ERP normally equates to relational planning, but it also plans and manages space or spatial relationships. For distribution, agriculture, warehousing, and construction, the ability to calculate, plan (schedule) and track the use of space and its contents is critical.

The emergence of WMS enriched the ERP spatial planning gene pool. Product is located and put into storage, field or staged on the shop floor. Spatial definition can be multi-dimensional. For example, isle, row, and location define a racking system.

A distributor ERP system focuses on the management of inventory, including staging areas, directed put-a-way, cross docking, location control, and the order to cash cycle. Picking logic is integral to all areas.

Network / Integration Complexity

All companies have networks and the addition of integrated layers increases complexity.

- Integrated shop floor reporting
- Multiple plants
- Plants with different ERP requirements
- Complex/international supply chains

Companies with simple processes and products are candidates for using an ERP SaaS or ASP option. The opposite is true for enterprises with highly developed digital nervous systems or those with a number of facilities tied together by intricate supply chains.

Another level of complexity is the degree of integration with third party or homegrown systems. BI and CRM systems often involve complex integration issues, but may be candidates for SaaS applications.

Transactional

All ERP systems are transaction intensive but some business verticals are more concerned about information status than relational or spatial factors. ERP systems for an insurance company or financial institution manage service information, not products. They require processing high volumes of real time transactions for updating multiple status files.

The speed and frequency of updates and the accuracy of processing are factors in all ERP systems. Manufacturing ERP systems are becoming real-time with shop floor reporting and integration, but many organizations still batch and process transactions overnight. The information reality is hours, unacceptable for transaction intensive organizations.

Real-time

Real-time information is quickly becoming a prerequisite, but some business models demand it. Use this metric for evaluating current and future needs, as business information and processes speed up the business reality.

Business Shape Charts

Following are flowcharts illustrating the difference in business structure. Please note on the chart how features and functions vary based on characteristics. What also becomes apparent is the difference in complexity between the various models. These differences equate to software supplier tiers and the associated cost of the software system.

There are various types of businesses with different functional requirements.

- Discrete - repetitive, make to order, make to stock, and engineer to order
- Process – make to order, make to stock
- Distributor – kit to order, kit to stock, and repack

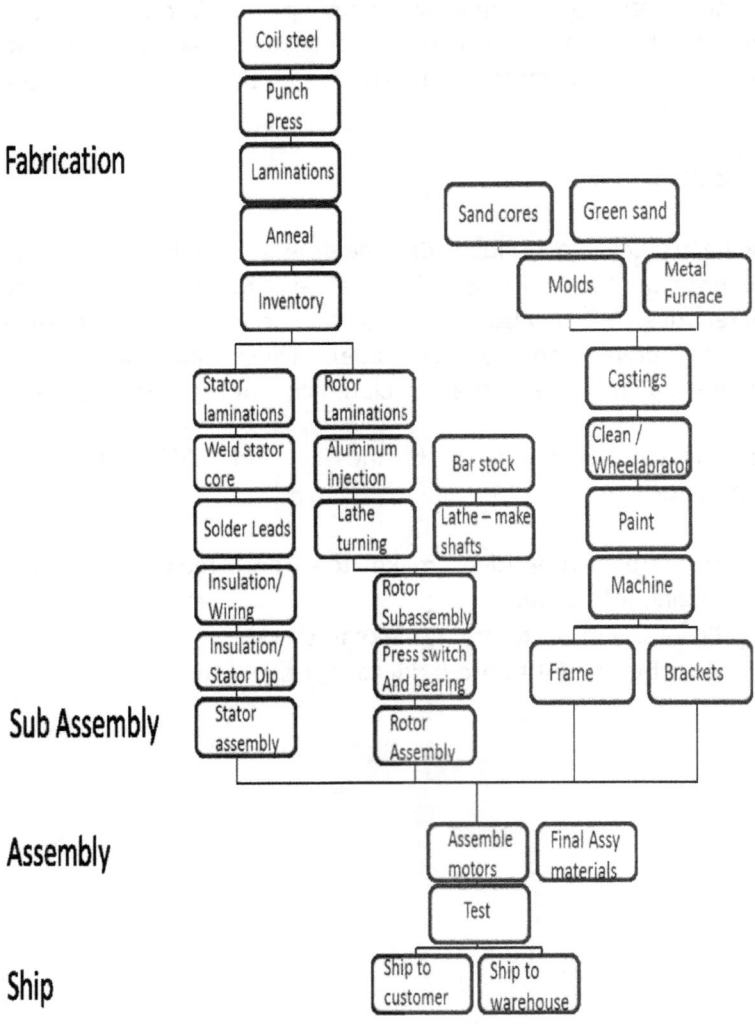

Illustration - Complex Manufacturing

Functional Requirements of Complex Manufacturing – Cast Iron Electric Motor:

- Complex multi-tier Bills of Material – highly engineered
- BOM version control
- Full level pegging
- Multiple process steps per part number
- Process and repetitive production
- Complex routings and work centers
- Combination of process and repetitive operations
- Difficult schedule management
- Cycle time management is an imperative
- High quality requirements
- May be ETO, BTO, ATO or BTS- BTO may also be standard stock or custom designs
- Ability to trace all materials, components and SKU's
- Complex vertical and horizontal functionality
- May have complex distribution requirements
- Transportation planning may be important

Decorative Trees and Shrubs

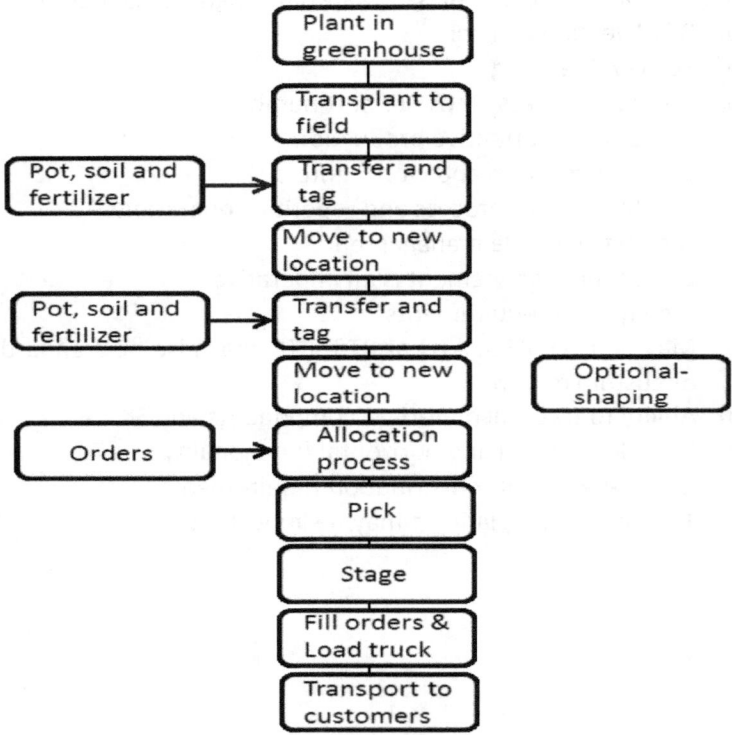

Illustration - Decorative Trees and Shrubs

Functional Requirements of Decorative Trees and Shrubs:

- o Simple Bills of Material
- o Precise process steps
- o Tracking required at each stage
- o Process timing is critical
- o The production cycle is years
- o Allocation process may be required
- o Product moves sequentially between controlled areas throughout the cycle

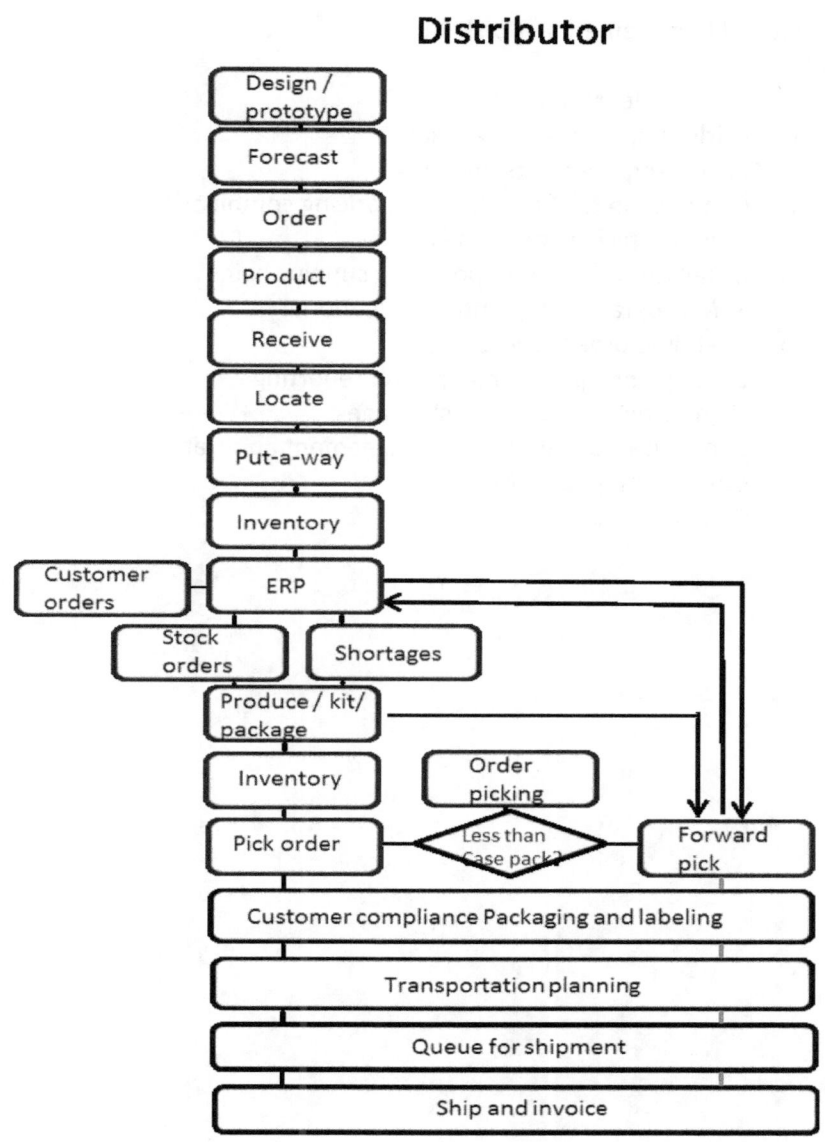

Illustration - Distributor

Functional Requirements of Distributor:

- Product development
- Fairly simple bills of material
- Kitting requirements planning
- Complex units of measure and pricing combinations
- Complex picking processes
- Detail forecasts to support long supply chains
- SCM programs frequently international
- Real time order processing
- Labor planning, assignment and reporting
- High velocity reaction to shortages
- Sophisticated warehouse management applications
- Customer compliance
- Tracing/tracking

Wire

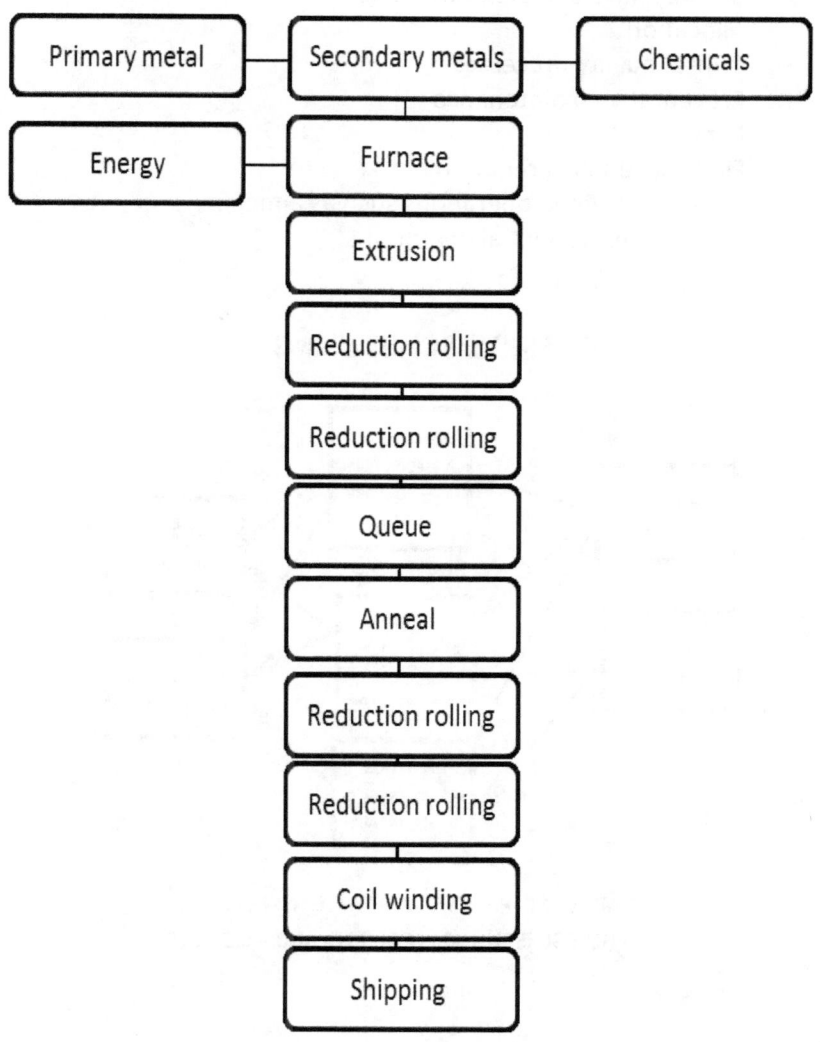

Illustration-Wire Manufacturing

Functional requirements for manufacturing wire

- Orders for correct alloy structures
- Bill may have complex variations
- Allocation
- Critical quality processes
- Preventative maintenance
- In process tracking
- Finite scheduling requirement
- Time constrained operations such as annealing
- Dependent sequential operations

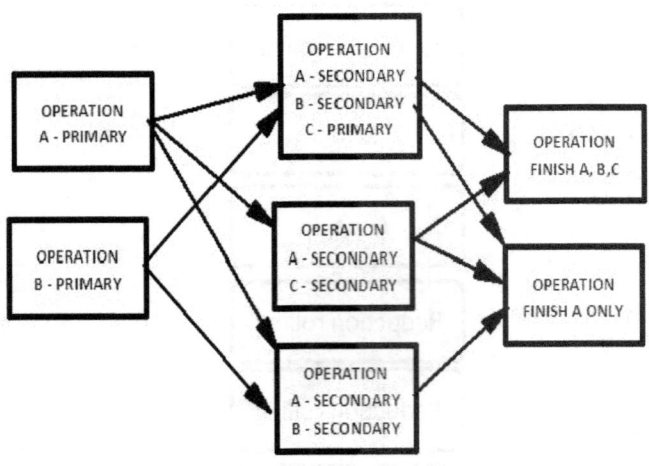

TIME AND CAPACITY CONSTRAINED OPERATIONS
WHERE SCHEDULING IS COMPLEX AND FREQUENT

Illustration - Finite Scheduling

Spider Diagram

Filling out the spider diagram allows matching the business complexity to the software chart on page 226.

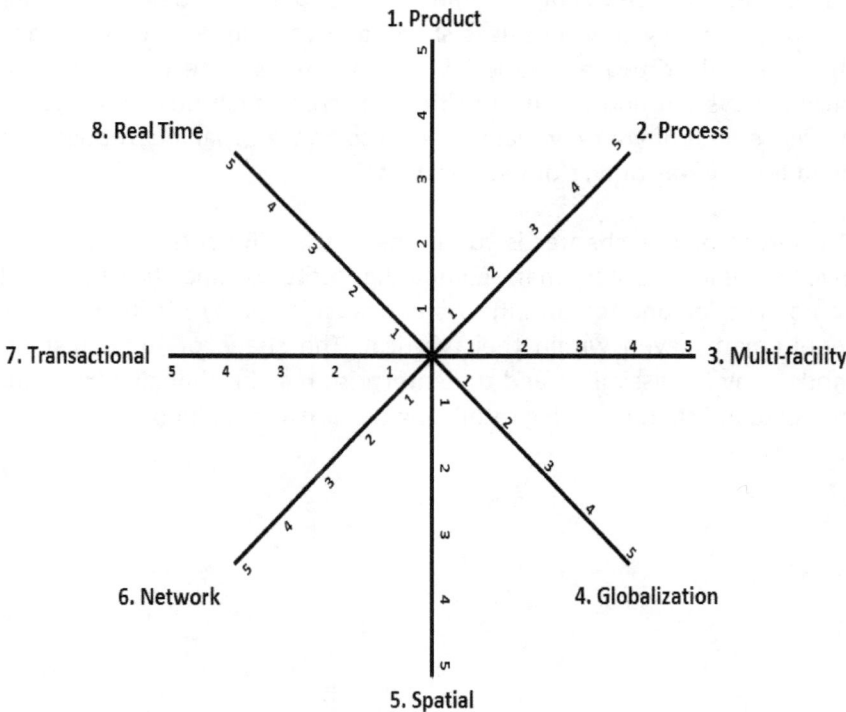

Think carefully about each leg and score it accordingly. One represents the least and five the most complex factor. Show this chart to your potential supplier. Does their functionality free your enterprise to focus on its core purpose? In addition, answer the question "will our system support current and future critical business mission and strategies?"

Summary

Companies must be willing to commit time and money to understanding and documenting their business shape and complexity profile. Ideally, the selected software solution will superimpose precisely over the business system and roll up the finances from each business layer. A precise match of your company type to software capability reduces the need for work-a-round's or modifications.

The intent of this chapter is to emphasis that ERP software selection involves issues other than comparing features and functions. All companies looking for an ERP System must carefully distinguish their requirements even within their vertical. The shape of their business model may be dissimilar, and the enterprise may be changing from one model to another, requiring rethinking the software solution.

9 Just-In-Time (JIT)

In the 1980's the Toyota Production system, based upon a pull system concept, Just-In-Time (JIT) using Kanban and other process management methodologies, threw the ERP movement into confusion. The simplicity and power of JIT caused the reexamination of ERP. Had ERP run its course? Would it follow formulas to the scrap pile?

ERP and JIT operate on different philosophies. ERP concerns itself about relational planning calculations and reporting. Premised on a cycle concept, where usage determines the rate of replenishment, JIT is the philosophical opposite of ERP. There are applications where each is superior to the other, but combined and correctly used, they are powerful partners for managing and controlling operations.

One premise of JIT involves information sharing. Customers provide their suppliers with forecasts, often in the form of their ERP outputs. These forecasts place planned orders in the supplier system.

When forecasts cover the planning horizon, they trigger purchasing and the start of manufacturing operations, such as fabrication. If they are accurate, the product is output just in time for shipment to the customer. If the supplier groups the orders to gain an economy of scale production and overcome system deficiencies, such as long setup times, the resulting inventory is their responsibility.

In the absence of forecasts, fast delivery to customers constitutes short lead-time programs where the customer or the supplier (often both) must carry inventory or break setups. This is not JIT.

Kanban, an original JIT concept, is one of the execution tools.

Kanban

Kanban is a system concept reengineered by Toyota into a useful and powerful planning and control mechanism. Conceptually, Kanban is a cycle, as shown in the illustration below.

KANBAN ROTATION

```
  PART A              PART A             WITHDRAWAL
  CARD 3              CARD 2             TRIGGERED
                                         BY RETURN OF
  A  100       ⇨      A  100     ⇨       EMPTY BIN
       STORES                            PULL SYSTEM

      ⇧                PRIORITY
                       BOARD
                       PART B
  B   50    ⇦          CARD 1
       ACQUIRE
                       PART A            PART A
                       CARD 4            CARD 1
      ⇧
  A  100    ⇦                        A  100
       QUEUE                              USE
```

Illustration - Kanban

In Kanban, transactions and containers rotate between the user and the supplier. The cards (transactions) contain production information and the quantity per container (or any other unit of measurement) needed to produce the part. The cards travel along with the container. When one card/unit is used, it cycles back to the supplier and communicates demand for additional parts production.

The pull concept is a key Kanban feature. The using operation goes to the producing operation for the parts, or they may signal a need by presenting a card with an empty container. Production never pushes parts to the next operation. The Kanban card triggers all activities.

In contemporary ERP systems, electronic signals replace the cards. Kanban requires specific order rules in the ERP system.

The number of Kanban transactions in the cycle controls the total amount of inventory. The greater the requirements, the faster the replenishment demands on production, who must produce higher frequently demands in a shorter production cycle.

Kanban presumes production to inventory. One to one production lot sizes are the core of the Toyota system. While one of the JIT concepts is zero inventories, it is not practical to discard inventory as a tool, and Kanban employs a tightly controlled rotational inventory process. Given the appropriate planning, Kanban has application through the entire supply chain.

Kanban has three major drawbacks. First, all container quantities have to be calculated. Second, Kanban is "blind" to ERP requirements. When an abnormally high-demand order hits the system, the Kanban may be under-planned. When demand drops, it takes time for the Kanban system to reflect the change. Third, Kanban works fine without reporting production or disbursements while ERP needs these transactions for accounting and material's planning. Bar coding Kanban transactions is one solution. As manufacturing moves ever closer to "reality now" and demand-pull, everyone needs access to the information. The financial department and auditors must be involved in all discussions about this issue.

To compensate for these shortcomings, most ERP systems calculate the Kanban quantities and produce the transactions. The system automatically issues or recalls cards rotating through the shop. ERP runs in the background, passing the requirements to a Kanban subsystem.

There are applications where using Kanban cards is superior to electronic methods. This happens where low cost parts requirements are repetitive and highly predictable, but vary considerably in demand at any point. Control is often loose and planning difficult. Putting the information on the cards saves the constant printing and distribution of orders, eliminating paper and electronic work schedules. Here is how one system works:

Using a rack, a worker files the Kanban cards in priority sequence. The quantity has been predetermined and does not change. After using the parts in one Kanban container, the worker takes another to replace it. Refilling the empty container puts it in a queue, waiting for the demand (pull) signal.

There are circumstances where Kanban transactions are required. Smart planning reduces the pain of processing extra transactions. A bar-coding system, (see photo below) automates the process.

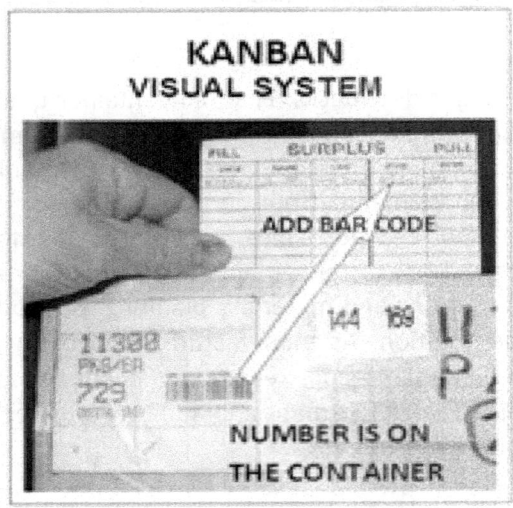

Illustration - Kanban Visual System

The photographs are from one of our distributor clients. The system was operational long before we arrived, but it is classic. The client used the system to manage an active less than case pack picking area with up to forty thousand SKU's. These cards rotated to the case pack storage area or kitting department for replenishment. This area was cycle counted and maintained a 98-99% record accuracy. While installing their new

ERP system, the client modified the package and automated the highly successful techniques.

Another of our clients worked diligently to eliminate ERP and replace it with Kanban. While not successful, they became highly sophisticated in applying the technique. They successfully extended the use of Kanban to manage a high percentage of their purchased parts and components, forming a partial demand pull system. In most cases, they have managed to avoid inventory, other than demand from the cards in the rotation, at both their plants and their suppliers. This eliminated purchase orders, receiving and incoming inspection creating significant savings. All members of this collaboration are zealots for the system. They achieve One to One Production, and the customer never runs out of components.

Summary

JIT and its component, Kanban, are powerful tools for the external and internal SCM. Expanding the tool to demand pull increases its value. In any event, the cyclic functions of JIT blend with the relational functions of ERP, making both stronger and more productive.

10 Third Party Software

Third party software suppliers using best practices are a competitive challenge to ERP suppliers. These companies offer WMS, CRM, logistics, and many other specialized solutions. They focus their investment, research, and time exclusively on their core competence.

Third party systems will contain options and greater sophistication than general-purpose ERP suppliers who have tacked on functionality to increase sales. Third party suppliers frequently have more expertise in their area than ERP suppliers. The key issues are:

- Does the general-purpose package have sufficient functionality?
- How successfully does the third party bolt-on package integrate with the ERP system you are considering?
- How much does it cost?
- What are the integration issues?

Forecast Systems

Forecasts bridge the lead-time gap connecting product acquisition and sale. The most elementary forecast systems use historic demand uploaded into a matrix. The second type uses formulas and exponential smoothing to calculate future demand. The third type uses inventory analysis instead of sales. Service level factors are established by classification or discrete model, MAD (or mean average deviation), service factor, lead-time and the lead-time factor.

Alternative Systems

Third party providers, like IQR International, offer inventory reduction and inventory performance software to both manufacturing and distribution enterprises. These programs often work with SAP, Oracle and other ERP systems. Used by many big companies, including Cummins, Sherwin-Williams, and Kellogg's, the software selection team needs to investigate its possibilities.

It is up to the company evaluating the system to determine the forecasting methodology. Many ERP systems do not include this application, relying instead on third-party suppliers. An assortment of excellent packages exists, capably interfacing with a variety of ERP suppliers. All are subject to the same third party rules.

Sales History

Forecasting systems normally require three to five years of history, which is a data conversion issue. The redefinition of part numbers, short fast lifecycles, and high product turnover rates may force a high level of manual record cleansing.

Most companies maintain sales history based on order shipment instead of the customer request (demand) date. They may be critically different. Some companies include lost sales. Aligning demand and supply to the correct periods is essential to obtain valid forecast results. Examine all the facts before making a decision on the value of converting historical data.

Plan-O-Grams

When shoppers go into Wal-Mart, Target of other retail stores, they find product arranged by SKU. The merchandise is on racks, hooks, boards or other types of displays. How the product gets on the shelf is important because it is labor intensive. A store associate has to take the product out of containers and put it on racks, hooks, or exact positions on the shelf. Many of the retailers demand that supplier's prepackage and precisely sequence product to facilitate replenishment. Businesses servicing large merchandisers need this functionality. Few ERP systems, unless designed specifically for a distribution company, have this type of functionality. The most common software product is Plan-O-Grams.

Manufacturing Execution Systems

Forty years ago, a cartoonist named J. R. Williams joked about workers and bosses in much the same way that Scott Adam shares humor through his comic strip Dilbert. The difference is that William's characters worked on the shop floor while Dilbert develops high-tech software. The depiction, while funny, is of the shop floor as a dirty place where less intelligent people find jobs working for bumbling bosses.

The shop floor of the twenty-first century is not a black hole. It is an increasingly modern and sophisticated place, demanding high levels of technical work skills.

A friend owns a custom machining company, Marten Machining Company, in Steven Point, Wi, that is so clean one could eat from the floor. Multi-axis computer driven machines turn out complex geometric parts in fractions of the time needed for conventional methods. They use integrated engineering design and computer-aided manufacturing software. They run an automated work cell where a robot takes parts from one multi-axis machine and feeds it to another, each in sequence, and then moves the completed part to a conveyor. The operator turns down the lights, and the cell makes parts by itself. This is the new world of manufacturing.

All manufacturing operations are highly variable, with machine breakdowns, worker absences, material shortages, and quality issues occurring on a real-time basis. The ERP planning modules, programmed relationally to bring the ordered components together at the right time, have difficulty with these variables. Supervisors and workers scramble to find alternate solutions while dealing with the domino effect on the schedules. These activities introduce significant waste into the system as people react to change. Late orders result from the inability to see the whole picture and reroute critical orders.

MES replace the operational routing, work center and reporting functions of PAC, moving it to a real-time environment. They process transactions from sources like robots and computer-controlled machines, as well as traditional manual data entry sources. MES systems are mathematics based and require a high degree of definition and rule development. Most MES systems are linear and deterministic, meaning they react to a chain of prior occurrences in response to causal events such as machine breakdowns or rescheduling decisions. Even the best of these systems can only report on the status of operations, and the history of work completed. The better systems use Artificial Intelligence to break the dependence on determinism and replace it with a stochastic process, using probabilistic methods to calculate solutions. This considers both predictive actions and randomness, providing the most effective result, and parallels the way humans deal with complex shop floor problems, and consider all the factors while providing solutions in real-time.

MES Systems are in the providence of VMP. The same selection rules used for ERP apply to MES. Both call for high levels of due diligence and capability analysis. An improperly selected or used MES can penalize operations.

Many companies cannot afford a sophisticated MES and need to look at optional methods to construct highly responsive shop floor systems. Without proper systems, they may build a smart enterprise but one unable to respond to the new intelligence.

Customer Relationship Management

Marketing and sales organizations are reducing the granularity of marketplace and customer specific intelligence. Companies have found data warehouses to be essential applications. Various report writer software extract data and convert it into actionable information.

CRM includes data warehousing. Data warehousing processes information into ever-smaller granularity. CRM provides a foundation for understanding the needs of the customer, supporting the sales force, and gathering intelligence.

CRM applications are gaining popularity, acting as the voice of the customer. Companies offering services and products over the Internet initially embraced it. More companies are demanding sharper marketing intelligence. The use of CRM is pervasive in all industries needing to increase marketing and customer intelligence.

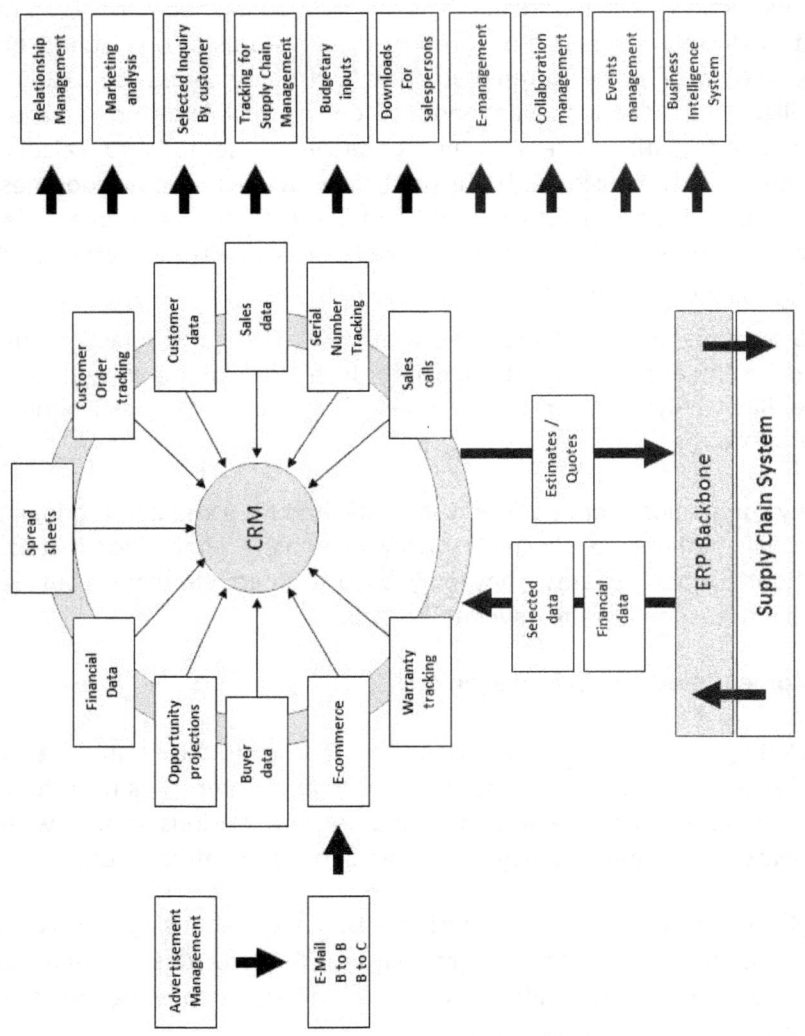

Illustration: Customer Relationship Management Chart

CRM helps a business understand and address customer needs. A complete CRM system provides interface and integration with ERP, feeds and takes information from the supply chain, and breaks down the silos, allowing the free and rapid exchange of information. All the data must be available to sales, marketing, and finance.

ERP companies have added CRM functionality, but some of the best systems are third party, so bundling may not be an advantage. If not, find a CRM designed to easily integrates into the ERP.

Warehouse Management Systems (WMS)

WMS automates warehouse activities. They provide the framework for executing fast response programs with customers, such as JIT.

WMS activity separates manufacturing from distribution ERP systems. Conventional ERP provides tools to manage inventory with transactions and ABC analysis to segment product for control and sales purposes. Location control is included in some systems. Computer assisted put-a-way and comprehensive location management are rare in manufacturing and frequently missing in distribution ERP.

Distributors use a number of sophisticated order picking processes. One of these is "less than case pack"; where product is "pulled" from forward pick areas. Others are wave picking and program pulls. The replenishment system for a forward pick area is unique. Most ERP systems plan the replenishment of the entire warehouse. Distribution manages forward pick areas independently, resulting in two levels of replenishment. Few manufacturing systems provide this capability.

Include WMS functionality like:

- ☐ Data collection systems
- ☐ Real time ordering
- ☐ Location control
- ☐ Picking sequences
- ☐ Bar coding

- ☐ EDI and real time response to customers
- ☐ JIT support
- ☐ Directed pick by item within order

Some ERP packages incorporate a third party WMS to complement the ERP. As with all third parties, make sure it meets the business and budget requirements. In the end however, if the ERP fails to meet operational criteria, it poorly serves the enterprise. Manufacturing companies may have these types of WMS system's requirements.

- ☐ Directed put-away
- ☐ Location control
- ☐ Cycle counting
- ☐ Wave picking
- ☐ Less than case pack
- ☐ Auto replenishment of picking areas from general warehouse
- ☐ Auto placement of replenishment orders total organization
- ☐ Auto replenishment dependent distribution locations
- ☐ Cross docking
- ☐ Palletizing
- ☐ Directed put-a-way
- ☐ Directed picking by SKU within order
- ☐ Program picking
- ☐ Paperless picking
- ☐ Bar code scanning
- ☐ RFID

Summary

There are third-party software packages available for virtually any application. Make sure integration issues with the primary ERP package are resolved. At the same time, fixation on ease of integration may cause you to bypass powerful tools better fitting your needs.

11 Supply Chain Management

Contemporary ERP systems include supply chain management, which has two major components.

SCM is the physical planning and control of logistics, materials ordering and movement. SCM is the focal point for understanding traditional systems functionality.

Supply Chain Collaboration (SCC) is working with customers and suppliers on programs that integrate and manage information and process. For example, product planning and design, trading forecasts, direct inquiry into ERP systems and managing JIT programs. There are four levels defining the degree of collaboration. These are traditional, coordination, cooperation, and collaboration. Many companies have taken the concept to extremely sophisticated levels. Most ERP and CRM systems provide the tools for collaboration. Define your needs prior to purchasing a system.

Vertical Integration

Until the nineteen eighties vertical integration was the core business model for manufacturing. The enterprise was tightly structured. Raw materials were steel, copper, aluminum – base metals and components.

Time was important but synchronizing production was difficult, resulting in long lead-times, high inventories, and marginal delivery performance. The vertical, layered model was a perfect application for a relational planning method like Material Requirements Planning (MRP) and the more advanced Enterprise Resource Planning (ERP). The benefit of MRP was the ability to perform integrated planning and to re-plan operations as conditions changed.

Core Competency

Companies gained success by sticking to core competencies. They farmed out other types of work, or bought from supplier's fitting their core competency criteria.

The core competency model broke the vertical integration model but fragmented the ERP requirement. Specialty companies need software applicable to their business. Companies pouring iron need process-oriented software. Fabrication and custom shops needed order pegging. Assemblers needed to be able to pull parts together "just-in-time."

Horizontal

The global economy and outsourcing altered the model. Business needs include complex logistics, planning, and tracking products from fragmented global supply chains. Control moved from a vertical model and spread to horizontal models. The manufacturing and purchasing relationship changed, shifting greater weight to SCM. In most cases, a hybrid emerged requiring ERP systems that support internal vertical production and complex supply chains.

Manufacturers and distributors have some differences in their view of supply chains. Manufacturers tend to track SKU's. Distribution companies track orders, which may be quite large in terms of quantities and the number of SKU's.

Vertical companies need software capable of planning and controlling a wide range of complex processes, from foundry, to fabrication, machine shop, annealing processes, sub-assembly, and final assembly.

The management and control of supply chains have become as complex as the vertical business model. Expeditors can no longer run around departments and facilities to "put their hands" on the parts. It is imperative that parts and schedules be precise, controlled, and communicated.

The ERP effects from globalization are pervasive. Nearly all enterprises use automated SCM technology, with varying levels of sophistication. Ideally, the functionality allows for international connectivity over the Internet, and provides for order and SKU tracking from supplier to customers, supported by systems where products and information flow fast enough to create a vertically integrated effect.

Given the capabilities of technology to integrate and synchronize demand and supply, an internal supply chain mentality will extend the global model. The key methodology for future success will include the demand-pull principles facilitated by WMS and CRM systems, tied together with integrated information and mobile technology. New MES and SCM using Artificial Intelligence (AI) have the capability to coordinate these complex environments with less human intervention. This portfolio of systems is expensive, but they form the smart shop floor and flexible supply chain.

Compliance Issues

Customers, like Wal-Mart and Target establish compliance issues for both distribution and manufacturing companies. Their strategy is supplying a product at the lowest cost to consumer, meaning paying their suppliers less. Excellent performance means products are available when the customer wants them. Programs include RFID, containers, packaging and display requirements.

Complex Tracking Requirements

UPS, FedEx and many of the Internet stores can track orders anywhere in the system. The days of transporting product to the shipping area and losing track until the product arrives is over. The internal nervous system and the Internet provide tools to track orders/products from the cradle to grave. These tracking and feedback mechanisms are vital to the use of demand flow techniques and manage shipping, cross-docking, and instant feedback from the point of sale.

Barcodes

In many applications, a UPC code is required on the package and/or label. The barcode has applications for reporting from the shop floor, logistics, shipping, and inventory management. Codes include the SKU number, but other embedded codes are used. There are multiple barcode formats, including UPC-A, UPC-E, EAN-8, and EAN-13. Standard barcodes require line of sight scanning one at a time

Define the scanning requirements before selecting a system. If scanning technology is for external use, label printers (output from the ERP system) still must meet quality standards. For internal scanning, install a wireless infrastructure.

Radio Frequency Identification

RFID is not a new technology. The Department Of Defense and Wal-Mart require the use of RFID tags. RFID systems can read multiple tags at one time without a direct scan and contain more information than standard barcodes.

There are many types of RFID tags, broken down into active, with a small power source, and passive, without power. RFID applications include toll road passes, supply chain tracking, inventory control, warehouse management, and cross docking.

Nearly all retail stores use RFID to prevent theft, capture data, and populating POS (Point of Sale) data back through the supply chain. The sales clerk at the store or worker on the line disables the tag before the product passes through the outbound scanning devices. If a tag has not been disabled an alarm sounds.

RFID has asset-management application. The military medical organizations use RFID to reduce inventories and deploy the right resources anywhere in the world. The management of a construction company has the ability to know where every expensive piece of equipment is located.

RFID tags have excellent application in Kanban and JIT environments. The rotating containers can have embedded RFID tags carrying the information needed to manufacture and route the product.

RFID allows rapid cross docking. It facilitates the use of automated sorting and material handling systems. To the provider, RFID means added cost and complexity.

RFID functionality in ERP has nearly become pervasive, but it will not replace traditional bar coding. Carefully determine your company's requirement for scanning technology before selecting a package.

Evaluate the need for scanning equipment and add it to the technology plan. Note: if the plan is to install both ERP and bar coding, the ERP system takes priority.

Master and Inner Pack Configurations

Customers are increasingly specifying detailed packaging requirements and compliance is a significant customer benefit.

The units of measure on each product are in multiples, allowing nesting smaller sales units into larger multiples. While the product within the packages does not change, the SKU number does. It is identifying a unique product. Each customer uses a different configuration. Another variation occurs when the product base packaging is also different. The process provides easy serialization.

These requirements affect ERP, for example, the units of measure for one customer may not be the same as for another. An inner pack for one customer may be four, and for the second customer it is six. Two different containers will be required. In theory, each configuration will require a new Bill of Material. They both require a unique part number.

1. **PACKAGING**

   A. MASTER BOX NUMBER
      dimensions
      quantity per box
      UPC or relevant codes
      box weight

   B. INTERMEDIATE BOX NUMBER
      dimensions
      quantity per box
      UPC or relevant codes
      box weight

   C. SUB INTER BOX NUMBER
      dimensions
      quantity per box
      UPC or relevant codes
      box weight

   D. INTER-PACK BOX NUMBER
      dimensions
      quantity per box
      UPC or relevant codes
      box weight

2. **PRODUCT WEIGHT**

   Calculate weight and accumulated weight for each level

Illustration: Packaging Considerations

Serialization and nesting control functionality are required. Companies dealing with different packaging configurations need to carefully analyze and think through the logic of how they will deal with the issue. This can be a project roadblock if not resolved. You will not want it to become an issue once implementation is in process.

Palletizing Guidelines

The requirements for configuration extend beyond packaging, dictating the palletizing method and location for the different types of labels. An automated warehouse application will require resolution to all of these issues.

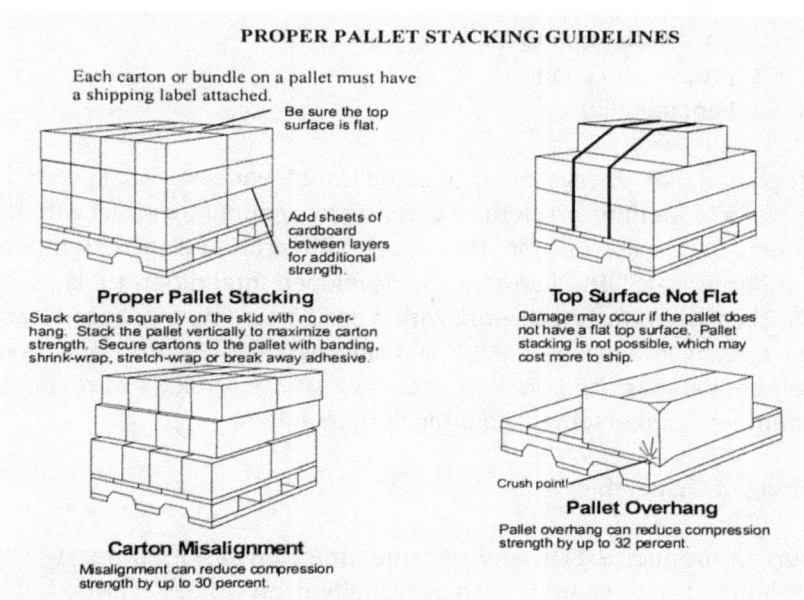

Illustration: Pallet Configurations

Many ERP systems do not adequately handle RFID, complex unit of measures and Plan-O-Gram picking sequences. Nor do they handle pallet stacking as shown in the above illustration. Few older systems will have the functionality. For those using homegrown systems, the problem is greater. These are not simple programming applications. For distributor's, these processes are key to their success as well as a factor in their ERP decisions. The requirement will pass back through the supply chain and include manufacturers.

Integration with ERP

With the intensive move towards automation, systems integration is a prime issue.

1. Databases
2. Languages
3. Field sizes

4. Architecture
5. Hardware dependencies
6. Proprietary code
7. Functionality

Integration has always been a complicated endeavor. Ask your ERP suppliers to identify which third party systems integrate easily with their systems and which do not. The issue of integration is important when considering SaaS. The industry has developed integration tools such as ETS. These tools integrate work within design parameters, but not when one system is written in .NET and another in C++, or if one uses a Progress database and another uses DB 2. There is middleware, but it is expensive, cumbersome, and difficult to maintain.

Timing of Ownership

Sourced product is FOB and becomes the purchaser's property when put on the boat, where it is an availability dead zone. Received but not located product is a second dead zone. Many systems do not properly handle these situations.

Language

In the global workplace, supply chains cross countries, cultures and communication involves multiple countries and languages. Some ERP suppliers provide the ability to switch the actual data view to different languages, a powerful tool. The influx of Spanish speaking workers in the USA places new demands for bilingual ERP, making the workers, regardless of language, more productive.

Currency

Currency conversions follow the same types of requirements as language.

Legal and Compliance

Expecting an ERP system to provide legal functionality is a stretch. Understanding the requirement and how to integrate the functionality, either through modifications or through an interface, is smart due-diligence. Countries will have their specific compliance issues.

Accounting Practices

Countries have different accounting practices. Some are complex, like Sarbanes-Oxley. The ERP system must reflect the requirements in the locations where the business operates or the ERP system resides.

Branch Locations, Mergers and Acquisitions

Many companies have multiple facilities, often functionally different. A fabrication facility has different and greater ERP requirements than an assembly plant. Fabrication involves converting quantities per assembly into various yields or geometric dimensions. For example, a part stamped from coil metal. To place an order for the sheet metal (dependent to the requirements for punched parts) the system has to know how many parts relate to a given amount of metal. If you are a fabricator, due diligence on these capabilities is time well spent.

Mergers and acquisitions can be game changers. One of our clients was an investment company that purchased companies, turned them around and either sold them for a profit or kept them in their portfolio. Investments included manufacturing, distribution, ornamental trees and branded retail enterprises. These are very smart people. They did not try to create one integrated ERP system, recognizing the need for specific function ERP to improve planning and execution. They also implemented VMP aimed at optimizing the performance of each autonomous entity. This approach was marginally more expensive, but simplified future sale because all connections to the corporate entity were clean.

Many companies, limited in facility types, take the opposite approach. They want to integrate all the corporate entities through the ERP system.

The differences include fragmented supply chains, and the internationalism of production and distribution systems. Mergers and acquisitions marry different business units with disparate business types, changing the business dynamics and the software requirements.

Business integration may involve installing the same ERP as the parent company, facilitating corporate planning and the use of a common chart of accounts. The branch locations will lose the independence of their own system. They may also have to wait in a queue for their turn.

It is useful to put members from the branch locations on the project team. Preferably, this will occur before conducting the strategy discussions. Define and include specifications for branch locations as early as possible.

Summary

There are two different facets to SCM but only one system.

- **Supply Chain Management Systems**
    - Managed Inventory
    - Transparent demand processing
    - ERP Integration
    - Warehouse system integration
    - Transportation
    - Planning
    - Activity tracking for orders and events
    - Integrated SCM
    - Activities synchronization
    - Elimination of spreadsheets
    - Integration using scanning technology where applicable

- **Customer / Supplier Collaboration Programs**

  - Traditional – demand / supply issues
  - Coordination – trading information
  - Cooperation - joint product design, integrated forecasting
  - Collaboration – shared VMP (all the above)
  - Synergistic - full partner in demand flow

Decide which supply chain functionality to incorporate into your ERP specifications.

12 Parking lot lists, Modifications and Middleware

Modifications (mods) are one of the more serious issues in the selection process, as they are expensive, time-consuming and require perpetual technical support. When the parent software is updated or upgraded, it may dictate costly changes to the modification or middleware.

Some consulting and software companies apply the Pareto principle to ERP selection. While incorrectly attributed to Italian economist Vilfredo Pareto, Dr. Joseph M. Juran, used the principle to reinforce quality concepts.

He defined the Pareto principle as the vital few and the trivial many. In general, the principle states that focusing quality improvement on the top 20% of the issues will fix 80% of the problems. The principle has many applications, such as twenty percent of the SKU's generate eighty percent of the sales.

It helps to view The Pareto Principle from two perspectives, both insightful.

When matching business needs to ERP functionality, the team may agree that a certain percentage of matches, such as 80%, qualify a system for consideration. Implicit is the need to resolve the remaining 20% through workarounds, program modifications, or process changes.

The second part, the law of the trivial few, states that 20% of the issues are significant, and the rest are not. From this perspective, the company defines the thirty (arbitrary number) critical applications and functionality. If the package provides these critical functionalities, the other eighty percent are less necessary.

This concept has serious weaknesses and teams need to rethink how to apply the 80/20 rule to ERP selection. Any package must pass a reasonability test and contain the required functionality. In the first example, one of the 80% can be the equivalent of a vital few in the second example. Critical functionality has priority in either event.

During the software investigation and the demo, the ERP supplier must help identify the mismatches between your requirements and the software capabilities. If functionality is lacking or extensive modifications required, they must address the issue honestly or take a chance the truth will eventually eliminate their product. You have to decide if there is value in continuing to look at the system. Given correct information, clients tend to make the right decision.

Post the gap issues on a parking lot list at the start of the selection process and update it at every step. It is worth the price and space to devote one large marking board in the war room for problem visualization. Discuss and document proposed solutions and frequently visit progress on defining the solutions. Modifications become especially contentious when they are difficult and take a long time to program and implement. Constantly check if the vital few are covered.

Installing ERP systems improves productivity, but only when a process is changed for the better. Frequently, systems do not make a user's job simpler. It is easy to dismiss their complaints as "not adjusting" to change. Changing processes often complicates some work and reduces efficiency. The user community will point out these situations, but it only counts when someone listens. Increasing the difficulty in one part of the system will increase the efficiency in the rest. Communicate tradeoffs to the user community. If they understand the need, they will help implement the change.

There are numerous stories about software developers who ignore the user community when drawing up the specs for a system. Software programmers often think they have better solutions than users. Failure to listen to the voice of the user causes failure in all the previous categories. Do not let this happen on your project. Certainly, the IT example extends to management, consultants, supplier, and project management.

A West Coast distribution company liked a package, but it lacked full WMS functionality. They could investigate third party systems, or have the supplying company develop the modification. If they had chosen the modification, the business may have inadvertently become a beta site. This would mean underwriting the development and testing of significant new functionality for the supplier.

These are enhancements, not modifications. They can put the project in jeopardy, escalate the cost, and dramatically increase the risk of failure. Software development takes time, and the effect ripples through the project. For the most part, customers are not in the development business. For them, it is a non-value added activity.

Worse, a supplier is not going to make an investment for a specific solution. They might combine the requirements and produce a marketable product. This can extend the implementation, and the result may not be a precise solution. The finished product is an enhancement posing as a modification. When you see this situation unfolding, modify your contract to maximize your investment.

An option might be for the supplier to collaborate with and integrate third-party software. The solution may involve middleware. Evaluate and calculate the benefits and disadvantages of each approach.

The scheduled completion for modifications is often well into the project. This causes a chain reaction. Projects are time phased, and events scheduled in sequence. The hardware schedule may be firm, and equipment may have to wait for the modification.

Training schedules are impacted. The timing for the completion is seldom precise. Since learning is a building-block process, lack of training in one module will make some downstream training incomplete.

Once the modification is completed, the software may fail to perform the task exactly as required. One major cause is the failure to involve the user community in the definition. This is an egregious action.

Software Development Process

It took forty years for the software development cycle to mature. There is no excuse for ignoring it. The magnitude of the change and morphing into an enhancement will become clear in the process. Without resorting to any technical jargon, the iterative development cycle is:

1. User specification – A programmer, systems analyst, or consultant meets with the associates and documents the processes. This includes all inputs, processes, outputs, volumes, who, what, how and why it is done, why is it important, when it is used and where it applies. Define and document potential solutions.

2. Conceptual design - A plan, flow charts, and specifications list describing how the redesigned system will work. This is an iterative process involving the user community, consultant and software developer. The user must drive the definition and agree to the solution. Develop an action plan using checklists for each step. Define test scripts. Prepare three estimates: completion date, hours, and cost.

3. Approval process - Associates approve detail changes because they affect how formulas will function and how the product will work. The user community and project manager should approve all changes to the detail design.

4. Detailed design - The detail design uses the customer specification and the conceptual design to develop program specifics. Frequently, the detail design causes changes in the conceptual design. The user community must be involved in resolving all detail issues. Update the three estimates and document the reason for missed dates.

5. Programming methodologies - The programming conventions used by the supplier, such as language, are transparent. The client needs assurance the design will work, be on time, within budget, and of high quality. The user community must have test scripts prepared

by this time. Prepare and distribute updates: on time or late to schedule and variance to budgeted dollars and hours.

6. Structure the test with associates – Use a test database.

7. Test process - The developer will run a number of tests to debug a program before turning it over to the client for review. In reality, they cannot test all possible conditions. Testing is an iterative process involving the user and developer.

8. Documentation - Document the modification in two forms. Include programming, systems, and user instructions. Specifications for user approval, regardless of programming protocols, must be clear, relevant, and easy to read. Forcing an iterative development process assures that needed documentation will be available.

9. Fix all issues as they occur - Testing may reveal problems in the programming or the design. Heavy workloads and late project performance will create a temptation to avoid the additional work. Saying the system is good enough is not acceptable. Make sure it is a quality application. People will be living with the result for a long time, and flaws creating inefficiencies have long-term effects. The cost to fix it later will increase total cost. This is where the Lean mentality is useful – do it right the first time.

10. Update documentation – the supplier and user community must update the documentation. The supplier must provide written documentation stating the program tested successfully, and no further work is required. It still has to pass the full systems test. Update the three estimates with real data, showing the variance relative to the plan and actual performance. In some cases, this is an invoice.

11. Full systems test – Use the documentation and real data to test the modification. Sign off only after the modification has satisfied all the requirements. The signoff is complete when the user community and the Project Manager accept the modification.

Summary

It costs money to develop or modify software regardless of where it resides. SaaS systems modifications may be as expensive as on-premise applications if the provider allows modifications of any type. Where the software does not fit the business processes, a decision is required, "Do we change the process or modify the software?" Gather the evidence for internal sources and the software supplier before answering the question. Bake the evidence and the decision into the deliverables and the contract.

13 Software Success Factors

Projects have clearly documented deliverables, and failed projects miss due dates or are over budget. Affinity Systems defines failure as "the inability of the completed project to meet the needs and expectations of the enterprise."

It is useful to define common success factors. The law of the jungle postulates "survival of the fittest," stating that all creatures are either the predator or the prey and only the strongest or cleverest will survive. When entering into an ERP environment, keep the analogy in mind.

On the surface, ERP systems appear to be a technical issue, combining software and hardware to build a system where humans are merely components. Nothing is further from the truth. ERP success is dependent on people, not things.

People are the Competitive Advantage

Successful ERP implementations are about people skills. Technological systems do not make decisions, people do. People are responsible for the failure of the system and deserve credit for a successful project.

Personnel involved in an ERP project, from the top of the organization through the data entry clerk, are engaging in a risky career activity. It is important they are all aware of the risks and opportunities.

Following is an event that indelibly etched the importance of keeping associates involved and in the loop.

Some years ago a group of professional businesspersons participated in a supervisory training session. One of the exercises demonstrated how people react in a group environment based on the way they are treated. Eight participants sat at each round table. Per instructions, each attendee counted out a number from one through eight. The session leader sent the ones, threes, and eights out of the room, and then gave the balance of the participants the following directive.

"When the ones return, they are always correct regardless of what they say. Agree with them in every case. Listen to the number threes but regardless of what they say, disagree with them. They are wrong. Treat the number eights as non-persons. Move your chairs close together to keep them out of the group. Do not acknowledge their presence or listen to their input."

Upon returning, the groups brainstormed the key motivators for associates in the workplace.

The number ones, some completely wrong but exonerated and supported by the group, soon relaxed, becoming open and vocal. Some propped up their feet; all demonstrated secure positive body language. The number threes, many of them correct, were increasingly vocal and agitated, raising their voices as they passionately pleaded their cause. Some finally gave up in frustration.

The number eight members met silence when trying to rejoin the group, and were ignored entirely, their presence and input rejected. Before the session ended, in less than five minutes, some of the eights were angrily standing and screaming at their groups.

The Consequences

The experiment had consequences for every group and individual. Where the number three was a true leader, they cooled off. Where the ones had been wrong, the groups brought them back to reality. Most of the groups reassured the threes and eights when they were correct, and that they were wanted but our group's number eight, a friend, and a natural leader, never completely got over the rejection.

The message is that associates treated as number eights are unpredictable. Frustration has three clear outlets:

- Taking it out on others
- Taking it out on oneself
- Sublimate through a creative outlet

Associates will apply energy to your project or to personal purposes. Team members will have their own agenda and perception of the project. You want them to fully participate and contribute their creative energy, and your management style may hold the key. Regardless, specific associates are seldom the direct cause of failure. Properly directed, associates are frequently the reason for project success.

Another situation underscores the power of involvement.

A young man, promoted to Manager, Shop Operations, assumed responsibility for a fabrication complex that included a foundry, machine shop, die-casting, metal punching, and fabrication. With limited machine shop knowledge, he swallowed his pride, put up with the teasing of the operators, and listened as they relayed their knowledge. With little warning, the economy spiked and key customers created an overload of demand across the shop.

Production struggled but continued to fall behind schedule. On Monday, the MSO discovered the scheduler had spent most of the weekend trying to reschedule operations.

Recognizing it was time for drastic action; the MSO called a meeting with the machine operators, and asked for their help. He gave each operator a copy of his schedule. In less than two weeks, the operators had zeroed the late list, and the following week production was stable and on time. How did they succeed when management could not? They had detail knowledge of setups, how to optimize processes, and how to rapidly transition between parts. They eliminated what was normally wasted time.

Associates do not fail when they are trusted and involved. They want to succeed as much as you do. Let them.

From a positive perspective, ERP initiatives are rewarding learning experiences. Projects involve all functions, and team members have the opportunity to learn how activities are integrated. They get to work with other members of the organization in a multi-functional environment. This applies to managers, often insulated from the details, through all team members. History chronicles the bloody trail of good people with truncated careers due to failed ERP projects. Conversely, people from all levels of the shop and office elevate their positions through their contributions, and knowledge gained.

When ERP projects go wrong, there is the inevitable search for someone to blame. Unfortunately, this person is not always the guilty party but often the most vulnerable. It is sometimes difficult, given the high number of activities involved in a project, to determine precisely who is responsible for the failure. Confusion surrounding the activities facilitates blaming the wrong people. This is a horrible approach. Indiscriminate sacrifices violate trust and produce unintended consequences.

The casualties are normally project managers, consultants and persons perceived to be roadblocks. On all projects, some people get the reputation as "being negative." A smart project leader tries to understand their concerns. Start with the premise that associates want to succeed, but they must live with the conversion and make it work.

Executive Leadership

Executive leadership is the key success factor. If the president/CEO is not actively backing the program, park it. Until the leaders are willing to invest time and deal with the expense, personnel shortages, and occasional chaos, the project will not succeed.

A Clear Corporate Direction

ERP projects need a clear corporate direction. Peter Drucker states that:

"Strategic planning is the continuous process of making present entrepreneurial (risk-taking) decisions systematically and with the greatest knowledge of their futurity; organizing systematically the efforts needed to carry out these decisions; and measuring the results of these decisions against the expectations through organized, systematic feedback."

Strategy is the root source for the steps needed to accomplish the vision and mission. There are enterprises failing to strategize for a number of reasons. At the positive extreme, there are executives that clearly understand and share the direction of the enterprise. The issue is having appropriate strategies, not how they are developed. Communicate precise strategies to facilitate the matching process.

Establish a Matching Process

A successful process matching resource and capabilities to the strategy are imperative. The matching process is a series of iterative, GAP analysis.

"A technique that businesses use to determine what steps need to be taken in order to move from its current state to its desired, future state. Also called need-gap analysis, needs analysis, and needs assessment. http://www.businessdictionary.com/

Enterprises considering ERP systems need to work through the organization from one level to another, aligning requirements to capability, and identifying any shortfalls.

Priority

Following a strategic planning meeting, people want instant action. This will not work. If it did, implementation of easy solutions would immediately follow definition. Tactics are plans to bridge the gaps between strategy and capability.

The sequence for developing tactics is critical. There are relationships to other systems, and some steps precede others. For example, if a new

ERP system and Lean Six Sigma are both on the list, which has priority? There is not an easy decision. ERP systems provide infrastructure elements for Lean. Conversely, a Lean Six Sigma may change functionality, requiring different ERP features.

Following are four of the major resource issues. They are:

- o   Availability of qualified team members
- o   Availability of investment capital
- o   Consequences of doing versus not doing
- o   Availability of time
- o   Priority

Larger companies with larger work forces can do multiple projects concurrently. Most small to midsize companies will have to prioritize people and financial resources.

Understand the Business Shape

Buy the right package for the right business:
- Special purpose software where applicable
- One size does not fit all
- Must be scalable
- The more comprehensive the package, the greater the expense and complexity
- Consider all purpose and industry specific software
- Integrate through middleware at critical functions – understanding that middleware creates processing overhead
- Open standards
- Following are types of businesses with different functional needs:
    - Discrete - Repetitive – make to order –make to stock
    - Discrete – Engineer to Order, high quality
    - Process – Make to order, make to stock
    - Distributor – Kit to order, kit to stock, repack
    - Construction – Build projects

Process Mapping

Value Stream Mapping is a Lean concept, partially replacing the old-fashioned flowchart. Regardless of the label, document the processes prior to ERP selection and/or as a part of the VMP. For enterprises determining a direction, this is an excellent place to start. Review current documentation because it is probably outdated.

Team Formation

Put your best people on the program. They all have to be decision makers. One can argue about process owners and stakeholders but select people who will involve their specific sub-teams.

Data Integrity

Make a commitment to Six Sigma quality data conversion, the establishment of procedures and reporting processes. Remember, Garbage in, garbage out (GIGO).

Training

Train everyone. Saving training dollars is a false economy. When buying high capability ERP, companies must train the people on how to use it. This seems obvious but poor training dramatically increases risk factors. You may have to examine new ways to approach the training issue. Young people today use Facebook, Twitter and other social networks. They are literally on-line real time. Some ERP training is classroom oriented and boring. Work with your ERP supplier to find interesting ways to train these demographics.

Sometimes it is difficult to adjust schedules, juggle around children's school hours, or leave earlier in the morning. People make sacrifices to attend training sessions or to read material about how the system works. There are consequences for not making sacrifices. ERP installations frequently result in job losses. The ERP system may simplify the entire workload requiring fewer people. At the end of the project, high performers have a greater chance of keeping their jobs or getting new opportunities.

Improperly trained personnel increase project failure and cause inefficient systems usage. Learning how systems work before installation is the preferred approach. A knowledgeable user community, not all of them project members, is critical to successful implementations. Get the associates involved at the earliest possible time. When converting the systems, they must validate the information, normally on a weekend when their part of the system goes live.

A Proven Selection Process

There are many documented selection processes. Use one that is comprehensive but suited to your needs. There are ERP selection companies providing web services. Several companies provided us with significant input for this book. The selection process should be:

- Business needs driven
- Completely documented steps
- Non-ERP company specific

Part 2 of this manuscript is a generic selection process.

Quality Project Management with Executive Overview

ERP and VMP are not for beginners. These are complex projects, and good project management skills are required. Executive management has a highly vested interest in a successful result. They must stay involved.

There is an old adage, "Those who don't know history are destined to repeat it." Edmund Burke.

While you must know and understand what causes failure, it is just as important to understand the reasons for success.

- ☐ Top management was actively involved in all aspects of the project.
- ☐ The program was a top corporate priority.
- ☐ Training was extensive and included executive management.
- ☐ The project followed a structured process.
- ☐ Execution was relentless and thorough.

The executive staff must interact with the project team and determine realistic expectations. Normally, ERP projects require VMP to achieve planned ROI. Factor this reality into the expectations. Project ROI may be greater inventory turns, improved customer service, higher shop efficiency, overall reduced cost and increased profits. The metrics used to justify the project become the performance measurements.

Summary

ERP projects are serious and complicated undertakings. Set realistic goals and expectations for the project. Prepare the organization. People are responsible for the strategies, assessment, future state, and the selection. Associates know if the ERP system matches with company needs. People are responsible for project failures. Blaming the system is futile and useless. A pig's ear will never make a classy purse, but someone bought the pig's ear and paid for the attempt.

14 Lessons Learned – Stories from the Dark Side

This was a contentious and fun chapter to write. For many it is the most important because it deals with actual situations. They are the other side of the previous chapter.

These stories involve the groups of key project players. It is important to understand the relationships. These cases must not distract from the positive and necessary role each group plays. Executives have authority because they have earned it by making the right decisions for their companies. The majority of consultants, both independent and those representing the supplier are committed and capable. The user community is normally dedicated "and gets the job done."

Individuals are human with egos. Complex system theory tells us the same thing our grandparents did, "mix people all together (in a team), and you're never certain what will come out." Self-organization will occur and some self-destruction. Ego and authority clashes can destroy ERP projects, but also keep them from failing. No one likes to lose.

Executive Management

The importance of top management involvement cannot be overstated. The argument is that once management has agreed to the program with funds, staff and delegated responsibilities, they have completed their task. This is a perilous path filled with pitfalls. Executive management must own the program. This means backing the program, establishing priorities, frequent and consistent monitoring of progress and attendance at team meetings.

Executive Priorities

A group of investors acquired a large company in the western part of the United States. The previous owner, who disliked computer systems, remained president of the organization. The investors made the decision that a new ERP system was essential. The president, unconvinced, was quite disruptive, pulling team members from training sessions and preventing others from working on the project. It took months for ownership and the executive champion to force the right priority into the project. In the end, the president became a believer, convinced the system would improve, not harm customer service, and actively participated in its successful implementation. The reason for the major delay was not the president; it was the misrepresentation of functional capability by the supplier.

There are frequently casualties in ERP projects. In the example above, the executive champion (the CFO), the consultant, director IT, project leader, and the programmer responsible for data conversion lost their jobs.

Free Consulting Services

One game played by clients is trying to get something for nothing from consultants. It is humorous to observe the amount of ingenuity expended in this effort.

One version involves individually interviewing consultants, getting solutions without spending money. Some executives think it is a smart technique but most understand the game. It causes problems only among those who believe they are getting something for nothing.

Consultants and other service providers limit information. While discussing tentative solutions, they will not spell out the dimensions of the solution, what knowledge is required to implement it, the inherent dangers, or the process required to achieve it. Lacking accountability for the recommendation, consultants may provide misleading direction. Most walk away but word gets around.

This game has numerous variations and one is worth mentioning. Our policy is to make a site visit, including an exhaustive plant tour, and meet their people. It is our due diligence to find how to help, and determine if potential clients will be good business partners.

A manufacturing company contacted us explaining the CEO "had a problem" even talking about investing in ERP. Affinity Systems LLC agreed to the sales visit. Later, their team called to set up the meeting, admitting they had a prepared plan. When asked if they intended to bid the project. The answer was no. The obvious intent was obtaining a free plan validation. It was a non-value adding activity; a waste of our resources, and we declined. It does speak to some company's mentality. Would you accept the advice of someone who has not studied the situation? As a consulting company, would you have so little integrity as to validate a million-dollar plan without understanding the business situation? We want companies to succeed regardless of any games and attempts at self-destruction, but we do not waste our resources on non-value adding games.

Game playing raises other integrity questions such as:

- What other games will the client play?
- Will they pay for services received?
- If so, how long will service providers have to wait for payment?
- Will you be subject to lawsuits?
- Will our reputations suffer from remarks made by the client company to other companies?
- Will they post unfair reviews on line?

Our advice to client companies is to play games at your own risk. As in most things, you get what you pay for.

Culture

Culture plays an important role in ERP selection and the success of Lean Six Sigma programs. Culture dictates how companies think, what actions they take, and how they react to variables. It plays a direct role in the success of system's projects.

Executive management sets the company culture. Some companies are fixated on the way they do business and cultural paradigms become ingrained. Some companies are family-owned and in transition to control by other family members. Others companies have narrow perspectives of ownership. The employees are unexposed to alternative systems and techniques. They have literally passed the knowledge, with its suppositions, internal myths, and traditions, from one generation to another or from one employee to another. Outsiders joining the company must conform or be pushed out. Sometimes, with enough outside influence, the knowledge and habits of the group slowly change.

A friend, Fr. Alan Sloviak, uses a wonderful analogy to illustrate the narrowness of our perceptions. It is variation of "The larger the island of knowledge, the longer the shore of wonder," by Ralph W. Stockman.

"If our personal knowledge is an island, and all the knowledge in the world the ocean, the shoreline represents our appreciation for what we do not know. Consequently, as we learn and gain knowledge, our island becomes bigger. At the same time, our shoreline grows and there is even more we know we don't know."

Here is an example of how culture can influence the process.

The executive staff of a farming implement-manufacturing company felt the need to install a new ERP system. The problem was that three years prior the company had hired a consulting group to reengineer their core processes. The project was a dismal failure, resulting in inefficiencies and hard feelings among the workers. The president/owner of the company was angry and disappointed. He decided all ERP technology was unnecessary, expensive, and untested. After all, the business had grown steadily, its products were highly acceptable in the marketplace, and they made money.

The president consistently rejected the pleas of the executive staff to fix the systems. ERP and consulting companies visiting the company instantly saw the need for a new ERP system and understood the opportunity loss. Eventually, the company floundered and a larger firm bought them. The acquiring company took immediate steps to increase efficiency by installing a new ERP system and implementing Lean, but it was too late. The company dropped the agricultural line, unable to compete in the global economy.

Our experience has shown that companies with closed cultures believe they have the expertise to choose an ERP system, but set themselves up for failure by making decisions based on false premises. They frequently do not understand the failure is a self-inflicted consequence.

When visiting China, at a University in Beijing with an APICS contingency, our groups discussed closed cultures. The professors stated that Chinese management distrusted formal systems, making the software decision without performing due diligence. The failure rate for ERP projects was very high, estimated by the professors at greater than 70%. The blogs from consultants around the world indicate they repeatedly encounter this situation.

ERP projects will meet significant resistance in cultures not geared to change and innovation. Some of the problems are:

- Presumed knowledge
- People not willing to change
- Lack of trained personnel to do the project
- Personnel trained to task and not to system
- Fixation on current processes

It is ownership's responsibility to recognize fixation and the need to implement a business transformation process aimed at cultural change. Contemporary businesses in the global economy are knowledge driven. Significant waste in terms of time, money, and resources may occur before ownership realizes the business is moving in the wrong direction.

Obviously, culture influences the ERP process. If the cultural imperatives become a roadblock, management must determine how to eliminate the constraint through training and/or transformation.

Software Companies

Like every business, software products range from simple to complex. The number of programmed features and depth of functionality determine complexity, which in turn increases implementation costs.

Due diligence may feel like a waste of time and money, but weighed against the high cost of failure, it is imperative. If necessary, hire a knowledgeable consultant to speed up the process and point out subtle pitfalls.

ERP selection involves the formation of a partnership. It is important to establish trust and confidence in both the relationship and the process. The ERP industry mirrors the integrity of society in general. This includes subtle or explicit bribes, half-truths, and outright lying about capabilities and support. Following are some unfortunately true stories.

Bribes and Kickbacks

A high-ranking executive for a distribution company in Los Angeles enjoyed going to Las Vegas. A software company told him to select their product and "those trips could be frequent." The executive immediately took the supplier off the list, although prior to the bribe, the supplier was the top choice.

At a vertically integrated forest products company, the ERP supplier told the IT director, "If a particular ERP supplier is picked, some money will be transferred to your checking account each month." Executive management was informed, who in turn told the supplier to "get lost."

An independent consultant was offered a month of schooling "all expenses paid" as an incentive to pick a specific system. While this is a common practice, it compromised finding the best ERP solution to meet the needs of the client. The software company withdrew from the evaluation.

Deceptive

Responses to RFPs can be deceptive. While claims may not be a lie, they can be misleading.

A Midwestern glove company purchased a textile industry specific package. The ERP provided a bill of material, work center, and routing processes as advertised. The supplier failed to mention no one had been able to make the engineering applications work effectively. The bill of material and ERP functions were complex, convoluted, and unmanageable.

The client fired the consulting company then hired another to finish the project. When installed, the system proved useful for the office and accounting functions but not for operations. It failed to meet its original objectives and expectations. This is an example of how industry-specific packages may not fit all companies in a "vertical." A standard generalized and less-expensive system would have provided this manufacturer with excellent functionality.

Ease of use is often a selling point. A multi-plant company located in Los Angeles was installing a complex ERP in the headquarters plant. One of the branch plants, located in Arkansas, needed an inventory solution and did not want to wait for the corporate system. They purchased a third party inventory location system, premised on ease of installation. Out of the mainstream, due diligence was bypassed. The software never worked correctly, resulting in chaos and absorbing vital resources needed by the ERP team, wasting time, talent, and money.

The successful implementation of the new ERP with integrated warehouse functionality finally put down the non-functional package. The moral of the story is to be careful about "temporary fixes." They can destroy priorities and schedules. There are many temporary systems that no one has the time or courage to seek out and replace.

Often, systems are not what they appear to be, and are harder to install than thought. It will always take longer to get it done than planned.

Details, Details

A distribution company selected software based on its automated picking capability. It supposedly provided the ability to back flush shipped product and automatically reorder shelf replenishment. The supplier programmed the feature, disguised as a modification, for a sister manufacturing plant. To get the general functionality, they converted the system to use bar coding at the item level, preventing the automatic allocation of product to an order, a frequent distributor requirement. The functionality was incapable of advancing item by item within an order to facilitate directed picking. Worse, the system would not support the "less than a case pack" application, a significant disadvantage for a distribution company.

Lying

An ERP supplier made a presentation promising multi-plant processing capability.

The client needed to integrate business units in different states, and share information on receiving, inventory availability, shipping, and production requirements by location. All business activity would fold into the divisional level. At the end of the month summarized data needed to roll up into consolidated statements. The complicating factor was multiple charts of accounts.

The solution proved to be individual plant codes and the team members charted the precise method, and one supplier signed off on the capability. After a serious debate, the team chose their package, inferior to the shop but ideal for finance. A competitor, heavy on operation's functionality, honestly stated they did not have multi-plant capability. They lost the sale. When the customer started working through the system's codes, multi-plant only applied to the financial module.

Was this a half-truth, a lie, or just a misrepresentation of the software? The system was not capable of meeting an important strategy.

Fortunately, the software company was rewriting the package, and they included true multi-plant capability, solving the problem.

Some ERP companies use these tactics because they work. When false claims or actions affect implementation or operational effectiveness, legal actions are an option. The problem is that lawsuits are disruptive, time-consuming, and expensive. The business suffers in multiple ways. It fails to get performance from the software and consumes resources trying to recover damages. When failure becomes public information, it may cause embarrassment or even affect the value of the company. Alternative arrangements may partially satisfy the needs of both companies. The solution is due diligence and using a structured program process to select and install complex information systems. In other words, prevention is the best solution.

Consultants

Consultants make convenient and easy targets, sometimes bringing it on themselves. Here are few examples.

Charging by the Pound

Consultants perform assessments and advise management. The longer it takes to perform the assignment, the larger the pile of paper and the fees. At the end of the assessment period, consultants present a large binder report stating, "Here are our results." The report meets management expectations, and they read only the executive summary. The assumption is the thicker the report, the greater the "due diligence." This may actually be measuring waste, not actionable information.

Credit

The large assessment report is traditional. The sad reality is many associates devote time and energy defining the current state and developing solutions. Their ideas are bundled into the recommendations and the consultant gets the credit. When it is time to implement the same people roll their eyes and gripe. "We've been telling management about this problem for years. Now some smart-ass consultant takes our ideas to the boss, and they love it. Look who gets the reward and who has to work extra hours to implement it?"

The chapter on business assessments defines a superior way.

The Consultant as the Project Manager

A convention management company hired an outside consulting firm to head up an ERP project. The board member responsible for hiring the consultant had facilitated the selection of the ERP solution. While the technical capability of the IT manager was never in question, his ability to manage and control the project was in doubt. The IT manager attempted to undermine the authority of the consultant and conflicts proved constant, bitter, and disruptive. In discussions with other consultants, these conflicts are pervasive issues, bringing into question the use of a consultant as the project manager.

The Consultant as Facilitator

A paper converting company interviewed and hired an independent consultant to support and mentor an internal project manager with little ERP experience. In this case, the knowledge from the consultant facilitated a smooth and successful ERP implementation.

Frequently, the consultant helps perform the business needs assessment, builds the business case, and the action plan, and may be involved in preparing the team for evaluating ERP packages. When the selection is complete with a knowledgeable supplier team onsite, re-think the role of independent consultants.

There are conflicts among consultants, IT personnel and independent consultants. Each sees the other as a competitor for power and money. The executive champion must strongly exert authority and make sure actions benefit the client.

Ability to Work with the Company Employees

Consultants must work with the user community. As the project unfolds, the consultant will be a significant voice for the user while protecting top management interests. Consultants need user involvement to make positive change and must look out for the best interest of their client. One of the key challenges is to make sure the ERP supplier follows a proper project protocol. (See the chapter on "Modifications)."

Billing Hours

Stories abound about consulting companies deliberately extending project steps to increase billing hours. The RFP process, discussed later in the book, is open to abuse. Most consultants bill by time, materials, and expenses. A few pad the hours they work. A frequent technique is doing unnecessary work. Avoid this by having a clear agreement on project scope and rates prior to hiring. Some consultants charge travel time, an expensive proposition. Others charge for hours worked while in the airplane, a negotiable accommodation. Set up internal support people to do clerical jobs consultants perform as revenue streams.

Some companies invite abuse with consultants. Scheduling a two-hour meeting is an example. If the consultant has to travel, it cuts hours of potential billing. Discuss billing hours up front. This helps prevent abuse from both sides of the desk. Agree on hours, rates, and situations. Many consultants avoid the problem by charging by the day, other by charging a minimum of four hours, a few by simply overbilling. An increasingly popular method is to charge by total project.

Normally, consultants bill for all expenses but there are logical limitations. Picking up a large bar tab causes extreme tensions. Conversely, fleabag hotels and bickering over meal receipts causes unnecessary hard feelings on both sides. These represent extremes, but the situation underscores the message. Agree on all the parameters ahead of time and treat each other with respect. Clearly spell out the deliverables, scope, and expectations of the contract.

Once In and Never Out

Once in and never out occurs when consultants extend their revenue streams by failing to pass ownership to the users, adding cost, and dependence as well. The consulting firm is responsible for making the client independent. When the job is completed, so are the consultants.

ERP Company Consultants

ERP consultants run the gambit from good to beginners. They may lack systems and operational experience in your business type. Many consultants wrongly act like the project manager, working to the best interest of their employer first and the client second.

The executive champion and project manager must manage the performance of all consultants. When the project experiences problems and it will, the finger pointing will start, often at the ERP consultant, who will point right back. When a system is in trouble, identify and fix the problem quickly. This is one reason for internal project managers. Even when the person lacks experience, they can get the job done with the backing of a competent consultant, and involved top management. Internal leadership keeps the power and knowledge within the business.

Safeguards

Make sure the consultant has experience with your business type and model. If affiliated with an ERP company, including multiple favorable experiences with a specific ERP supplier, they may favor that software supplier. Why pay them for a complicated selection and RFP process, demos, and taking team members away from work and making site visits when the result is predetermined? Your consultant must have only one-goal – to find the best ERP solution for your business. You do not need a highly paid pseudo-sales representative.

While not logical to most, these activities may be part of an act to prove "due diligence" to executive management or the Board of Directors.

Change the role of the independent consultant to audit progress for management. The project leader and the ERP consultant may take undesirable shortcuts. An independent consultant reporting to the executive champion can be a great leveler.

Failures caused primarily by ERP suppliers are:

- Failure to understand the needs of the client
- ERP software unable to support the business and strategic plans
- Mistimed training
- ERP suppliers who bribe, lie or misrepresent the product
- Failure to admit problems while blaming others
- Inadequate modification process
- It is on the way (vaporware)
- Pricing policies
- Not listening to the associates
- Failure to use the ERP development process

While appearing to paint consultants in negative terms, Affinity Systems LLC is a consulting company. Most consultants are committed to finding the best solution and treat clients fairly. While often blamed for poor implementations, the failure rate would be much higher without us. In addition, it is easier to tell the Board of Directors "our consultants led us down the wrong path" than admit that internal conflicts caused the failure. Consultants are a useful and vibrant resource bringing experience and knowledge to the process. Like any resource, you must understand and appropriately work with them. From our experience, companies installing ERP systems need to hire a proven consultant partner. Problems occur when:

- Consultants are used instead of an internal project leader
- Unknowingly using consultants who also represent ERP providers
- They fail to understand the needs of the business
- Failure to translate the business needs into software requirements

- Failure to admit problems
- Abuse the relationship
- Failure to establish implementation method –Phased or Big Bang
- Failure to listen to the user community

User Community

The user community is frequently the largest variable in the ERP implementation. Consultants teach executive management and project teams that good people can make a bad system work and poorly motivated and untrained people can make the best system fail. Our experience reinforces that this observation as true.

15 Failure to Look Beyond the Status Quo

Technology generates change and dynamic organizations encourage and promote it. In other companies, there is an ingrained adherence to the status quo, with resistance to changing how people work. Use the need's assessment phase to determine how people will react. There is some truth in the statement that people are not afraid of change but only afraid it will negatively affect them. In other cases, they simply do not know any better or have different agendas.

An agricultural business in the Northwest decided to implement a new ERP system. One of the owners, a graduate from a prestigious school and proponent of large business, had project responsibility. The executive staff had predetermined the need for a classic ERP system. They hired a consulting firm and began the assessment process.

Several facts became immediately apparent. They had lightweight engineering and capacity planning requirements, with shallow bills of material. The core issue was managing product from one location to another. Overall product demand consistently exceeded supply. They used an elaborate allocation system to control sales. The executive staff firmly believed the business would be out of control without it.

All the reviewed ERP software provided allocation routines, but involved rethinking and changing the way they viewed information. They were unable to make the leap from one method to another. We call this fixation, narrowing the perspective and ability to deal with problems outside of their comfort level.

A training program designed to address the limited knowledge and cultural aversion to change proved fruitless. They displayed little interest. The company fired the consulting firm because "they didn't understand the business," then installed a tier one system at much greater cost and internal effort than necessary.

We pursued the question. If they wanted a tier one ERP solution, why did they take an alternate path? The answer was interesting. The president wanted the prestige of working with a specific tier one software supplier. He first had to satisfy the board of directors that "all steps had been taken" to find a less costly solution.

It is important to prepare the organization for change by using communication meetings, change management classes, involvement of functional team members in the business assessment process.

Problem Employees

Most installations have employees who fail to do their jobs. Managers or supervisors must convince these employees to participate positively. If they do not, move them outside of the program or the organization.

Some people solve problems, but others lack this ability. It is important to work with team members and the user community to resolve problems affecting their areas of responsibility. There are associates who will not take responsibility for solving problems. They wait for someone to either supply a solution or engage them in finding a solution. Individually address these situations.

Commitments

Nearly all members of the project team and user community will have to perform all or part of their regular job. Only the most enlightened or cash flush organization backfills their project team. Projects drag because associates fail to keep commitments. The weekly follow-up meeting keeps the project moving, but daily communications are required to make things happen. Determine why tasks are not completed. Isolate and address the person or situation immediately. If work backs up, find a way to catch up.

Experience has shown that in-house project leaders enforce commitments effectively and retain a positive performance. Internal management has the power to hire, fire, promote, reprimand, or otherwise directly affect employees. The consultant only has positional power and not direct authority. In conflicts, internal personnel nearly always win over the consultant project leaders. In general, fewer conflicts occur when the company uses a strong company project leader interested in getting a project done and not in playing politics.

Trashing Ignorance

Thrashing ignorance (Ladder of Inference) is one of the most wasteful occurrences in any project. For example, someone brings up a problem, real or implied. Participants feed additional assumptions into the discussion. Someone else acts on the assumption, suggesting solutions. They debate the solutions and agree on a fix.

The consequence is the creation of an assumed solution for a hypothetical problem. Thrashing ignorance is deeply rooted in the workplace and society in general. It is a waste of time, and an indulgence in procrastination.

When signs of thrashing occur in team meetings, test for fact or assumption. If dealing with verifiable facts, ask if you have the right forum. If not, set up a future meeting to focus on the issue. Do your homework and get the facts, then define solutions for real problems.

Not Me Coach

Events go wrong in every project, such as late or poor-quality task completion. Management is going to override priorities. The lists of things that can go wrong are endless. Remember Murphy's Law that if something can go wrong it will, but strongly adhere to O'Tooles interpretation, that "Murphy is an optimist." Do not let situations slide or escalate. Address and fix the problems immediately.

No one wants to take the blame for errors or problems. The project manager must develop plans, assign responsibilities, and clearly define activities. This establishes responsibility and accountability throughout the project. Team based reward systems help prevent "not me, Coach" responses. The failure of an individual affects the reward system for all members, bringing pressure on non-performing persons.

Summary

The selection process provides some protection from negative effects.

- Top Management involvement
- Hire knowledgeable consultants
- Proper leadership structure
- Due diligence
- Perform a thorough GAP analysis
- Build a knowledgeable and skillful ERP evaluation team
- Ask the right questions
- Get into the details
- Keep everyone focused
- Insist on the involvement of the associates
- Write modification agreements into the contract

16 Security

Data security is a high-level responsibility. The world of IT and the Internet is replete with data and identity theft. Competitors, foreign companies, and governments swipe critical business secrets. The biggest problem, however, has not been data stolen over the Internet, but loss of millions of records through internal theft and sloppy security.

Management seems to know about computer viruses, worms, adware, Trojans, and other threats to information systems. Security issues with software, including recovery, prevention, loss of proprietary information, cost billions of dollars each year. Loss of intellectual property rights (IPO) is beyond calculation.

Every enterprise must implement a security plan supported by the ERP solution. Start with security levels and limited record access. Establish policies to control what people can take home, data encryption methodologies, mobile devices, and daily accountability.

The cloud presents special security problems since the data is not directly under your control. In fact, the major providers have created layers of security far beyond those normally established and used on premise, but others do not. Like every other ERP issue, there are the beautiful, good, and ugly. Sorting out the facts by supplier and SaaS provider are part of the due diligence process.

Before selecting the ERP solution, establish a security administration policy stating who will have the authority to provide access. If data is limited to specific passwords, there must be a menu for each one, for example, specific password usage on one computer at a time. When mapping the old system to the new one, determine who has access to records or files. During implementation, prepare a "sandbox" system to test without affecting the live system. This is a good place to start refining who needs what information.

In this age of SCC, it may be necessary to allow customers or suppliers to inquire into the system. Make sure there is sufficient firewall functionality to protect data and the entire system from abuse by all connected parties.

Big data will increase integration and security requirements. Develop specific policies regarding mobile technology, including personal and company provided equipment.

Summary

Attending security seminars was part of the due diligence for this book, then analyzing volumes of information, including horror stories. Security and safety can be an alarming topic, and the unprepared or arrogant enterprise is flirting with disaster. Security is an executive-level responsibility. From a stockholder perspective, the president/CEO, and other executives are probably legally liable for business losses attributed to data theft. Security is not an afterthought, and we recommend security audits by a reputable firm.

17 Process Improvement -Value Management Programs

Business systems equate to highway systems. In the early nineteenth century, the automobile replaced horse-drawn buggies but cars needed level and paved roads to operate effectively. VMP paves and builds interchanges on business highways, the infrastructure for integrated planning and operations.

Business operates most efficiently in companies with documented, carefully thought out, practical and effective systems. Workflows are clean and sharp. Process documents spell out capability. The people are trained and cross-trained. The reporting systems have integrity. In Lean terminology, this is standard work. The company conducts business with speed and high performance.

Multiple decision points are in the process. One involves choosing a software solution, or installing VMP. The priority decision is not an easy one, because they are separate endeavors.

Business improvement programs take two basic forms, revolutionary and evolutionary.

Revolutionary

Revolutionary change occurs when the entire business, starting with the business model, undergoes dramatic change. This is process reengineering as defined by Michael Hammer in his books "The Engineering Revolution" and "Beyond Reengineering." Augmenting these concepts is "Breakthrough Thinking," expanding the boundaries of conventional methods.

Reengineering fell into disfavor when blamed for downsizing, resulting in job loss, instead of receiving the deserved credit for increasing productivity. The loss of jobs is an unfortunate consequence of increased productivity. Companies attempt to avoid layoffs by increasing business volume to offset the effect of productivity. The problem is that reengineering normally reduces costs and jobs faster than volume increases. Cost-cutting and productivity programs get special attention in the down cycles, and volume receives greater attention when the economy is favorable. It is difficult to change the momentum of either extreme.

Enterprises considering any type of transformation process will evaluate the level of change required. Transformational programs place extremely heavy demands on the organization. Reengineering significantly increases both opportunity and risk.

Business reengineering would normally take precedence over an ERP project because it potentially changes the system requirements. Both should be components of the future state.

Evolutionary

Programs like Lean Six Sigma are evolutionary and used to make current processes efficient and less wasteful. While reengineering techniques are used, evolutionary change is issue focused.

Lean Six Sigma programs put demands on the enterprise for priority and resources. Virtually, all ERP implementations will require process changes. The issue will not be whether a change is required but to what extent and how the change process is controlled.

Lean Six Sigma deals with the grunt world of work and quality. Be less concerned with labels than principles driving these philosophies. The probability is that these labels will morph into something else, but the core principles will remain constant.

Principles of Lean Six Sigma

Lean Six Sigma is a continuous improvement methodology devoted to chopping out waste by empowering associates to innovate. Lean Six Sigma promotes methodologies to document, analyze and determine root causes for problems and then define solutions. The focus for this book is to select an ERP system and Lean techniques are subordinate to our objective. Abundant information on Lean is available from multiple sources.

Some companies may want to take the time to teach Lean Six Sigma documentation techniques before performing the current state study. This action may distract from the objective. We do not advocate implementing ERP and Lean Six Sigma in parallel. Each is a significant project that demands its own priority. We do advocate inclusion as part of the needs assessment.

Here is a test to evaluate the effectiveness of your Lean program.

Do you have a Lean Six Sigma System? Take this test

Ask the program administrator for a list of projects.

There will be active tasks with planned completion dates. Completed projects have attached savings and completion dates.

Failure to find a log directly equates to a lack of program or a poorly managed one.

If the data are available, the rest is math.

- *Number of completed events*
- *How long it took to do them*
- *Payback dollars*

Compare the result to the administrative cost of the program, both internal and external. Armed with this information, assess whether you have a Lean program.

If the answer is yes, ask a follow-up question. Have the associates been empowered to participate in the program, or simply to go along? True Lean programs have empowered team members actively making positive change.

The first step of the software selection process is establishing the current business state by performing a need's assessment. ERP and lean Six Sigma require a problem identification and resolution methodology.

Affinity Systems has developed one called ACTION, originally presented in our book "Crunch Time for Health Care," dealing with VMP in hospitals and other medical facilities. We carry these principles through the structured process.

Analyze

Use situational analysis to increase awareness, define, and isolate opportunities for improvements.

- Separate situations from the background
- Bring components sharply into focus

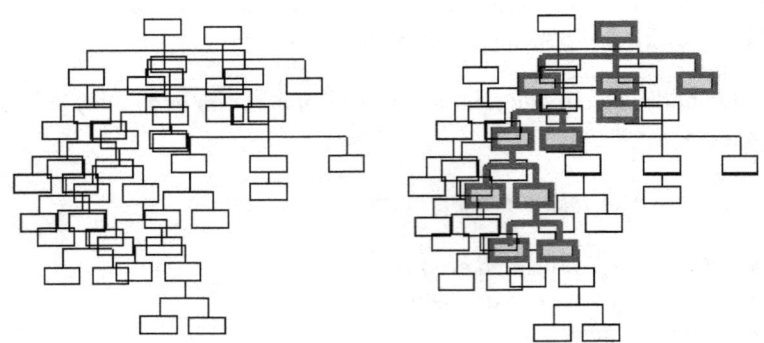

After target identification:

- Quantify the issue
- Test your interpretation

Ask:

- Is it a real problem?
- Does it justify an additional study?

- Is it small enough to make the change simple?
- Just do it or start a formal process?
- Is it critical, if yes take appropriate action?

Cause

Perform a root cause analysis to identify the true cause of the problem.

Following are the principles for getting at the facts:

- Define the problem in writing
- Gather evidence
- Illustrate in visual terms – flowchart, photograph, illustration, video
- State in mathematical terms if possible
- Separate the symptoms from the problems
- Ask if it is a real problem
- Document the problem and the systems it feeds (Input-process-output)
- Document who does it and how the work is performed
- Work through each layer up and down, ask 'WHY' multiple times to get to the root cause
- Document obvious solutions and alternatives
- Make sure the problem is worth solving
- Define the impact on performance and possible unintended consequences
- Define the impact on revenue stream
- Define impact on corporate values
- Define the impact on the mission
- Additional definition may be required to gain proper focus

Think

Analyze the problem and potential solutions. Apply the principles for thinking and develop future state solutions. Test the future state solutions.

- Work beyond the obvious and the quick fix
- Overcome bias
- Force yourself to get information that may prove you wrong
- Acquire additional knowledge
- Use tools for problem solving
- Seek expert opinion
- Research – if and how was this problem solved before (perhaps in a different environment or industry)
- Collaborative evaluation
- Team evaluation of evidence, cause and effect
- Analyze a problem in reverse
- Extrapolate a solution – can you backfill facts and logic
- Defeat path most traveled (fixation)
- Define how to make the solution visual
- Test solution with customer
- Experiment
- Critical review
- Ask what if, why not and so what
- Think through consequences of potential solutions
- Make a decision to fix, ignore or postpone problem resolution

Break all of the observations into time elements.

Innovate

Innovation is a trained process that follows a simple format. There must first be knowledge, followed by creativity, then thinking and finally, innovation. Enlightened governance sets the team free to work the magic.

The steps to innovation are:
- Process knowledge
- Curiosity
- Thinking and analyzing
- Collaboration and networking
- Trial and error (Proof of Concept)
- Positive results

- Honest feedback
- Test solution
- Communicate to all involved
- Implement solutions
- Measure
- Correct and re-test if necessary

Ownership

Correctly done, ownership starts and ends with the project team. Make sure there are names on the project plan to identify champions, leaders, and team members. Develop a sense of priority and purpose across the team. Empower the team, so they own the project.

Following the implementation and correction of a new process, departmental personnel, individually and collectively, must take process ownership. Using the functional team approach, this step is nearly automatic. When management or consultants install the new process, this is a specific set of predefined actions.

- Operational state
- Ownership
- Follow-up
- Measurement is ongoing
- Keep looking for new opportunities to improve

Normalize

Once ownership is established and the team starts the documentation step, they will find ways to simplify and standardize the process.

Make the improvements stick by designating them "the way" until it is superseded with a new iteration. This step is necessary. It holds the gains and creates a platform for future improvement, while creating a culture of quality and continuous improvement.

- Document and make the change transparent across the organization
- Simplify
- Standardize
- Communicate the new process and train as needed
- Continually measure the new way and improve as needed

Summary

A core premise of Lean Six Sigma is the rapid completion of multiple events, called Kaizen. It is our observation, based on feedback at numerous seminars and shop visits, that far more companies think they are doing Lean Six Sigma than are actually accomplishing anything.

We like to ask, "How many of your companies have Lean programs?"

Normally most attendees will raise their hands.

Our follow-up question is "How many of you completed a Kaizen event this week?"

We may see one or two hands, and often none.

Reviewing the program can be disappointing. Companies waste enormous amounts of money on formal programs that fail to meet expectation.

One of the benefits of the needs' assessment is identifying systems and processes opportunities for the decision-making process in Step Four.

18 Metrics

Metrics provide knowledge about performance to plan. They are better tools when parameters of acceptable and unacceptable performance (upper and lower control limits), or KPI's are established. This allows management by exception with nonconforming metrics getting the appropriate attention.

Business metrics are integral to process evaluation and tracking performance to plan. They monitor critical processes, assets, and program progress. For example, does the company need to take steps to improve productivity or to redefine their business model before selecting an ERP system? Without metrics, it is difficult to determine the best solution.

ERP demands high levels of accuracy. Establish a metric for each component and monitor performance. A properly constructed set of metrics will show the business tradeoffs and support finer granularity for drill down purposes.

A business cannot reasonably take major actions to improve a single metric. Problems need separation from symptoms. For example, measuring shipping orders to acknowledgement dates is a core metric. The causes for failure can be diverse. Operations may be late or materials defective or unavailable, or many other potential causes.

Key Performance Indicators (KPI)

The use of Key Performance Indicators became popular during the quality movements of the 1990s. Improvement programs make extensive use of KPI's and they are excellent metrics for project management. The format accurately supports the measurement of strategies and tactics. The indicators are ratios, fractions, or discrete numbers. For example:

- Estimated project hours - actual hours
- On time completion – projects completed

- Elapsed project time – elapsed actual time
- Number of modules scheduled – actual number of modules completed
- Number of people scheduled to be trained – actual number trained
- Number of issues on the parking lot list – number of issues actually resolved

Unlike score keeping, KPI's require careful development. They must be goal-oriented indices. Plot the actual performance against the indices.

Systems proponents advocate using KPI's. The major drawback is that organizations often need training on how to establish and use them. Once developed, KPI's must integrate into the business programs.

Dashboards

Dashboards provide graphical snapshots of the key metrics. They may be managerial, operational, or analytical. The best-designed systems use data warehouses to provide drill down capability on virtually any set of numbers. There are numerous applications available to automate this activity, as functionality within many packages, and as SaaS.

Most ERP packages provide a data warehouse with drill down capability. Dashboards are increasingly important, but not a core decision point for ERP selection. ERP systems are the informational backbone, and the dashboard is part of intelligence gathering. Without accurate and timely information from the ERP system, the dashboard provides misleading information.

Summary

Metrics can provide comprehensive views. Each business must establish systems that measure the health and performance of the business. When production performance is inadequate, a metric provides a valuable pointer to the root cause. If production is constrained, solve the root problem to increase output.

Part 2

ERP Lessons Learned Structured Process

"No matter how good the team or how efficient the methodology, if we're not solving the right problem, the project fails."
                                                            Woody Williams

19 Structured Process

Part 1, Due Diligence, addressed broad but important issues. This part presents a process based on the practical application of ERP project and VMP principles.

Many approaches separate information technology and VMP. In today's integrated business environment, they are complementary, and properly approached, are synergistic.

When marching into battle, a map is required. Lacking a plan of attack, resource deployment is uneducated, random, and reactionary. Given this scenario, victory will be elusive.

Take a Total Systems Approach

The following chart shows the enterprise input/process/output structure. It helps visualize the activities required in the nine-step selection and implementation process. It decomposes the enterprise into specific functions.

The enterprise is a complex cause and effect system comprised of subordinate complex systems and cycles. Addressing one specific area, such as the production process, has consequences in all the other systems. Products may require reengineering to fit new processes. Capability affects what product will be available for sales. Waste and energy consumption add cost and become opportunities for improvement.

An enterprise is top down with domino like effects. The driving force shapes the mission, which sets up strategy, tactics, and business plans, which in turn determines the resources required to achieve the mission. The consequence of each may be unpredictable or planned but there are always unintended consequences.

Given structure, the enterprise needs capital, materials, workers, machines, energy, and facilities. Engineering designs product and sales obtains orders, which feed ERP, calculating what to buy and make.

Production converts assets into products, which flow through the supply chain to the customer. The customer receives and pays for the product allowing the enterprise to pay for workers and additional assets, propelling the cycle.

Every process and activity throughout the cycle take time, and time is not just money; it is opportunity and risk. Both are process waste. The faster you drive the cycle the greater the ability to take advantage of opportunities, meet priorities, and avoid risk. Identify every source of waste through the business assessment

As you start this project, remember that success means understanding exactly how these elements work and affect each other. You want to make the organization very efficient, but the ultimate objective is for the system to provide controlled speed, with every element of the enterprise working in sync. The rule is "efficiency never trumps effectiveness." With the ERP system installed, use VMP to step on the accelerator.

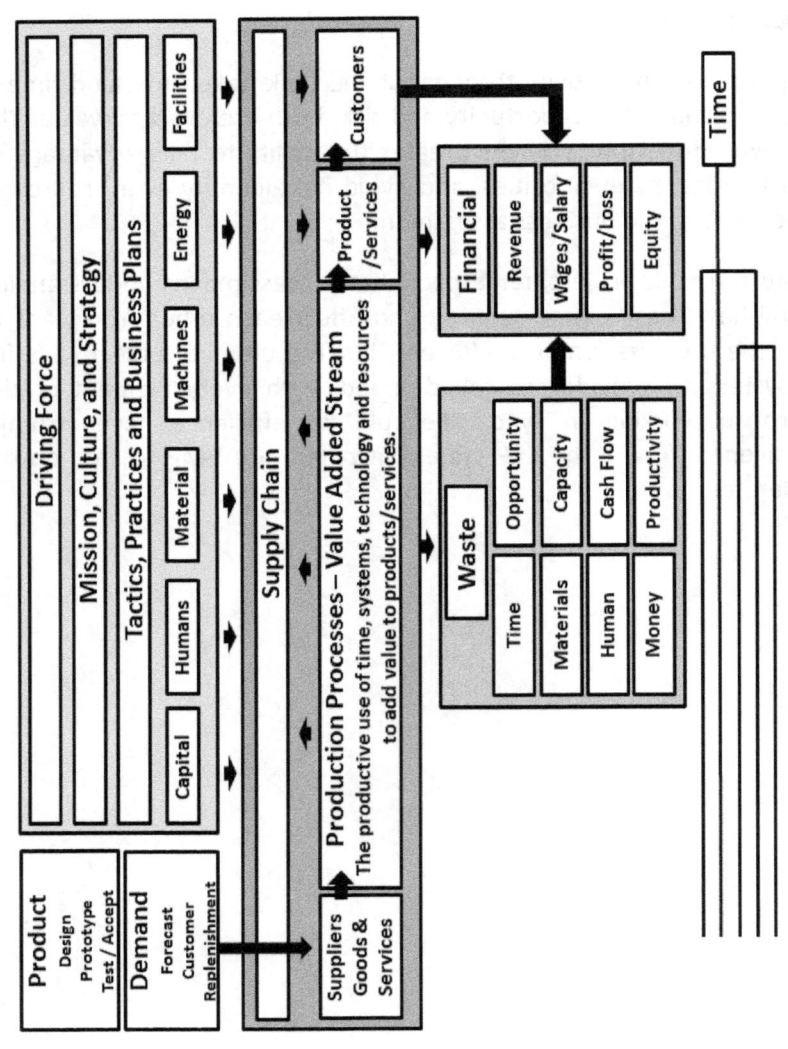

Enterprise I/O Chart

ERP Selection Method

Every project needs a structured process, but far too many projects reinvent one. It helps to have a hardcopy with check off lists, as this one does.

The selection of ERP and/or VMP can take different directions because in addition to the software, events drive actions. For various reasons, the chart and checklist may not be inclusive for your project. Following is our method, customized for each project.

This process has nine steps:

1. Current/Future Business State
2. Current Operational State
3. Planned Future State
4. Decision
5. Organize for the Project
6. ERP Software Selection Process
7. Implementation
8. Measure New Operational State
9. Continuous Improvement/Standardize

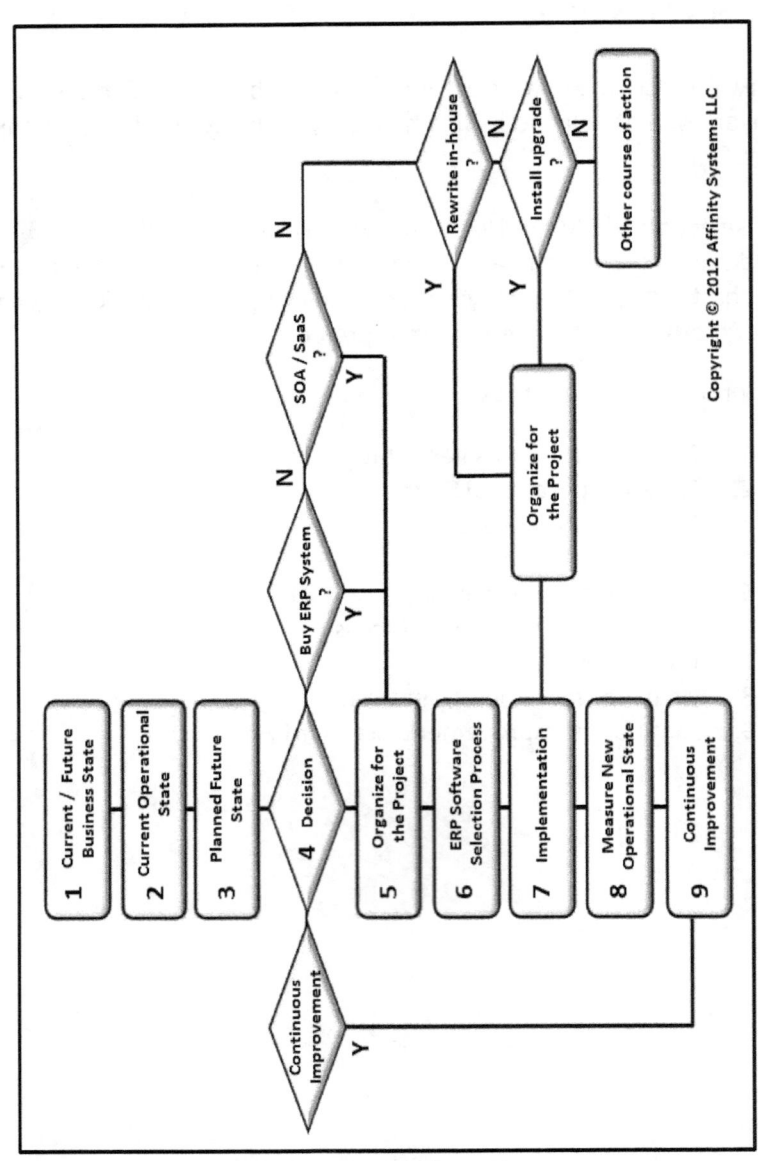

Illustration -ERP Project Chart

Step 1 Current / Future Business State (Strategic Direction)

Environmental Scanning is a component of the Systems and Technology approach used by APICS. Affinity Systems LLC personnel that have taught the certification class developed a modified program based on the core concepts.

Strategy formation evokes mixed emotions with executives. This process identifies ways to analyze and determine the direction of the company. Given today's dynamics and variables, assuming business as usual, is not a safe position.

Products and product development must be included in the evaluation. The move to make niche or special products faster will change business processes. Consequently, the specifics of the ERP package may vary.

The result of the strategic exercise must be a precise, documented direction. One truth is perfectly clear. Strategy belongs to the president/CEO, Executive staff, and the Board of Directors. ERP or VMP must have precise direction or risk failure.

It is interesting that implementation project plans are hundreds of pages long. Follow-up is in brutal detail with verbal admonition for missing scheduled tasks. Conversely, getting a one or two page strategic plan is often painfully difficult.

If a strategic plan is not available, it means:

- Executive management is uncertain of business direction.
- They are afraid to communicate it to the organization.
- They are concerned that competitors will use their strategies against them.

If strategies are not available, consider delaying major projects until they are. A company must know what programs to plan and fund.

It is frustrating when strategy is not available. In fairness, while difficult, it is leadership's top priority. Members of the Board should insist upon a copy of this document and know what direction executive management is taking the company. Board members serve to establish business direction and monitor progress. If they are not performing this role, what is their purpose?

In the book "The Art of War," Sun Tzu (ca. 500 BC) states:

"Strategy without tactics is the slowest route to victory. Tactics without strategy is the noise before defeat."

Sun Tzu may have lived 2500 years ago, but he clearly understood you must know what war to fight before deciding how to fight it, who to lead the effort, who the troops will be and what resources to acquire and deploy. ERP is both strategic and tactical.

Few companies are going to execute a full-blown strategic exercise to establish the optimal direction needed for selecting ERP systems or establishing Lean Six Sigma programs. Companies clearly understanding and articulating their strategic direction will bypass this step. Companies uncertain about future direction or unable to state their strategic direction must engage in some level of planning to establish the right business direction.

The understanding of new business direction or opportunities normally takes time to unfold. Realization occurs as an accumulation of events rather than a sudden revelation. Awareness frequently happens when talking to customers or reviewing production problems. A new product or extreme external conditions like high gasoline prices, emerging markets, competitors, recession, or governmental regulations may precipitate the epiphany.

Excellent tools are available for analyzing enterprise performance, products, marketplace, and customers. In general, executive management knows if their customers are happy, if their products are competitive, and if their operations are efficient. Normal business metrics and financial reporting provide the basic intelligence to decide if the business is going in the right direction.

There are multiple methods to analyze and establish strategic direction, and we have used them all. Affinity Systems has frequently led or participated in planning sessions as a business owner, member of management, board member, or facilitator, exploring the options and pitfalls of various strategies.

Business Rationalization

The rapid pace of technology, expansion of the global economy and constant drumbeat of time compression in the marketplace has changed the nature of strategic planning. In the past, it was desirable to construct plans projecting years into the future, and refreshed annually. In today's accelerated world, the strategic effect is a dynamic, real time process. Flexibility is central to its successful execution.

Strategic Conference

The first method of strategy development is the traditional full-blown strategic planning session. The executive staff performs homework assignments, isolates themselves, and establishes precisely where the company needs to go. This normally involves or is the result of extensive research and intelligence gathering.

The business rationalization may precede and dictate the need to execute a current operational state study. This type of strategic conference is a significant effort and expense on the part of the enterprise. It frequently takes place on an annual basis.

In some enterprises, strategic planning starts with layering up the results. The Current Operational State is determined before the strategic planning session. A top-down analysis of the external business environment supplements this study. Map the current strategies against the Current Operational State to develop:

1. Opportunities and Risks
2. Strengths and Weaknesses
3. Competitive analysis
4. Financial implications
5. Gaps between capability and current objectives

These studies provide the intelligence to re-justify or modify business strategies and programs, which may include new ERP, VMP, or a business transformation process. Convert perceptions and needs into strategies, objectives, and tactics.

Strategic Planning – Intensive Planning Session

The second method to plan strategy involves intensive planning sessions. While understanding their strategic direction, most companies have not translated it into software terms. Having agreement among members of management on specific interpretations is important. As consultants, Affinity Systems uses different approaches but find one-day brainstorming or intense planning sessions to be excellent for developing strategies and definitions. They:

- Bring associates together to focus on core issues
- Condense the amount of time required for the planning activity
- Are highly interactive, causing tough problems to surface
- An excellent opportunity to discover how individuals think
- Find out how much disagreement there is to planned directions

The executive staff, selected board members, the leader of the operational state study and the consultant normally attends. A consultant with strategic planning expertise will bring a fresh perspective and ask questions relevant to business direction.

The result will be a greater number of options or expansion of current ones.

The intensive planning session works to gain buy-in, support the strategies, and make sure all the issues are on the table.

Executive Statement

The third way is by proclamation. The president/CEO will dictate the strategic direction to the executive staff. They will provide a go or no go decision for conducting the current state operational study. If the strategies are translatable, the purpose is accomplished.

Interview

There are times when only one method works, interviewing the executive staff.

- Interview all members of the executive staff and directors
- Compile and analyze strategies
- Synthesize into strategic statements
- Executive approval
- Restate into ERP features

Interviews take place in preparation for intensive planning sessions. If the current state study precedes the strategy development, the interview is an integral component. It develops content for a subsequent planning session.

Best Practices or Assumed Strategies

The worst method for obtaining strategies is to apply a best practice or assumed strategy approach. Here is a partial compilation of presumed strategies gleaned from companies over the years.

Our strategic direction will be:

- World class customer service
- Statement of quality standards
- Improved business intelligence
- Increased process flexibility
- Reduced waste
- High velocity production throughput

- ☐ High velocity order to cash cycle
- ☐ Improved asset management
- ☐ Corporate integration
- ☐ Adaptability
- ☐ Higher profit margins
- ☐ Improved productivity

The above results are enlightening. It is a restatement of the obvious. What company does not want to improve in these areas? This particular list does not say anything about mergers and acquisitions, growth, markets, competitive actions, process changes or product development.

Presumption is a high-risk activity when dealing with strategy. The impact in the real world could lead to improper ERP selection or a poorly implemented VMP. Worse, poor strategy escapes into the marketplace, where it can profoundly affect the sustainability of the enterprise.

From our perspective, using best practice or assumed strategies is risky and we have never seen it succeed. If executive management is unwilling or unable to provide strategies, advise them of the consequences. If strategy is not forthcoming, cancel or delay the project. If you do proceed, be warned of the high risk of joining the forty percent of failed implementations.

After completing the business needs assessment, future strategies become increasingly obvious. If the decision is performing a needs assessment without a strategy statement, it is imperative to revisit the strategy before developing the Planned Future State. This helps ensure a translatable strategy will be in place before making the decisions in Step 4 of the process.

Process Outputs

Companies executing the strategic planning exercise must decide at some point if they have exercised sufficient environmental scanning.

- ☐ Evaluate and calculate the risks and opportunities of regulatory constraints, macroeconomics, and the political landscape
- ☐ Analysis of customer needs
- ☐ Finalize a competitive product analysis - include lifecycles
- ☐ Resolve need for a breakthrough strategy
- ☐ Determine the need for transformational processes facilitating change, increased flexibility, innovation, competitive advantage, and operational reengineering

To facilitate the project, strategic planning must result in:

- ☐ Restatement of vision and mission
- ☐ Business model validation
- ☐ Current strategies/future strategies
- ☐ Gap analysis future strategies to current capabilities
- ☐ New strategies and tactics to fill the gap between current and planned capabilities

Following are expectations from the strategic planning process:

- ☐ Clear-cut executive commitment to perform a current state operational study - if not done prior to strategic planning
- ☐ Vertical, core competence or distributed operational capability
- ☐ Mergers and acquisitions
- ☐ Changes in product
- ☐ Outsource definitions
- ☐ Export plans
- ☐ Planned capacity expansions
- ☐ Programmable and/or computer controlled equipment
- ☐ Changes in the business model
- ☐ Significant operational changes
- ☐ Definition of requirements to build the smart enterprise

Critical Decision

If there is no strategy by this point, call it quits and have a cold beer. The party is over – or should be.

Translatable Strategic Definitions

All strategy influences the information system. Translate strategies into sets of ERP functionality. Following are four examples:

Example 1 Strategy Statement: Mergers and Acquisitions

We will purchase at least one additional operation each year and integrate the information systems within six months of the acquisition.

Translation: the system will be more complex and must provide multi-plant/company processing and the tools for easy integration. The chart of accounts will be a critical issue. The development of integration tools is required. The project team may be semi-permanent or permanent.

Example 2 Strategy Statement: Products

We will manufacture a product line offering customizable features using assemble to order concepts.

Translation: if the enterprise currently has a build to order or engineer to order fulfillment model, the information system must be able to support assemble to order. This is a major change affecting the information system, engineering, manufacturing, processes, and distribution.

Example 3 Strategy Statement: Procurement

We will outsource 50% of our purchased materials and components from China, India, Indonesia, and Mexico.

Translation: full supply chain functionality is required, supporting multiple languages and currencies. Companies engaged in supply chain programs need lot size traceability and order tracking.

Example 4 Strategy Statement: Customer

We will immediately begin using SCC as a tool for customer service and for future product development.

Translation: the system must support at least two levels of SCC, information sharing and product development.

The information sharing functionality must be a part of the ERP system. Selected customers must be able to access information in the database regarding order and shipping status. This means real-time operations reporting. In addition, supply chain partners are collaborating in demand flow projects.

The requirement for product development includes electronic exchange of design criteria, color matching, engineering drawings, sharing bills of material and other relevant information.

A CRM solution appears to be a viable consideration covering all of these functions and big data is on the horizon.

Strategy Requirements Stated for ERP Purposes

- Summary of strategies requiring computer based information support (e.g. use of a business intelligence model)
- The objective for this planning function is to synchronize the business systems to the various strategies
- There are frequently multiple business units, each with their own strategic and operational requirements that require integration
- Correlate these inputs to understand how a total system will work

Summary

Clarify strategies and match them to capabilities to develop solutions. If strategies are not available now, put the project on hold or agree to perform this step immediately after the business assessment and prior to the development of the future state.

Step 2 Current Operational State-Business Systems Assessment

Developing and analyzing the Current Operational State is one of the most difficult steps in the process. This formal business-planning step logically follows the strategy definition. Its purpose is to evaluate the capability of the organization and its systems to accomplish the strategies. The system assessment may precede strategy development, or become inputs to help establish them.

The risk factor of an ERP project dictates an in-depth study. When installing specific duty software like CRM, the assessment is more restricted. On the other hand, if the goal is to install supplementary software and the enterprise systems are inaccurate or broken, this is an opportunity to do the job right.

Business needs assessments are expensive and time-consuming but there are ways to manage the cost while accelerating the completion.

Internal Leadership

Assessments require executive authorization. This person may be the president/CEO, or appointed executive with the authority to get the job done right. The process is both enlightening and disruptive.

Traditionally, organizations assign responsibility to the financial and information technology departments. The most important leadership qualifications are the level of authority, working well in team environments, and business knowledge. Other consultants may downplay authority, but all projects have points requiring executive intervention. Even highly skilled project leaders will experience covert and overt authority challenges. Heading up a major systems study and project implementation is not a popularity contest nor is it a job for the fainthearted.

An executive task force is advisable because the study will touch all corners of the business.

Responsibilities

- ☐ Executive sponsor
- ☐ Executed by end associates
- ☐ Outside consultants

Consultants

Consider hiring a consultant for this stage. They have been through this process many times, and they are able to anticipate many of the problems.

Most consulting companies, including ours, have established checklists used to ensure focused assessment. Checklists provide useful and necessary insight about business interworks and its employees. Our checklists have nearly a thousand questions, many of which depend on answers to other questions. They are put together to determine how a process works plus its relationship to other processes. The thousand questions go unasked. Our practice is to fill them out as we conduct the assessment and not distract from or belabor the process. The shop tour and interviews will provide some answers, but raise new questions because details vary. Even if not specifically asked, we check off each answer in the quiet of our office.

If a consulting firm is used it is important to establish the ground rules.

- ☐ Qualifications
- ☐ Affiliations
- ☐ Project scope
- ☐ Schedules
- ☐ Accurate and precise billing process and inclusions
- ☐ Deliverables

Project Plan

Executive management must establish the project framework.

- ☐ Study of business and information flow
- ☐ Internal leadership
- ☐ State of training
- ☐ Strength of systems
- ☐ Ability of the enterprise to achieve the strategies
- ☐ Define opportunities to improve the business
- ☐ Capability of the employees

Organize the Project

- ☐ Assign tasks and responsibilities
- ☐ Establish how to compose the work teams
- ☐ Establish metrics
- ☐ Develop Key Performance Indicators
- ☐ Provide strategic guidance
- ☐ Put together a project plan
- ☐ Determine who will do the process mapping and how will it be accomplished
    - o Manually
    - o Business process mapping software
- ☐ Prepare a list of the documents to be gathered
- ☐ Establish dates for completion
- ☐ Assign interviewee
- ☐ Set up the intensive planning sessions

Establish and Communicate the Project Philosophy

There are optional ways to conduct the system study, covered in Part 1. They reappear here because this part stands alone as a check-off list. All of the techniques apply in the appropriate environment.

Management needs cohesion on how to approach and accomplish the project. Until the study is completed, it is hard to answer the question "how many will lose their jobs", if any. Be prepared to answer the question at the project kickoff meeting for software selection. Experience has shown that honesty and leveling with staff and employees produces the best results.

There are two basic approaches, both used on the project but philosophically different. Affinity Systems prefers the second method, because it invites the associates into the process. This accomplishes two goals. First, the associates are involved very early, in what may be a long process. Second, they associates deserve credit for their work and contributions. Inclusion invites positive participation.

Method 1 - Sequential (Traditional)

- One thousand questionnaires resulting in three-inch studies
- Credit goes to consultant or team performing the study instead of the associates who supplied the information

Method 2 - Interactive
- Team flowcharting (Value Stream Processing)
    - What is the process
    - Why is it done
    - How is it done
    - Who is doing it
    - How long does it take
    - Where is it being done
    - What are the linkages
    - Material and work flows

- Team Intensive Planning (brainstorming) sessions at multiple levels
    - Executive, if possible, otherwise interview
    - Management

- ☐ User or process owner
    - ☐ General tools
    - ☐ Interviews
    - ☐ Surveys
    - ☐ Research (e.g.-comparative external data)
    - ☐ Photography/video

- ☐ The team gets the credit

Inform the Organization

If the team approach is used, most employees will be involved in some activities. It is important to enlist their aid.

Communicate the project, scope, reason, and expectations to the organization. Failure to achieve buy-in is an obstacle.

Train Team Members on Assessment Tools

Conduct assessments at the appropriate level of detail (granularity). A high-level assessment provides decision information for selecting software or VMP. High-quality process documentation and deep granularity will determine functional requirements.

Team members must know how to perform the study, and use the available tools.

Tools for Assessment

- ☐ Process charting (by whatever name), manual or program
- ☐ Volume analysis
- ☐ Transaction analysis and volume by type
- ☐ Document bottlenecks
- ☐ User needs surveys and analysis
- ☐ Capability analysis of current staff
- ☐ Interfaces with customers
- ☐ Interfaces with suppliers

Many of the tools used for systems assessments have equal application in VMP.

Methods

The intent of the study is to create a body of company knowledge: what, why and how it performs work. The performance data on critical activities establishes the base for the evaluation. If the strategic planning precedes the study, it can focus on how well the capabilities of the enterprise support the strategies.

Use the ACTION process identified in Chapter 17, Process Improvement. Enterprises involved in Lean are normally familiar with tool usage.

- Use functional teams
- Interview executive and key management personnel
- Define the 20-30 top core business processes
- Review metrics and create new ones where they are needed
- Define what is unique (soul) about the enterprise
- Build a series of lead-time and cycle-time charts to time phase the critical business cycles.
- Use process maps (by any name, e.g. Value Stream Mapping)) to document systems and processes.
- Pareto diagrams
- Affinity Charts
- Ask why, why, why then look past the answers to separate symptoms from problems

Assessment of Current Information and Operational Systems

The outcome of the exercise is to analyze the business as a process. The result will allow management to make decisions about future directions.

The worst thing is for employees to withhold information on how they do their job and what problems or issues they live with. The people have significant knowledge about what is working well and what is broken. Rooting out these systems and productivity problems, issues and concerns, are precisely the reason for doing the assessment. Gaining full cooperation is where associate involvement pays off.

Following is a process outline. It is not complete (remember the thousand questions) but these should provide some structure.

Need to address non-solution issues such as:

- ☐ Document the peak business cycle
- ☐ Actions to keep the business running
- ☐ Business metrics
- ☐ Manpower to maintain
- ☐ Financial requirements
- ☐ Organizational responsibilities
- ☐ Stockholder expectations
- ☐ Financial reports
- ☐ Surveys

Areas of Focus:

- ☐ Understanding the business
    - ☐ Current business processes
    - ☐ Operations
    - ☐ Office
    - ☐ Branch locations where integration is either a given or a possibility
    - ☐ Distribution

- ☐ Customer requirements and expectations
    - ☐ Level of customer satisfaction
    - ☐ Service metrics
    - ☐ Order fulfillment
    - ☐ Ability to meet compliance specifications
    - ☐ Available to promise
    - ☐ Order tracking

- ☐ On-line ordering capability

☐ Legal
- ☐ Sarbanes-Oxley
- ☐ Other regulatory compliance such as OSHA, EPA

☐ Packaging requirements
- ☐ Unique organizational requirements
- ☐ RFID
- ☐ Bar codes

☐ Record accuracy
- ☐ Bills of Material
- ☐ Routings
- ☐ Work centers
- ☐ Price
- ☐ Cost
- ☐ Inventory
- ☐ Billing
- ☐ Shipments
- ☐ All Master Files

Two Examples – Areas of Focus

1. Customer Service

- ☐ Determine accuracy of "Available to Promise"
- ☐ Document the order fulfillment process
- ☐ Document the level of delivery performance units ordered to units shipped
- ☐ Document delivery performance level on complete orders
- ☐ Document the lead-time to customers on critical products
- ☐ Work all flows through the office, shop and shipping

2. Inventory Management

- [ ] Process map all systems and processes
- [ ] Document the replenishment times from suppliers through production to customer
- [ ] Document the number of transactions by type
- [ ] Calculate the rate of inventory turnover
    - [ ] Domestically produced by the enterprise
    - [ ] International
    - [ ] Intransit
- [ ] Sourced from international
- [ ] Shipping errors
- [ ] Ratio of right product to wrong product in stock
- [ ] Shrinkage in inventory
- [ ] Level of stock outs
- [ ] Level of expediting
- [ ] Analyze amount of write off at the end of year
- [ ] Determine need for annual physical inventory
- [ ] Receiving put away picking and shipping errors
- [ ] The accuracy of information on future receipts
- [ ] Does the location system accommodate - lot, containers, skids, part numbers, batch in relationship to rack, shelf, location
- [ ] Interfaces with customers (e.g. collaboration programs, JIT programs)
- [ ] Interfaces with suppliers
- [ ] Types of software in use
    - [ ] ERP
    - [ ] SRM
    - [ ] MES
    - [ ] Engineering
- [ ] Build optimum solution
- [ ] Support of the business strategies
- [ ] Management of costs
- [ ] Study education needs of end associates
- [ ] Find the best solutions:
    - [ ] Formal systems

- ☐ Informal systems

- ☐ Corporate culture
  - ☐ Unions
  - ☐ Existing paradigms
  - ☐ Management
    - ☐ Management style
    - ☐ Agendas

Assessment of Current ERP System Functionality

- ☐ Are there are hot lists on the shop floor?
- ☐ Are orders promptly processed?
- ☐ Do the workers trust the prints, process, and paperwork?
- ☐ Can you build a quality product using only formal, documented processes?
- ☐ Are the schedules executable?
- ☐ Are the reporting methods reliable and simple?
- ☐ Are the cutoffs logical?
- ☐ How many people are expediting materials?
- ☐ Are feeder departments on time with parts and components?
- ☐ Does the final assembly schedule freeze long enough to retain accuracy or it a moving target?
- ☐ Is the system fast enough to support information at the speed of reality?
- ☐ Does it incorporate mobile technology or integrate with available applications?

Information Systems Assessment

- ☐ Software
  - ☐ Applications
  - ☐ Program quality
  - ☐ ERP packages
  - ☐ Licenses

- ☐ Files and structures
    - ☐ Languages
    - ☐ Inventory by user (P.C.)
    - ☐ Identify associates by system
    - ☐ Upgrades

- ☐ Authorized or unauthorized
    - ☐ Security applications
    - ☐ Reports and other user complied status data

- ☐ Document the ERP system
    - ☐ Hardware
    - ☐ Inventory of equipment
    - ☐ Age
    - ☐ Capability
    - ☐ Upgrades/ Updates
    - ☐ Facility
    - ☐ Air conditioning
    - ☐ Mainframe
    - ☐ Distributed
    - ☐ Remote support requirements

- ☐ Integration with other systems
    - ☐ Internet
    - ☐ Telephone
    - ☐ Fax
    - ☐ EDI
    - ☐ Machine tools
    - ☐ Support tools
    - ☐ Third party software
    - ☐ Mobile applications

- ☐ Client server vs. mainframe
    - ☐ Number of associates
    - ☐ State of the database
    - ☐ Functionality of the programs and the hardware

- Data collection

- Data
  - Test record accuracy – office and operations
  - Gather samples of all documents and define precisely how they are used
  - Gather transaction volumes
  - Record accuracy – test counts paperwork and real world
  - Test record accuracy including BOM, inventory, routings, work center, etc.

Areas to be Included in the Study

- Accounting and Finance
- Marketing Information
- Human Resource systems
- Administrative functions
- Sales and Customer Service
- Order Processing / allocation
- Master scheduling
- Engineering
- Products – lifecycle management (PLM), new product development
- Inventory management
- Manufacturing
- Warehousing
- Distribution
- SCM
- Business intelligence
- Customer Relationship Management
- Purchasing
- Forecasting
- Inbound logistics
- Supplier relationship management (e.g. deals, collaboration)
- Transportation – outbound logistics

Analyze the Data

Compile the results into an informative report for executive management. Define how the current state supports/falls short on the strategies.

The analysis will determine if the system is capable of achieving business continuity. It maps the strategic plan against current operations to determine what programs are required to reach the strategic goals.

- ☐ The situation is known or presumed
    - ☐ External pressures
    - ☐ Internal pressures
    - ☐ Executive direction

- ☐ Information needs presumed
    - ☐ Cause and effect to other systems
    - ☐ Strategy definition
    - ☐ Interviews
    - ☐ Intensive planning sessions

There will be contradictory information. Many issues stated as problems are symptoms, and you must find, and expose the root cause. Remove emotion from the process. The data must support all conclusions.

The second part of the report includes team recommendations to executive management, who must authorize/participate in the future state development. The report may indicate how much trouble the company is in and the cost of correction.

Include in the analysis:

- ☐ Problem statements
- ☐ Metrics
- ☐ Survey results
- ☐ Interviews
- ☐ Questionnaires
- ☐ Capability analysis of current equipment to perform job

There may be political pressures to exclude unfavorable information. Those persons preparing the document must not participate in a cover-up for several reasons. First, it is a matter of personal integrity. Second, executive management cannot fix unknown situations. Third, when the truth emerges, there will be consequences and ruined reputations. Make sure the executive staff gets the whole picture.

If the pressure becomes too great, or the authority level is high, submit a confidential report to the executive champion and president/CEO.

There is an alternative. The consultant can play an important role in getting critical data to the right place. We are not, or should not be concerned with internal politics or hiding information, nor do we have to live with offended persons after project completion. We view it as important to make sure executive management has accurate and complete facts.

Analysis

- ☐ Build optimal solutions
- ☐ Support the broad needs of the business – build in adaptability
- ☐ Improve the customer service systems
    - ☐ Speed of production
    - ☐ Speed of information
    - ☐ Product quality
    - ☐ Timeliness
    - ☐ Customer relationships

- Management of costs
    - Smart, fast operational systems
    - Productivity improvement base

- Find the best solutions
    - Formal systems
    - Informal systems

- Resolve non-ERP issues
    - Workers to maintain security and data integrity
    - Workers to support day-to-day operations
    - Remote support requirements

The System is Broken

The inability of business processes to support the strategies and operations of the business indicate the system is broken in some way. Some ERP systems are not, nor were ever capable of supporting the business requirements. The two choices are to live with or replace it.

Step 3 Planned Future State - Conceptual Plan

The future state has many labels, including conceptual plan, future vision, and business process modeling. Look past the labels and focus on the desired objectives.

Mapping Future to Current States

The future state plan maps the business capabilities, determined by the need's assessment, to the business strategies. It identifies gaps between the two and provides actionable solutions to achieve the strategies.

It is remarkable given the 40-year history of ERP systems that numerous projects move into implementation without a future state plan. There are many reasons. Some companies think it is a non-value added activity. Others view it as an opportunity to avoid a cost. Regardless of the reason, bypassing the step is a false economy.

The future state is the business system blueprint, defining each component, how it will function, interact, and perform work. It sets up the project plan. Properly done, it supports the ROI, business plan, ERP selection criteria and establishes the type of Lean Six Sigma program.

It is useful to review the process from step one to this point. Check off the completed activities.

Environmental Scanning - Results

- ☐ Establish the current and future business states.
- ☐ Is the business model still correct?
- ☐ What is the driving force? Exercise great caution in defining and changing the driving force. We recommend acquiring a copy of "Top Management Strategy, What it is, and How to Make It Work', written by Benjamin B. Tregoe and John W. Zimmerman.

- ☐ If not what is the new model?
- ☐ Review the mission – is it still the target for directing asset utilization and marketing efforts?
- ☐ Is the enterprise agile (able to react quickly), Lean (efficient) and adaptive (intelligent, proactive and change oriented)?

Build a Conceptual Plan

- ☐ Complete needs assessment
- ☐ Statement of systems objectives
- ☐ Map the future state
- ☐ Map future to current states – gap analysis
- ☐ Design and document the future systems elements
- ☐ Determine how the plan will work in operations
- ☐ Define the actions required to convert the systems based on the various gap analyses
- ☐ Prepare a preliminary plan
- ☐ Assign responsibility for each activity

Conceptual Systems Design

- ☐ Translation of strategy into ERP terms
- ☐ Analysis of gap between strategy and capability
- ☐ A conceptual plan to bridge the gap
- ☐ Prepare an integration plan to support the conceptual plan
- ☐ Project recommendations and options - a formal plan in outline form
- ☐ Suggested priorities
- ☐ Rough-cut financial impact

Statement of the System's Objectives (Examples)

- ☐ Use Lean Six Sigma methodologies throughout the organization
- ☐ 24-hour shipment on 90% of the orders
- ☐ One-minute visibility of all orders and quotes
- ☐ Rapid prototyping/sampling to support sales efforts

- 98% on time delivery performance as measured by completed orders
- The elimination of an annual physical inventory
- Inventory turns increased by two turns each year with less than 2% stock outs
- Productivity will be improved by a 15% annual average for the next five years
- All records of the business maintained at 98% accuracy
- Cycle time consistently cut until it is equal to customer lead-time
- Fully integrated financial reporting
- One to one production where possible
- High velocity, highly flexible manufacturing capability
- Build supply chains with full, real-time access to information
- Build collaboration programs supporting product design and Lean Six Sigma
- Define potential and costs for future outsourcing and insourcing
- Develop convergence plan for information and process
- Install ERP system as infrastructure
- Install other software when the ERP system is operational
- Rapid but limited product modification in the distribution centers
- Redefinition of product numbers (SKU's) to facilitate sales over the Internet
- Development of group technology codes
- Use of cells
- Eliminate shop and distribution paperwork

Map of the Future State

The future state map is a conceptualization of the system components, per the series of illustrations developed with various clients. We have found that putting the plan in a visual form helps document and communicate the process. An actual future state is complex with greater granularity than the one shown. Each of these illustrations communicates the design and its implications throughout the organization.

Distribution System

This is a visualization of the distribution system, as planned after the changes. This chart details the distribution layout and the required systems features.

- Directed put away at receiving
- Directed order picking using multiple picking methods
- Less than case pack forward picking areas replenished from full case pack area
- ERP controlled components storage for kitting area
- Modification center
- Kanban for kitted inventory replenishment and to fill "less than case pack" orders
- Flow-through quality control checks
- Case pack area

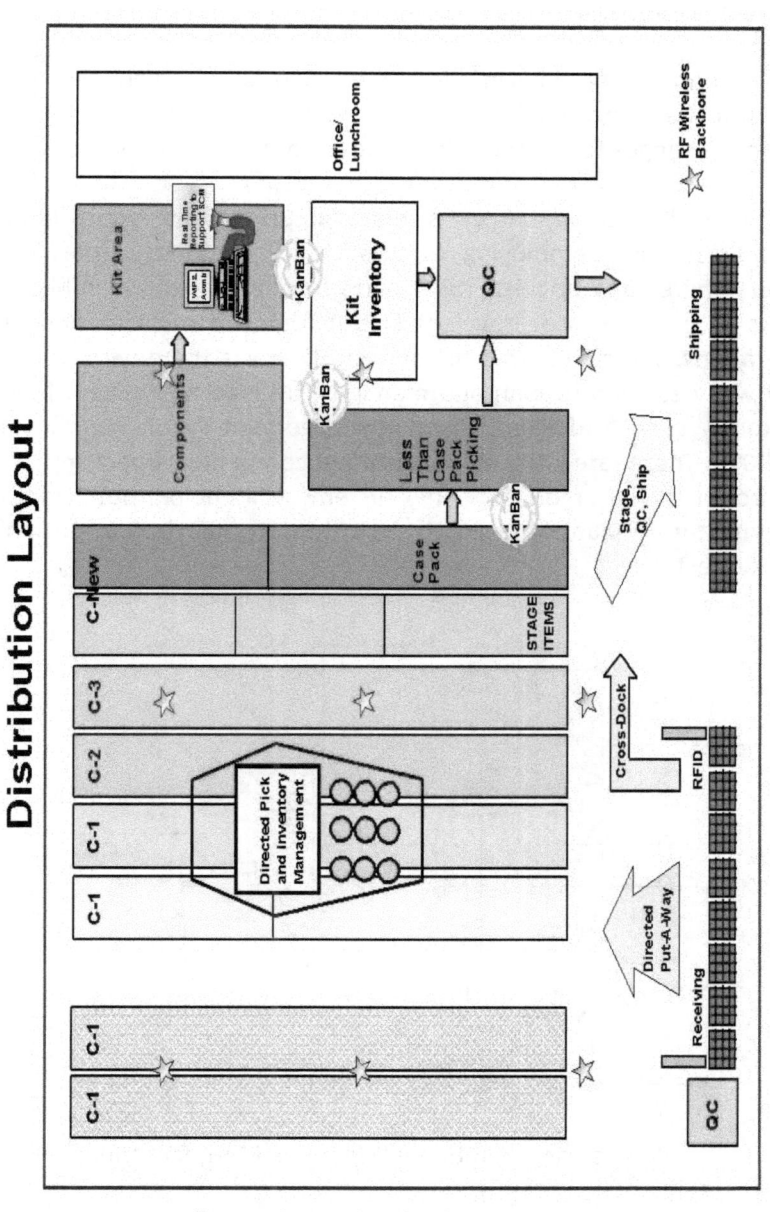

Illustration - Distribution Layout

Manufacturing System

The manufacturing flow in each illustration is at a high-level view. It illustrates a conceptual process instead of a precise method. Any planned changes to the shop floor layout normally occur in stages.

The first illustration shows a manufacturing flow often found in companies not employing sophisticated methods. Inventory is "everywhere" and hot lists drive parts to queue final assembly. Thirty years ago, this was a prevalent layout found in most manufacturing operations. We call it "traditional," and this was the environment that ERP was designed to plan and manage. The lead-times were long and customer service (delivery to acknowledgement date), was frequently 85-90%. There are still manufacturing companies operating in this environment. A modern ERP system will help, but traditional manufacturing plants frequently lack the internal disciple to make it work effectively.

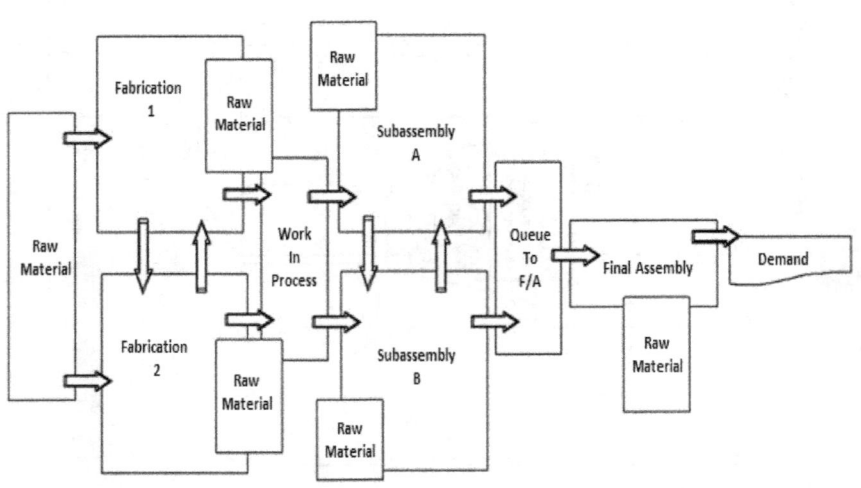

Illustration- Traditional Repetitive Manufacturing

The second illustration is similar, but faced with increased pressure from customers and long purchase to cash cycles. Manufacturing began working in different ways to increase throughput. One of these was to drive the plant to customer priorities, now possible through ERP systems. Management focused on shop flow, and reduced inventory by reducing queue.

Close coupling operations helped companies reduce work in process. Those with long lead times added safety stock formulas, which inflated inventories. These rules were/are put into ERP systems. Today, companies flatten bills of material, shorten lead-times, and work on JIT programs with suppliers to keep raw material at tight, hardworking levels. To accommodate these techniques, ERP incorporated JIT techniques, such as Kanban and demand pull. Many companies still operate in this mode.

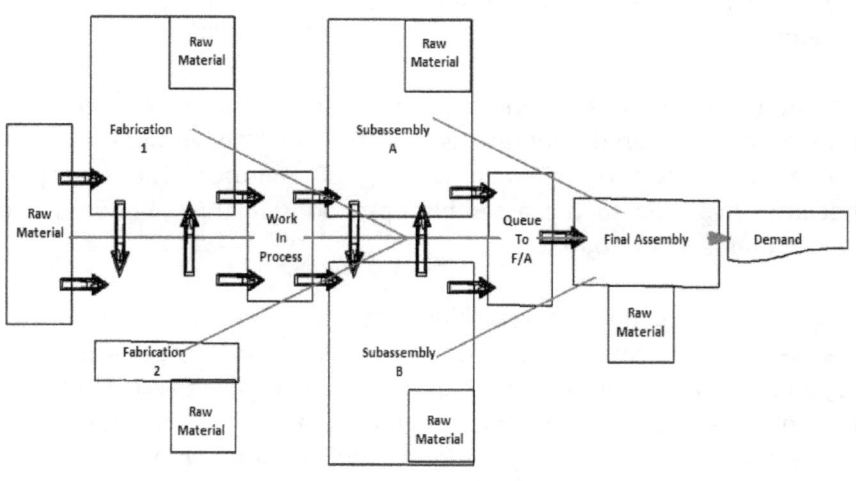

Illustration-Plant in Transition

Two JIT concepts, Kanban (covered in Part 1), and cellular manufacturing are used to refine the plant layouts.

Cellular Manufacturing

Old school production sequenced machines and operators together to produce parts. This division of labor technique reduces work to smaller units where the operator only needs to perform specific tasks within their three-square feet of responsibility.

The following defines the process:

One hundred parts, each rough machined at Operation A, go into a container. When all one hundred are completed, (less if, there is scrap), they are queued (pushed) to the next operator. Completion occurs at Operation C. When the parts are finished, a fork truck takes the output container with one hundred finished parts to subassembly and/or final assembly operations.

Assuming each part takes one minute at each operation, the total run time is three hundred minutes. Assume the batch move time between operations is twenty minutes, totaling 60 minutes. The first part becomes available to the assembly operations in three hundred and sixty minutes or six hours.

In cellular production, the machines are organized (normally but not always, in a "U" shape per the illustration. One or more operators, each capable of running multiple machines, perform work within the cell. The raw parts are queued at Operation A. The part is processed and immediately given to the Operation B, which upon completion passes the part to Operation C. When done, the part is available (although not yet accessible) to final assembly.

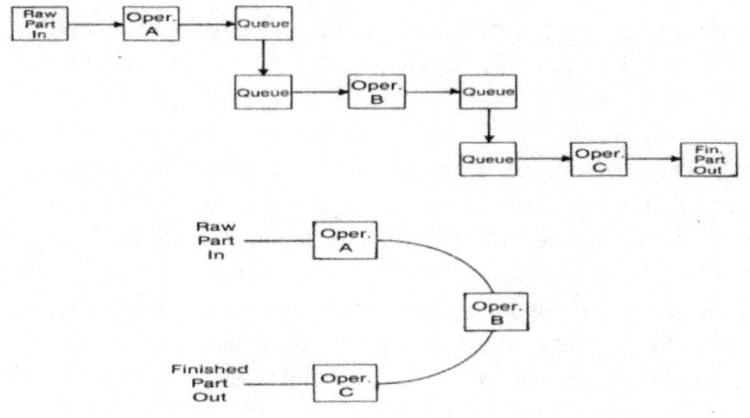

Illustration - Manufacturing Cells

Assuming one minute per operation per part, the total time to produce one part from stop to finish is three minutes. Parts, accumulated during the operation, move en mass to the next operation.

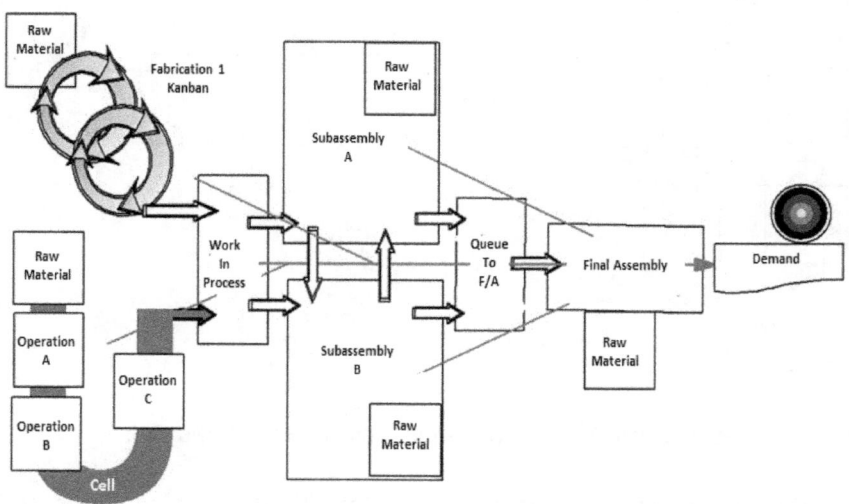

Illustration -Traditional Repetitive Manufacturing using cells and Kanban

Using Kanban and cellular production drastically reduces all inventories. They are special tools for dramatically increasing throughput and chopping lead-times.

The following system uses many of the concepts discussed in this manuscript. Manufacturing cells feed a small work-in-process area, primarily to buffer different output rates. In carefully thought-out flows, the production and use of parts occur rapidly, making inventory irrelevant. The following chart converts the above repetitive manufacturing process into a continuous flow layout using all the tools except inventory. Close coupling or "clustering" is one of the JIT concepts. It involves moving operations close together and reducing or eliminating move and queue time.

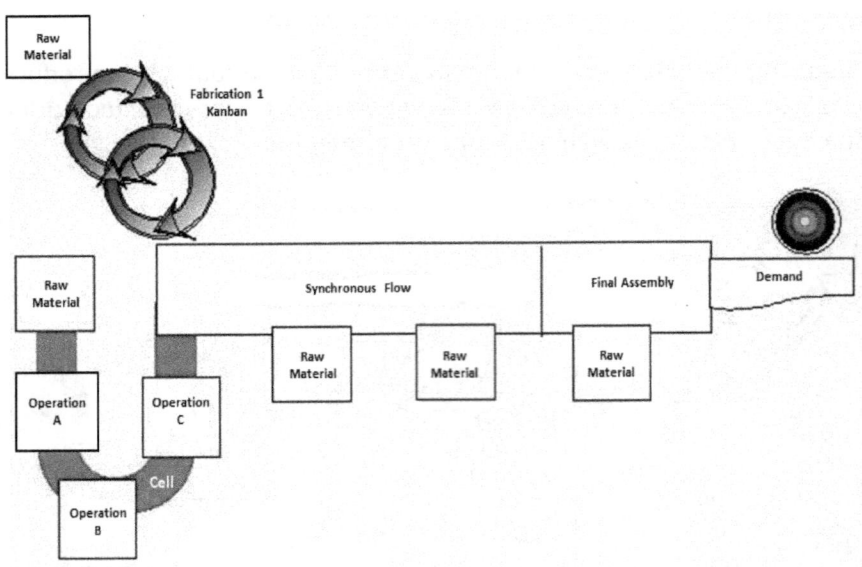

Illustration- Synchronous Flow with Kanban and Cells

The distance and time a part or activity takes between completion and availability to the next operation is important. In the first two manufacturing layouts, parts go into an inventory. The completed basket of parts is not available to the next operation for the twenty minutes it takes to move the container from the final operation to assembly. Regardless, there is savings of forty minutes in total queue time.

The third manufacturing layout shows a close-coupled operation, virtually eliminating move times. The first finished part is now available in three minutes.

	Minutes	Savings	Improvement Ratio
Traditional batch	360	0	0
Cell (not close-coupled)	320	40	12.5
Cell (close coupled)	3	317	105.7

Understanding planned shop floor iterations allows the team to analyze software with the knowledge of future requirements. The four production layouts shown require increasingly sophisticated functionality.

Spending time analyzing and rationalizing shop floor processes reflects a commitment to contemporary manufacturing techniques, including:

- Force multiplier concept used to drive all activities to the fulfillment of demand. The intent is to be demand driven using one-to-one manufacturing principles and pull concepts in an applicable process.

- Synchronous flow where applicable.

- Final assembly planning pulls components from feeder departments, with raw materials, into assembly queue per the schedule.

- There is minimal WIP inventory at subassembly.

- ☐ Use manufacturing cells where possible. Analyze flow throughout the value chain and determine cell potential. Ensure the ERP has the needed functionality to manage cells with schedules and techniques for planning, loading, and reporting.

- ☐ Use electronic/card Kanban systems where applicable. The Kanban cycle has the potential to extend into the supplier's inventory and into the customer's warehouse.

Until manufacturing is using all the available tools to compress time, faster information may prove to be an expense. Take the time to plan for fast, accurate physical and information realities. The task may require multiple steps, re-engineering, ERP tools, and VMS.

Future State – Demand Pull

Demand-pull is a JIT/Kanban derivative using integrated information instead of containers. All the suppliers and customers share information about orders, product movement, and sales. If sales of a given product suddenly increase, that information populates through each level of the supply chain. Each link has the information needed to adapt to changing conditions. The key focus of demand-pull is instant status/event sharing, giving all links more time to react.

Although we have not discussed supply chains in Part 2, professionals are currently focusing heavily on the collaboration opportunities presented by demand flow. With this increased emphasis, discuss its use internally.

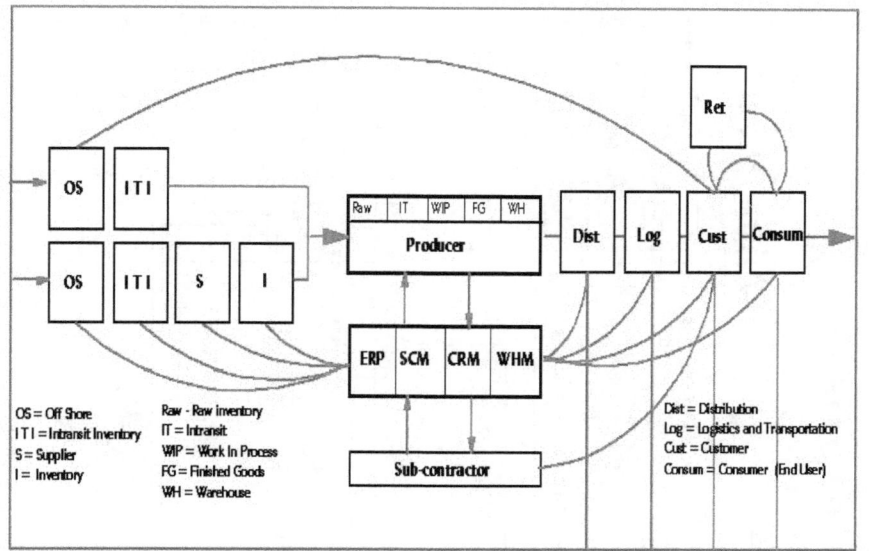

Illustration - Demand Flow

ERP System

This chart on the next page shows an ERP system for a manufacturing company. The sales forecasts, order files, bills of material, routings and work centers are fed into the ERP calculation where purchase and production requirements are generated. Purchase products normally show as recommended orders. The purchasing department analyzes this set of information and releases orders based on that evaluation.

Using the above ERP design for the smart enterprise, draw a chart that fits your future state. This chart is for a complex, multi-plant organization using advanced functionality, such as CRM, MES, and BI.

The plan should contain layers of detail on how the system works and how the design supports the objectives.

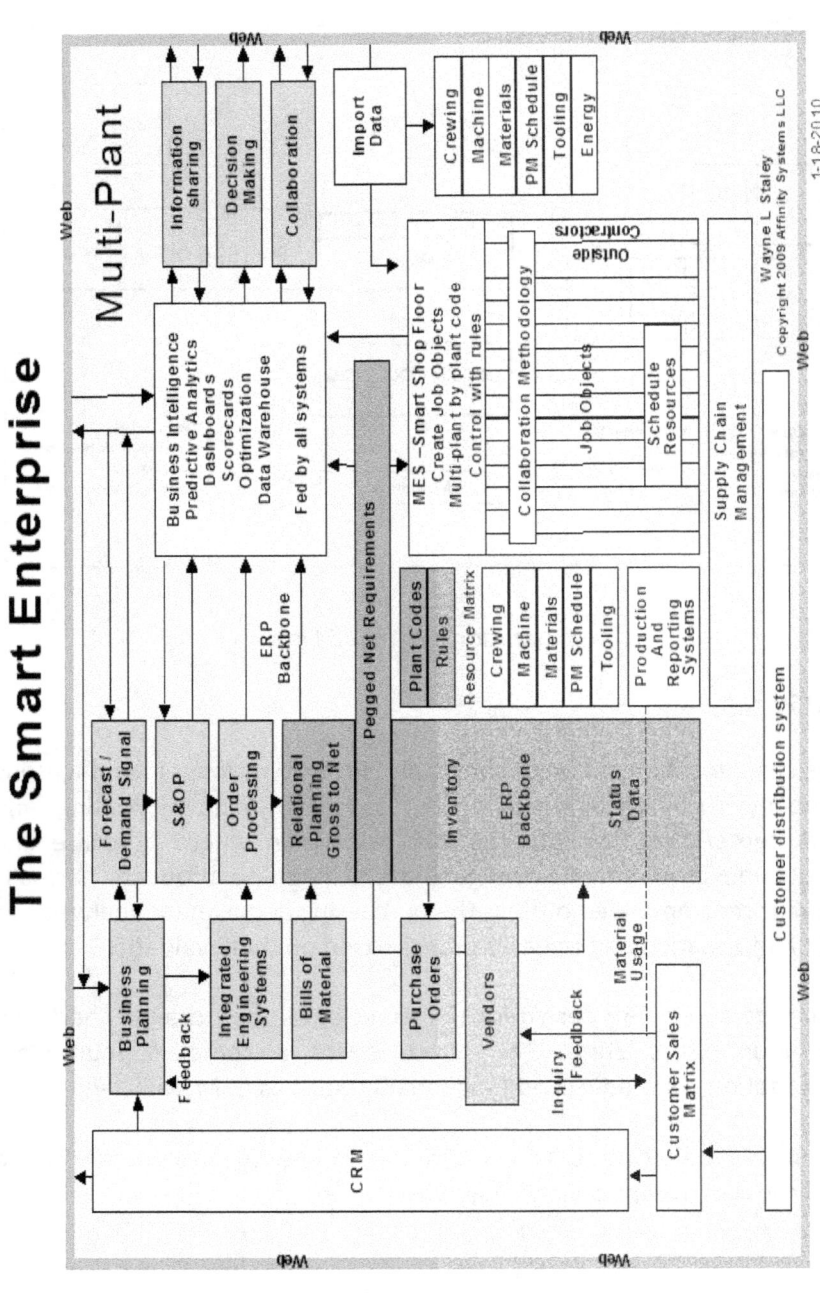

Illustration - The Smart Enterprise

Future State Plan

The future state plan, developed through the business analysis, includes all the business systems. Support strategy statements with tactics, using techniques similar to those translating strategies into software terms, as discussed in Step 1. The Future State Plan contains a consolidated overview, and is broken into prioritized subordinate plans, such as the ERP Project Plan. Other plans may exist for changes at the distribution center, time-phased changes in the shop layout, SCM programs, or any number of business activities. The business analysis will nearly always isolate opportunities for improvement in both process and information.

Following are the broad outputs for the future state:

- Financial objective
    - Investment strategy
    - Risk/opportunity assessment
    - Profit growth
    - Return on investment
    - Return on assets
    - Least risks
    - Total cost management

- Marketing (Customers)
    - Planned penetration percent – market share
    - Define areas of real or potential competitive advantage
    - Define areas of real or potential comparative advantage
    - Definition of current and future markets to serve
    - Definition of products required to service markets
    - Definition of strategic programs such as customer collaboration
    - Definition of other customer/supplier programs such as demand pull

- ☐ Statement of information technology requirements such as CRM Software, and/or business intelligence functionality
- ☐ Sales growth
- ☐ New product identification
- ☐ New product introduction
- ☐ Market niche growth
- ☐ Steps to make each interaction with customers a positive one
- ☐ Technological customer interfaces

☐ Product

- ☐ Modular design where possible
- ☐ Design for life cycle (production through recycle)
- ☐ Design for energy efficiency
- ☐ Design for reparability
- ☐ Design for manufacturability
- ☐ Design for minimal environmental impact
- ☐ Establish quality requirements
- ☐ Flexibility of use
- ☐ Adaptability
- ☐ Functionality
- ☐ Technological level

☐ Operations

- ☐ Document changes to ETO, ATO or other core paradigm
- ☐ Supply chains
- ☐ Distribution
- ☐ Document current and requested capital expenditures and their impact on the information and operational systems
- ☐ Document outsourcing plans
- ☐ Systems capability to support the smart enterprise
- ☐ State vertical horizontal or hybrid organization

- ☐ State need for continuous improvement programs such as Lean
- ☐ Document contingency plans for acquiring product
- ☐ Document energy saving opportunities

☐ Order winners (from the APICS Systems and Technology Review Course)

- ☐ Price
- ☐ Quality
- ☐ Delivery
- ☐ Flexibility
- ☐ Product design
- ☐ Service

The balance of this chapter will focus on the ERP Project Plan and Integration Plan.

ERP Project Plan

The plan requires an ERP solution, the integration of the ERP supplier's implementation process, and a preliminary schedule for the selection process. It includes training the team on ERP selection techniques, and makes the business case for a new ERP system. A schedule of events with estimated timing is required. If the study finds there a pervasive resistance to change, a transformation process may be required. For example, training focused on a culture change.

This is an opportunity to detail the critical project organization steps, including how crewing issues will be resolved.

Assign initial due dates to all activities. They will change as specific information becomes available, and all the relationships and timing between events unfolds.

The use of project management programs such as Microsoft Project is highly recommended. There are a number of programs, including open source, using the company intranet while providing mobile views of the information. Key among them is the individual task list. Several team members must learn how to establish, maintain, and use the program. Spreadsheet programs can get the job done, but they are time-consuming, less effective, and difficult to share.

Conduct review sessions with all associates to validate the accuracy of the data and the conclusions. Address all of their needs. Conduct a project approval meeting with the executive staff. Establish a budget, assign a priority, and properly staff the program.

Integration Plan

This plan interprets and time phases the conceptual plan into hardware and ERP requirements. Until the selection process is completed, some of the details will be unavailable. The plan states what and when to acquire and install hardware, and identify the associated training.

The distribution and shop layout example identifies different technologies. These include bar coding, RFID, Kanban, equipment moves, and mobile technologies. They support the strategic plans and the implementation of the ERP system. The timing and expenses are scheduled. Each step has a subordinate implementation plan.

Following is a partial list of considerations:

- Resolve centralized vs. decentralized
- Hardware platform
- Operating System
    - Open source – Linux
    - UNIX
    - Microsoft
- Network plan
- PCs and software
- Mobile devices and supporting technologies
- Need to address non-solution issues
    - Availability of security and data

- ☐ Remote support requirements
- ☐ Integration with other systems
- ☐ Telephone/Fax
- ☐ Machine and process tools and software interface
- ☐ Support tools
- ☐ Known process changes
- ☐ Key phases with estimated completion dates
- ☐ Mobile communications integration

Systems Impact Considerations:

- ☐ Other economies achieved/lost
    - ☐ Air conditioning
    - ☐ Technological rollover
    - ☐ Keeping up to date
    - ☐ Security
    - ☐ Disaster recovery
    - ☐ Ongoing costs
- ☐ Multi-layering, usability
- ☐ Cabling, electrical
- ☐ Systems / server space, noise, heat
- ☐ Support personnel needed
- ☐ Networks of PC required
- ☐ Upgrades frequency
- ☐ Cost factor

Server Platform

Your new software will run on a given set of hardware/software platforms. These include IBM iSeries (AS/400), Linux (SUSE, Red Hat, Debian/Ubuntu), UNIX (Solaris or AIX), Microsoft server (Windows, NT/2003/Vista/etc.), Novell Netware, hosted solutions such as SaaS.

It is important to know which platform to use. This will be determined as part of the software selection process. If the decision is to use current platforms, it defines one selection parameter. Delegate the hardware issues to your IT department. They will know the implications of making changes. If you lack an IT department, consider hiring a hardware consultant.

Dialog once centered on the different capabilities of Windows and UNIX. Our firm has always favored the IBM platform because it is highly reliable and less susceptible to hackers, virus, and downtime. The rule is to ask what the native platform is.

Personal computers function independently or in networks. The software license applies to one or more PCs. Carefully think through the implications of non-integrated information inherent with PCs.

To streamline the approval process, obtain estimates. Prepare a spreadsheet showing the time phased expenditure for equipment, software, and consultants. Prepare a recommendation section. This will provide a first cut plan for managing the financial aspect of the project.

Once the project starts, force a decision on the legacy system. At some point, it becomes undesirable and non-productive to fix or maintain the old system. Force all legacy systems changes through the steering committee with a signoff by the executive champion. Prudently shift the resources to the new system.

Summary

Charting the shape and visualizing the business is a useful exercise. As shown in previous chapters this helps define the type of ERP solution needed to support the future state. It serves two purposes. The first is internal. If the chart cannot be prepared, the solution is still fuzzy and needs additional definition. The second is to reduce the number of potential ERP suppliers. A supplier shown these charts will know if their product matches your specifications.

The Future Vision helps establish a reasoned approach to accomplishing the business objectives. It is part of the Critical Path. Take the time to do it correctly, and it will serve as the foundation for the entire project.

Associates must know the plan and expectations. This minimizes surprises. Do a final review with the executive staff, management, teams, and key associates. Keeping everyone involved and current will go a long way towards putting the plan into action.

Step 4 Decision to Achieve the Future State

Given the Future State analysis, the company must address the issues and make decisions on how to achieve the future state. The project team and consultants must formally present the Future Plan to the executive staff, who must freely question any area of concern. This needs to be a moment of intense transparency.

Preliminary Budget -Estimated

- ☐ Time phased expenses synchronized to actions
- ☐ Internal personnel
- ☐ Consulting fees
- ☐ ERP software costs
- ☐ Maintenance fees
- ☐ Hardware integration plan
- ☐ Training
- ☐ Estimate process changes
- ☐ Other out of pocket

Return on Investment (ROI)

Since the future state contains recommendations and a preliminary ROI, it looks like a business justification. While serving that purpose, it is a working document used to keep associates involved, current and in agreement. Until the specific ERP, hardware, and implementation, costs are determined, the ROI is preliminary. Expand the ROI as the costs firm up.

- ☐ Understand what comprises the ROI. It will probably be overstated and unobtainable without process improvements. Has the team defined the changes?

- ☐ Most implementations do not yield substantial immediate paybacks. The VMS provides the majority of the ROI. Project the cost and benefits over three years. Show base savings on the third year, not the first.

- ☐ Advise the team not to use headcount reductions for the ROI. They seldom occur as planned. If headcount reductions are included, get specific positions from the team. Tell them the cuts will be part of the measurement for program success. Give the team members an opportunity to change their minds.

- ☐ The team must focus on productivity improvements, legitimate cost saving and/or improved service and profitability. It may be simply a case of building the infrastructure for a VMS, or because you need a new system "to stay in business."

- ☐ Do not use "funny money." Executive management and the Board will know exactly what is going on and question each number, legitimate or funny money.

- ☐ Prepare a time-phased plan and updated ROI after the ERP selection is complete.

- ☐ Build and present a high-level PERT chart to time phase the activities.

- ☐ Spell out
    - ☐ Benefits
    - ☐ Risks of doing or not doing
    - ☐ Scope
    - ☐ Hardware required
    - ☐ RF System and/or RFID

Project Review

- ☐ Project team meets with the executive staff and reviews the plan, benefits and ROI
- ☐ Ask the really tough questions
- ☐ The review will include:
  - ☐ The Future State
  - ☐ A plan to accomplish the Future State
  - ☐ The integration Plan
  - ☐ The Detail Plan
  - ☐ Project recommendations and options
  - ☐ Suggested priorities
  - ☐ Thorough preliminary financial impact

Warning

The danger at this point is attempting too much at one time. While the study may show the need for both an ERP and Lean Six Sigma initiative, doing them at the same time is not just ill-advised, but dangerous. Both programs require significant resources. Few companies have the enough talent to support both efforts.

Decisions

Given these inputs, executive management must decide on the future course of action. These include:

- ☐ Do nothing
- ☐ Business transformation
- ☐ Implement an enterprise system:
  - ☐ ERP
  - ☐ WMS
  - ☐ CRM
  - ☐ SCM
  - ☐ MES
  - ☐ BI

- ☐ Implement a VMS
- ☐ Outsource (requires detail plan)
- ☐ In source (requires detail plan)
- ☐ Implement other business programs as indicated by the Future State

Summary

If executive management does not like the plan or lacks the resources to make it happen, it is a waste of time working through the selection and justification process. Once approved it is essential for all associates to be on the same page.

If the decision is to implement an ERP system, the following is a subset of associated decisions on how to accomplish the project. For example:

- ☐ Purchase ERP and install it on premise
- ☐ Fix current system
- ☐ Reinstall
- ☐ Apply upgrades
- ☐ ASP
- ☐ SaaS or other cloud option
- ☐ Rewrite in-house

Given the decision, the project must receive a priority, budget, and a commitment to resources.

Step 5 Organize for the Project

Successful programs are well organized. This may seem obvious, but installing ERP is a disruptive process generating some level of chaos before restoring order by successfully completing the system. If unsuccessful, the chaos continues and broadens. Meanwhile, the business has to operate while working on the program.

The lesson learned is to anticipate the issues. There will be difficult situations. Now is the time to plan and develop a well-reasoned approach to problem resolution. It is executive management's responsibility to remove ambiguity.

Executive Role

Understand how long the project will take then add a generous chunk of time for miscalculation. The most probable guarantee is it will take longer than anyone's estimates, and it will consume more resources. Facing these realities upfront helps to avoid negative reactions while immersed in the heat of the project.

Team Formation
- ☐ Executive Steering Committee
- ☐ Executive Champion
- ☐ Project leader
- ☐ Project team

Clearly spell out associates role and the proper chain of command
- ☐ Explain expectations
- ☐ Outline compensation for team members (if any)
- ☐ Provide a plan
- ☐ Provide a budget
- ☐ Establish a high priority

Outline the reporting timing and method – update the project PERT chart each time an activity is completed.

- Monthly project report to president/CEO and the Board

Executive Commitment

The first issue is a level of commitment. This starts at the top and works its way down.

Every executive will make significant contributions to the program. This may be staff assigned, delaying pet projects, or the transfer of power into the project. Executive staff must walk the talk and understand their accountability for poor progress in areas of responsibility. While middle management and shop supervision will be the most actively involved, they cannot do the job without the support from their functional executives.

- The president/CEO must be committed. If not, stop the program.
- Take careful steps to confirm buy-in by the executive staff, middle management, line, and user communities.
- Have a change management class to help people adapt to change.
- Provide appropriate incentives.

Organize - Executive Role

- Provide all the necessary resources
    - A dedicated team or employee backfill
    - Determine the answer to, "What's in it for me?"
    - Hire consultants where necessary
    - Provide a "War Room."
    - Allocate training dollars and facilities.

ERP projects are high-priority projects. Do not give ERP members conflicting priorities. When everything is a priority, nothing is a priority. Is the priority high enough to get the job done? If not, stop the process or change the priority – and back it. Keep the priority problems in the executive arena, not in the project.

Appoint the Executive Steering Committee

The president/CEO will appoint a small group of executives to function as a steering committee. They are empowered to make the decisions for the project. The executive champion must be one of the members, and the president/CEO frequently fills the role of another. Their duties are:

- ☐ Court of appeals
- ☐ Review scope and progress
- ☐ Review and approve decisions
- ☐ Resolve cross-organizational conflicts
- ☐ Define the key drivers and business requirements
- ☐ Project approval / contract issues
- ☐ The big picture –ability to rise above the detail
- ☐ Provide priority
- ☐ Assess / resolve personnel issues
- ☐ Provide / resolve resource contention
- ☐ Project oversight
- ☐ Budget tracking approval:
    - ☐ Project changes
    - ☐ Process changes

Appoint the Executive Champion

The prime requirement for the executive champion is good leadership skills. We think of ERP systems in technical terms, but selecting, installing and making them work are people issues. The most useful skills are project management, followed by ERP knowledge, and good negotiating skills. The role of the executive champion is:

- ☐ Get company support for the team throughout the organization
- ☐ Keep the project on the management agenda
- ☐ Make the tough executive-level project decisions

- Help sells and implements needs
- Act as project conscience and sounding board
- Retain:
    - Open door policy
    - Solve problems not fire or punish people
    - Refuse to duck the problems
- Resolve conflicts when the Project Manager is unable to fix them (may involve the Project Manager)
- Own the process
- Act as security change authorization control point
- Establish project rules and expectations
- Define the need for and the role of a consultant/facilitator along with the executive steering committee
- Provide a good place for outside consultants to report

Outside Consultant

Decide on the use of an outside consultant to help with the process. Our experience indicates that consultants should not be the project manager. External project leaders cause authority conflicts, contention between team and ERP consultants (if different). At the end of the project, they go home while internal personnel must live with the results. Here are some tips for working with consultants.

- Define reporting relationships
- Define the scope

The consultant should be completely free of financial relationships to ERP suppliers. The objective is to find the right ERP for your company.

The advantages of a consultant working as facilitator are:

- Provide a structured approach, much like this one
- They have expertise at selecting and installing ERP systems
- Since they know the pitfalls, they can provide early warnings and direction

While not functioning in the role of the Project Manager they do participate in:

- ☐ Establishing the plan
- ☐ Finding the right ERP system
- ☐ Ensuring there is an executable implementation plan
- ☐ Act in support of project manager

The decision to retain the consultant for the ERP selection is contingent on project requirements. The executive champion may decide to use the consultant as a control against the implementers.

- ☐ Follow up to make sure of activity completion
- ☐ Assist Project Manager and making reports
- ☐ Help resolve the technical issues
- ☐ Eyes and ears for executive management

Immediately upon project completion, the contract is closed. Extend or rewrite the contact for additional work if justified.

Executive Team Work Issues

Management must decide how to deal with work issues. Disruptive events can occur when key people are on the project team.

The team members often do their regular jobs as well as install the new system. Prepare to add help if daily tasks suffer. In most companies, it is impractical to completely backfill team members because of talents, experience, skill sets, and importance to the business.

Systems are not cheap and money must be available for extra people. Following are places where temporary help may be useful:

- Data conversion/data entry
- Procedures/documentation
- Clerical support

There are temporary employment firms that can provide support at virtually any level. We have excellent results using University and Technical School students, with majors including IT, engineering, process engineering, and educators. They are smart and willing workers.

Will the team receive any special compensation? This issue often comes up. The question will be, "what is in it for me?" If it is "just a part of doing their jobs," or their reward is "they will keep their jobs," we suggest carefully thinking through the reaction to those questions.

When establishing incentives, individual rewards are less important than team awards. The effort requires teamwork not superstars gaining at the expense of the project. Build a team that continues interpersonal collaboration long after the project has ended.

- The team members will normally find a way to get critical daily functions completed. If they cannot deal with the increased workload, then rethink the composition of the team.
- Provide full information access to the associates.
- Get temporary help when needed.
- Run interference when it is required.

Select the Project Manager

There is a recent trend to make rookie IT people the ERP Project Leader. This reflects a serious lack of understanding how complex an ERP project can be. The Project Leader must be someone with both project and leadership skills. They may not have full knowledge of ERP systems, but the right consultant can help fill this gap. It is virtually impossible to overcome all the challenges a rookie will encounter. It is our recommendation that any organization who has taken this step seriously reconsider the risk they are exposing the business to and fix the problem they have created. Properly used, rookies can be tomorrow's stars, but they need a chance to learn and succeed. It serves no useful purpose to turn them off early in their careers.

Determine who the project leader will be:

- ☐ A strong internal person
- ☐ Someone who gets things done
- ☐ Knowledge of the ERP concepts and business processes is essential
- ☐ On ERP projects, the CIO is often the project manager

Responsibilities:

- ☐ Manage and control the project – leadership – day to day
- ☐ Resolve all issues
- ☐ Immerse in detail when required
- ☐ No shortcut mentality – do it right the first time
- ☐ Schedule and follow-up on all activities
- ☐ Perform or participate in the gap analysis (between the old and the new system)
- ☐ Be involved with the vendor partnering process
- ☐ Keep the project on schedule - keep up, not catch up
- ☐ Training
- ☐ Coordinate activities, events and reports with the team, executive team, and executive champion, outside consultant and software/hardware suppliers
- ☐ Promote, participate, and follow up on team and user training
- ☐ Progress assessment
- ☐ Preparation of the request for proposal
- ☐ ERP software selection
- ☐ Contribute input into the negotiation process
- ☐ Manage the implementation and migration to the new system
- ☐ Support ongoing operations
- ☐ Ensure testing / user acceptance
- ☐ Communicate system impact issues

Establish the Teams

The president/CEO, depending upon the size of the company, may participate in the selection of the project team manager and the members of the cross-functional project team. The team members are normally managerial or supervisory.

Team formation – select the team members – these must be some of the best people in the organization.

- They must be decision makers and experts in their areas
- Communicators, but doers, not talkers
- Know how and where of take shortcuts without causing adverse effects
- They must be open minded
- Dedicated to fight for the best business solution and then making it work
- Savvy to the inner-working of the company
- Either has or can quickly acquire needed technical skills
- Willing to make the final selection

People need to be open-minded and work as a team. Do not ignore the dissenters, especially if he/she is an expert in their area. Do not mistake a cry for help or a warning as dissention.

Technical Persons

Internal and external technical people will be required on the project. These members need a combination of good technical skills and communication skills. Their role is to:

- Active participation in all project phases
- Implement technical changes
- Control all program modifications
- Make changes tailored to the business needs
- Explain costs and options
- Lead data conversion / migration effort

- Strong voice in platform selection
- Ensure application of system codes
- Ensure systems security
- Protect the integrity of converted data and files
- Ensure maintenance of current systems until decision to discontinue and shift support to the new system

End Associates

The cross-functional project team is comprised of supervisors and key personnel from the user community. Some companies call them captains. Associates reporting to the team members must perform the work, becoming functional implementation teams. Fold these often-informal teams into the communication loops by holding frequent meetings with their team members. Keeping the functional team motivated will determine the success of the project.

The functional teams are the unsung heroes and the source of pragmatic solutions, so train them all. After the implementation follow up with each user, and makes sure they know precisely how to use the system. Take time to solve any problems they may be having.

End associates:

- A source of valuable inputs and support
- Know how and where to put efforts
- Know the processes
- Know how and where to develop functional workarounds
- Must want to do the job well
- Must work with the chosen solution

Vendors

Multiple vendors will play important roles in the implementation, including the ERP supplier, possible third parties, and data collection networks. Since the life cycle of an ERP system may be "years," it is important that associates work together.

- Honest relationship built on trust
- Assist in education
- Assist in the solution setup
- Custom options
- Hook to other legacy applications
- Product expertise

Team Meeting

It is useful to have the president/CEO, executive champion, and steering committee meet with the teams. Spell out expectations and long-range business strategies. Since the team will evaluate the ERP packages, top management needs to bring them up to speed and keep them informed. In most cases, the team will help guard against strategic mismatches if they know what they are.

- Future process changes – review the Future State.
- Explain the need for the project and its effect on the business
- Discuss the need to keep the business running efficiently during the project

Reporting

Define the reporting method for updating the steering committee and Board of Directors. Spell out the frequency of reports and the distribution list.

The Decision

Decide who makes the ERP decision. With a package selected, the team will take a consensus vote to confirm the ERP package. Will the vote stick or will the executive staff override the decision? Here is a hint, the executives in China select the package and then form the team. They have a 70% ERP failure rate. If the team is truly empowered and the associates are deeply involved, trust the team.

Putting the Project Plan into Place

Update the project plan with specific assignments and responsibilities.

Initial Team Training

Team training on the following subjects is required before the selection process can start. The steering committee must determine how knowledgeable the team is, and what additional training is required to ensure a positive project outcome.

- ☐ A functional review of the business
- ☐ Change management
- ☐ The fundamentals of ERP
- ☐ The fundamentals of Lean as applied to ERP selection
- ☐ ERP evaluation methodology

Training

At this level, the major consideration is to get a commitment from top management to train well and thoroughly. We often use the analogy of a 747. An airline does not buy an expensive and sophisticated aircraft and then train its pilots to a basic visual status. It is difficult to understand why enterprises fail to implement training programs that enable the comprehensive use of the ERP system.

Lean Six Sigma principles apply. Any potential paid for but unrealized is a waste. Not training, saving on, or not using all the training dollars is a false economy. It is simply amazing how many companies fail to grasp this basic principle. If the enterprise is not going to spend the money training the teams and associates, executive management should seriously consider delaying or canceling the project until they are ready to make that commitment. To take advantage of ERP capabilities, train all members of the organization including executive management.

Timing

All enterprises have their internal business cycles with peak demands. Scheduling the implementation to occur during a peak period makes little sense. The cycles should have been isolated and documented in the need's assessment. It is useful to reaffirm the impact of a planned date at this time.

Phased Rollout vs. Big Bang

ERP implementations take two basic forms. The first is a phased rollout, where the cutover occurs module by module per a time phased schedule. Nearly all-large enterprises follow this practice. It would be too disruptive and difficult to control if cutover occurred at one time.

The second approach is the Big Bang. All the work leads up to a one-time cut over, which normally takes place over the weekend at the end of the month. The decision of phased versus big bang may not be possible until the inputs from the ERP supplier are available. Cut over timing is an important consideration and deserves due diligence. Discuss the decision at a steering committee meeting.

A third method, parallel adoption (an adaptation of the phased rollout) occurs by module, business unit, or geographical location. This method applies to enterprises installing a pilot or corporate system, and executing a time phased implementation schedule for all facilities.

Establish a Data Conversion Program

Data conversion can be the longest critical path item and of greater complexity than anticipated. Unrealistic pressure to meet the deadline results in poor conversion, creating negative effects as data problem's plaque the implementation. The responsibility for data conversion, and who will do it must be determined early in the project. Mapping current data to the new system must wait until the software selection. Part numbers may be changed. Group technology codes assigned, and descriptions changed for Internet sales or multi-company codes applied.

While delegated to the technical personnel, it is important for the project manager and executive champion to meet daily and review the progress on data conversion.

Define and Establish the Change Process

Establish a change control process and make the Project Manager responsible. Changes must have proper justification and documentation, backed up by an impact analysis.

Establish a General Philosophy on Program Modifications

We recommend reviewing the chapter on "Parking Lot Lists, Modifications, and Middleware"

All implementations result in modification of some type, to processes and programs. It is unreasonable to expect a precise match to the requirements. People will have to change the way they view and process information.

As a rule it is useful to establish a policy stating there will be no modifications without the approval of the steering committee. Communicate this direction to the team, and then vigorously enforce it. The only way they can avoid coming back to the steering committee is to find the best match, work-a-round or process change.

Make Plans So Business Continues to Operate

- ☐ Disaster recovery plans
- ☐ Backup/Restore plans
- ☐ Documentation
- ☐ Change management process
- ☐ Implement technical service level agreement
- ☐ Management
- ☐ End associates

Report to the Executive Staff and Board of Directors

If the plan is properly prepared, it will be easy to extract a summary for executive management or the Board of Directors.

- ☐ Present the project plan and supporting documents
    - ☐ Purpose for new ERP
    - ☐ Project organization
    - ☐ Project team
    - ☐ Cost / Benefit Analysis with ROI
    - ☐ Prepare Project Pert Chart – high level to show timing for major steps, including cut over
    - ☐ Approve the timing
    - ☐ Phased rollout or big bang with justification for the decision
    - ☐ Data conversion plan
    - ☐ Plan to freeze non-critical activities on the current system
    - ☐ Ask the tough questions
- ☐ Alternative if the proposal is not accepted.
- ☐ Will the resources, budget, and priority be available to execute the plan?
- ☐ What are the restrictions?
- ☐ Is there a commitment to training?

Decision to Proceed

- ☐ Reject
- ☐ Increase study granularity
- ☐ Scrap
- ☐ Take a different direction
- ☐ Executive Approval to Proceed
    - ☐ Team consensus
    - ☐ Executive champion approval
    - ☐ Steering committee approval
    - ☐ Executive staff approval
    - ☐ Board of Director approval
- ☐ Go

Step 6 ERP Selection

With the project organization completed, ERP selection is the next step. This carries the matching process down another level. Build the system specifications around the approved future case. Sharply separate needs from wants. Regardless of the attractive enhancements demonstrated, focus on the needed functionality. The analogy we use is of a beautiful car with a poor engine. While it looks great, it is not going to get you very far. The analogy continues. An operational car constructed of parts from a variety of spare cars may work, but one manufactured with a system of parts will be more efficient, last longer, and have more functionality. Think about software as a system and not just as "chunks" of functionality. Middleware, whether it holds the software package together or integrates your applications into the system flow are never as efficient as fully integrated code. The middleware or "mashed" software concepts often introduce "gremlins," unexpected and difficult to fix glitches. Many of the older SaaS applications are very prone to this problem. If selecting that option, very carefully evaluate how the package is constructed. Get your IT department deeply involved in all aspects of the technical evaluation.

Functionality Check List

This following functionality checklist is an updated version of the IBM "The Production Information Control System." It provides tracking for how much ERP has changed over the years, yet remains conceptually the same.

Core Enterprise Resource Planning (ERP)

- ☐ Sales Forecasting
    - ☐ Model selection
    - ☐ Forecast plans
    - ☐ Evaluation and measurement

- ☐ Customer Order Processing

- [ ] Configuration inquiry / matrix
- [ ] Corporate wide available to promise
- [ ] Unlimited line items
- [ ] On-line credit checking/card processing
- [ ] Easy customer and ship-to process
- [ ] Quotes
- [ ] Revision tracking
- [ ] Commission processing
- [ ] Sales analysis
- [ ] Drill down capabilities

- [ ] Engineering Data Control
  - [ ] Basic records file organization
  - [ ] Engineering drawings
  - [ ] Engineering changes
  - [ ] Product structure and standard routing records maintenance
  - [ ] Full where used capabilities
  - [ ] Interface with production equipment

- [ ] Inventory Control
  - [ ] Stock status control
  - [ ] ABC inventory analysis
  - [ ] Order policy
  - [ ] Inventory maintenance and update
  - [ ] Physical inventory
  - [ ] Multi-location for domestic and international
  - [ ] Available to promise
  - [ ] Allocation
  - [ ] Cycle counting
  - [ ] Location/lot tracking
  - [ ] Product traceability

- [ ] Requirements
  - [ ] Finished production requirements – gross to net
  - [ ] Component requirements gross to net

- ☐ Special features
- ☐ Lot sizing
- ☐ Offset requirements
- ☐ Net change
- ☐ Pegged requirements
  - ☐ Full level
  - ☐ Single level

☐ Purchasing
- ☐ Requisition and PO preparation
- ☐ Purchase order follow-up
- ☐ Purchase evaluation
- ☐ Vendor evaluation and selection

☐ Capacity Planning
- ☐ Projected work center load report
- ☐ Planned order load
- ☐ Order start date calculations
- ☐ Load leveling
- ☐ Rough cut capacity planning
- ☐ Work center capacity planning

☐ Operation Scheduling
- ☐ Dispatching sequence
- ☐ Order estimator
- ☐ Load summary by work center
- ☐ Priority rules
- ☐ Queue time analysis
- ☐ Tool control

☐ Shop Floor Control
- ☐ Labor planning and reporting
- ☐ Material movement
- ☐ Work-in-process feedback
- ☐ Creation of factory paper/online production data
- ☐ Machine utilization

- ☐ Tool planning
- ☐ Special packaging
- ☐ RFID
- ☐ Bar Coding
- ☐ Plan-O-Grams
- ☐ Visual controls

Extended ERP

- ☐ Customer Relationship Management (CRM) – Marketing automation
- ☐ Sales Force Automation – (SFA) Customer support
- ☐ Product Lifecycle Management (PLM)
- ☐ Product Data Management (PDM)
- ☐ Supply Chain Management (SCM)
  - ☐ Language
  - ☐ Customs
  - ☐ Management of FOB timing
  - ☐ Comprehensive order tracking
- ☐ Supply Chain collaboration (SCC)
- ☐ Warehouse management System
  - ☐ Multiple picking methods
  - ☐ Forward pick replenishment
  - ☐ Transportation Management
  - ☐ Location control
- ☐ Field Service
- ☐ Financial Planning and Budgeting
  - ☐ Budgets
  - ☐ Simulations

- ☐ Multiple charts of accounts
- ☐ Currency conversion and management

☐ Manufacturing Execution Systems (MES)

☐ Document Management Systems
- ☐ Content Management Systems

☐ Quality Management Systems

☐ Asset Management Systems

☐ Multi-Plant processing

☐ Governance
- ☐ Risk Compliance
- ☐ Sustainability
- ☐ Project Management
- ☐ Enterprise Performance Management (EPM)

☐ Intelligence applications
- ☐ Business Intelligence (BI)
- ☐ Enterprise Manufacturing Intelligence (EMI)

☐ Energy management

☐ Mobile technology

The Matching Process (Gap Analysis)

- ☐ Restate strategies into ERP features and functionality
- ☐ Map the current state gap analysis to strategy restatement
- ☐ Match type, style and model to global ERP suppliers and reduce list
- ☐ Match the capabilities and functions of the ERP package to the future state features and functions requirements

Analyzing Potential ERP Suppliers

Each software provider offers a range of functionality. Part of the selection process is to construct a master list and grade each supplier on how well the functionality works for your company.

- ☐ Demonstrations
- ☐ Site visits
- ☐ Finalize ERP supplier deliverables
- ☐ Supplier proposal
- ☐ Gap analysis field by field, file by file matching current ERP to new
- ☐ Boardroom review

The first task is to reduce the number of potential suppliers. Use the business shape and complexity profiles defined on pages 67-82, and select the ratings for your company.

The objective is to match your organization to the large population of software suppliers and determine which potential providers fit your profile. At the same time, it is important not to become obsessed with the largest provider in each category, nor to stay within a respective tier. Software systems are very diverse with a considerable overlap in product functionality.

Your Business Profile - Quantify					
Revenue	250+	100-500m	25-250m	1-50m	0-5m
Number of employees	2000+	1000+	50-1000	20-200	1-25
Number of users	60-1000+	30-1000	5-200	1-40	1-5

Data from: The Right Choice Makes All the Difference – http://softresources.com

Product complexity	5	4	3	2	1
Process complexity	5	4	3	2	1
Multi-facility	5	4	3	2	1
Globalized	5	4	3	2	1
Spatial	5	4	3	2	1
Network complexity	5	4	3	2	1
Transactional volumes	5	4	3	2	1
Real Time	5	4	3	2	1

Five (5) = high   One (1) = low
Data from: Affinity Systems LLC

Illustration-Your Business Profile

Match the following software tiers to your profile.

ERP Software Profile		
Level	Type of software	Tier
5 Highly complex	Enterprise	Tier One
4 Complex	Upper market	Tier One and Two
3 Medium Complex	Mid-market	Tier One, Two and Three
2 Somewhat Complex	Small to mid-market	Tier Two, Three and Four
1 Not complex	Small	Tier Five and/or SaaS

Illustration-ERP Software Profile

Select the associated price range

Software Price Range	
Tier One	750K to 2M
Tier Two	250K to 1.5M
Tier Three	25K to 250K
Tier Four	5K to 50K
Tier Five	$100 to $500

Data from: The Right Choice Makes All the Difference – http://softresources.com

Illustration-Software Price Range

Fill in the following summary:

Your software profile
Your complexity _____
Tiers applicable _____
Price range   _____

Illustration-Your Software Profile

In addition to the number of optional tiers, note the wide range of prices. If your profile is upper market, the prices range from tier one through tier 2 is two million for a high and 250k for a low.

Your objective is to get all the functionalities needed at the lowest price from a reliable, solvent, and viable supplier. There are other charges in addition to software price, including maintenance, per user, etc., but these will sort themselves out as you work through the process.

Following is a partial list of the software suppliers by tier:

Tier One

- SAP
- Oracle
- Microsoft

Tiers Two and Three

- Infor/Lawson
- IFS
- MS Dynamics AX
- Oracle JD Edwards Enterprise One
- Sage
- Microsoft Dynamics NAV and Dynamics GP
- Sage 500 ERP

- Exact
- Exact Macola ES
- Infor 10 ERP Express
- SAP Business One
- Syspro
- NetSuite
- Epicor
- Consonal
- Aviant

Many of the ERP software suppliers have acquired other companies and incorporated their products. In addition, they have developed fully integrated systems for different markets.

As in prior discussions, having all the software from one developer does not mean the systems work together. They have multiple packages, developed using different languages, and protocols. Upgrading from one system to another is frequently the equal of installing a new system from any supplier.

Use the following resources to help with your search:

http://technologyevaluation.com/
http://panorama-consulting.com/
http://it.toolbox.com/
http://softresources.com/

- ☐ Internet searches
- ☐ Professional publications
- ☐ Professional organizations
- ☐ Industry specific chat rooms
- ☐ The use of search tools, such as those offered at TEC
- ☐ Using a consultant or consulting firm familiar with the industry, generalized ERP and industry specific ERP packages

Reduce the number of potential suppliers to a manageable level by using the following strategic RFP concept to refine the match:

The Multi-Step RFP Process

Our research and studies have determined the RFP is the most hated step in the process by both customer and supplier. Every software company surveyed felt significant changes were required in order to make it efficient.

Many respondents used the opportunity to lay the blame on consultants. Our research indicates no group occupies the moral high ground, but be aware of the problem. What is important is to recognize this can be the most wasteful, expensive and least value-adding step in the process.

In order to shorten the time and increase the efficiency, approach it like a Lean process and eliminate unnecessary steps. Break the process into smaller chunks focusing on the precise issues at each level. It makes little sense to get into the details of features of functions with suppliers without establishing higher-level requirements.

We suggest using a variation of the traditional RFP process.

Traditionally, customers prepare long detailed RFP's. ERP companies hate to fill them out. It takes a major time commitment to answer all the questions. In addition, few people know enough to respond to all issues. The ERP supplier does not know if this is a potential client or someone doing a preliminary justification. Consequently, the salesperson rapidly fills in the answers. They may write, "A modification is required," when the requirement or solution is not readily apparent, to avoid automatically losing the sale.

The process introduces ambiguity and error. You need a document that translates the strategic plan into ERP software requirements, not a full features and functions list.

Strategic RFP

The Strategic RFI (also called a mini-RFP) communicates the core business requirements.

- ☐ Take the unnecessary work (waste) out of the RFP process
- ☐ Make your proposal viable to the ERP suppliers
- ☐ Provide the relevant information
- ☐ Avoid unnecessary responses to long, complicated preliminary RFP
- ☐ Increase the quality of responses from the suppliers

Following is a check off list for a mini-RFP:

- ☐ Name
- ☐ Description of the company
- ☐ Number of plants and types
- ☐ Size of company – use a relative scale if can't give out the information
- ☐ Organization
- ☐ Hardware, software and network configuration
- ☐ Existing database structures
- ☐ Key dates
- ☐ Send copies of your business profile and spider diagrams
- ☐ Submission requirements and cutoff dates
- ☐ Transaction volumes
- ☐ Two page strategy statement translated into ERP terms
- ☐ Thirty key operational requirements - informational
- ☐ Electronic Data Interchange (EDI) requirements- who supplies and how
- ☐ Type of company (make a check off matrix)
- ☐ Multi-plant / multi-company
- ☐ Integrated accounting with logic for Sarbanes-Oxley
- ☐ Industry type - Distributor, ETO, BTO, ATO, process manufacturing, construction, health care
- ☐ SCM with automobile industry

- ☐ SCM with multi-language and country processing capability
- ☐ Names of countries in the supply chain
- ☐ Engineering interfaces
- ☐ Inventory location management in multiple locations
- ☐ Support a visual system
- ☐ Supports Lean principles
- ☐ Picking logic for wave, less than case pack, bin locations and auto replenishment of forward, less than case pack picking locations
- ☐ Supports radio frequency (Bar Code Scanning and/or RFID)
- ☐ Plan-O-Grams
- ☐ Customer shipping requirements

Send strategy translations to a "number of ERP companies." Since these are high-level, requirements the suppliers will respond in kind.

Telephone Interviews

Reduce the list to five before sending out the features and functions RFP. There are several ways to accomplish this:

- ☐ Telephone interviews
- ☐ Online demos
- ☐ Online chat rooms
- ☐ Online ERP evaluation web sites
- ☐ ERP company web site

Features and Functions Request for Proposal (RFP)

The features and functions RFP is synonymous with the traditional RFP proposal. It must be in sufficient detail and focused on the top 20 or 30 most important criteria. The RFP represents all the associates, who must agree that all central issues and criteria are sufficiently covered. Send the RFP/RFQ to the survivors of the strategic RFP process.

There are on line companies providing RFP services. Their capabilities range from poor to excellent. Visiting their websites and talking to ERP professionals will help you select the right candidates. Reliable services are not cheap, but they will work through the issues and send the RFP to the selected ERP suppliers.

Set priorities and assign weights to each selection criteria. If a Selection Service is used you may want to do simulations with different weights.

Get steering committee approval on the criteria before issuing the RFP. This reduces questions about the selection process.

Suppliers have qualified by filling out and submitting a strategic RFP. It does not make any sense to repeat information. It should come back in a summarized form through the deliverables, spell out the evaluation criteria, and restate the key dates.

Suppliers will ask who their competitors are. There are different schools of thought about how to respond. One side feels that knowing provides an incentive to prepare more thoroughly. Other companies will not divulge competitors because negative effects may occur. Suppliers use the information to compare their system favorably to their competitors and this frequently includes product bashing at the demo. You want the supplier to concentrate on their ERP system and how it solves your business issues. Vendors may feel they have a built-in disadvantage and drop out of the race. While troubling it aids in the reduction process. Draw your own conclusion about how to handle the question.

In RFP, terms should:

- ☐ Support the mission and strategies, not the glitz
    - ☐ Account information needs
    - ☐ Flow within the business
- ☐ Key field sizes
    - ☐ Item master
    - ☐ Description
    - ☐ Group technology number

- Product structure
- Multiple representations, e.g. SKU for multiple customers

- Features and functions:
    - Non-technology related
    - Solution Oriented

- Describes each business function:
    - In detail
    - Relationship between them

- Need to take into consideration:
    - Cost – want but not selection criteria until later in the process
    - Solution support needs
    - Life cycle solutions
    - Ongoing charges
    - Total cost of ownership
    - The effects of increased velocity (throughput) on asset management
    - Scalability
    - Frequency and method of ERP updates

- Address all facets of the solution
    - Project schedule
    - Phased or big bang implementation methodology
    - Database
    - Applications
    - Network
    - Security
    - Hardware
    - Vendor support
    - Education
    - Implementation time line
    - Modifications

- ☐ Detail "supported/not supported"
- ☐ Maintenance fees

Responses will become an addendum to the contract.

There is an option to the features and functions RFP titled "ERP Company Deliverables." After evaluating packages, ask the suppliers to submit the deliverable's document. If they reject the RFP but you like the product, they should not object to a document spelling out the deliverables in enough detail to establish accountability. Refusing to provide this document is a warning signal. If the supplier remains on your list, pursue other options establishing legal accountability, such as a super detailed contract (showing all the deliverables).

The danger to the ERP supplier using the deliverable process instead of the features and functions may be the lack of detail on specifics. This puts them at a disadvantage.

Some teams call suppliers to fill in the detail, but this may cause information gaps when evaluating one package against another. If obtained through the RFP, follow-up before ending the evaluation. If from the deliverable, there is not an obligation to achieve parity. If suppliers fail to provide the appropriate competitive information, it is their problem, not yours. If you feel responsible for giving suppliers the opportunity to respond to iterative questions, perhaps the RFP was insufficient or the needs were unclear. Get the answer and include it in the deliverables. Know what you want because iterations cost money and time. Include the following minimal deliverables:

- ☐ Specifically, how it satisfies the strategic requirements.
- ☐ Specifically address the 20-30 key issues
- ☐ How the gaps will be solved (solutions to the business problems not sufficiently resolved by the features and functions of the package). This could be modifications, work a rounds or manual processes (including PCs)
- ☐ How many and what type of modifications are required, how much they will cost and when will they be done

- ☐ Software supplier team assignment
- ☐ Document how to measure performance
- ☐ Completion date
- ☐ All costs broken down by type
- ☐ Projected schedule of expenses

Analyze Responses to the RFP's

One technique is to use a white board and layout a spreadsheet of the core requirements with a column for each ERP supplier across the top and a list of functions in rows. More sophisticated or larger companies use tablet and mobile applications but making it highly visible is a valuable project management technique. Grade the functionality of each with a score of 0-5. Use the Spider diagram as reference.

5 = Better than required
4 = Meets all requirements
3 = Meets minimal requirements – some work a round needed
2 = Questionable – some modifications required
1 = Significant modifications required
0 = Not available

Prepare the metric either visually or on-line. The responses to the RFP will provide a rough-cut look at the criteria. Each team member will fill out the scorecard immediately after any demo or site visit.

Multiply the weight of the feature/function rank to calculate the score. Update your board, on line or Excel program.

Leave room for comments. If the core functionality issues do not get a high score, reject the vendor. If you are uncertain about how to score or what a company meant with a certain response, call them. If they are near to you, ask them to stop by. This is not a demo. It is fact gathering. Score keeping is not a game. You are searching for the truth and there is not an obligation for equal time with other suppliers.

There is debate about which should come first, the site visit or the demo. Although the site visit can help reduce the number of suppliers on the list, it is time-consuming and expensive. The demo will provide the team with the knowledge needed to evaluate the ERP package. Save the site visits for the final selection process.

Call Current Customers

The vendor's customer list will provide insight into what type of companies use the software. Call them all. Make sure the system they are using matches the core requirements. If the clients are manufacturing running ERP Systems, and you are a distributor, be careful going forward with the vendor.

Call the contacts list to see how they feel about the ERP and how usable the product is.

Vendor Analysis

Get financial data and thoroughly check out the suppliers. Make sure they are profitable and will remain viable. Find out their history on updates and ease of use. If they cannot pass these qualifying steps, do not invite them to demo.

Some ERP suppliers are private companies, and they are not required to make their financial data public. They may be reluctant to share it. Inform them that proof of financial viability will be required before getting the order. They may wait until the executive visit to share it. If they choose not to divulge the information, you are not obligated to keep them on the list. You are the customer, and entitled to the affirmation needed for fulfillment of due diligence.

Cut the List

At this point, the project team has the knowledge to reduce competition to two or three suppliers. The team must reach a consensus, and then meet with the executive champion and a steering committee. All must agree before proceeding.

After gaining team consensus, contact the suppliers to ensure their continued interest. We define consensus as "I can live with the decision, support it, and make the system work."

Put together a demo schedule. No one will want to be first, and everyone wants to be last. There are several ways to determine the priority. One is to draw names. A second way is to poll the team. It may seem arbitrary and less fair, but fairness is not the issue. You are trying to get the right ERP for your business. Schedule the demo sequence your team wants, without any excuse.

Demo – Potential Combat Zone

Demos are fascinating affairs. Some presenters are brutally honest; others oversell functionality and some lie. It is a tough, highly competitive business. Accept that fact and prepare to deal with it. If suppliers try to lie, or misrepresent the product, and you know it, nail them to the wall. Be prepared for a dog and pony show but make them stick to your requirements. In general, ERP representatives cannot afford a failure. It hurts their sales effort at other accounts and can be expensive to rectify. They must also live up to the conditions in the contract. These are reasons to include RFP documents and deliverables in the contract as addendums. Establish and communicate the basis for scoring. Make sure they understand you will grade the demonstration on the live system only.

Demos are a problem for ERP suppliers. They must somehow summarize your business data into a structure allowing the demo of all your business conditions. They normally have an accumulation of customer data in their computers. Remember, they are demonstrating a capability so be patient and open-minded but cautious.

One sign of commitment is when supplier teams visit up to one week before the demo, tour the business, interview associates, and perform their own evaluation. After the assessment, they integrate your company data into their demo. If they are not willing to take this critical step, remove them from your list. A demo without your data is just show and tell.

Make a distinction between technical support and the salesperson. The technical person has no incentive to misstate functionality because if assigned to the project they have to make the system work. Uncover their agenda by asking whether they will be a part of the implementation team.

Cover all-important issues. Project leaders and executive champions, encourage your team to ask the tough questions, and do not hold it against them. It is not the time to be shy. We have seen far too many cases where members of the user community were afraid to ask good questions even when they needed answers.

- ☐ Look for the truth. Just because the presenters say it, does not make it true or false. In the final analysis, only the facts are important.
- ☐ No glitz, stick to the core issues until understood.
- ☐ Start a parking lot list and get answers to all issues.
- ☐ Remember, team members will have to live with the results – perhaps for a long time.
- ☐ Make sure they use your data in the presentation.
- ☐ If you cannot break the code, it is not real.
- ☐ Ask pointed, tough questions.
- ☐ Is functionality equal to or better than the requirement?
- ☐ Is the system scalable?
- ☐ Is the system easy to use? If yes, prove it.
- ☐ Does the system function as advertised?
- ☐ Are they willing to put the RFP into the contract without change?
- ☐ Are they willing to submit a set of deliverables?
- ☐ Can you work with them?
- ☐ Does the system fulfill the requirements on the list?

- ☐ Does the system support the strategies?
- ☐ Were business critical functionality properly demonstrated?
- ☐ Does the system support real-time processing?
- ☐ Make sure the system supports mobile communications technology.
- ☐ How willing is the supplier to make modifications, and at what cost?

If suppliers use a demo program, it defeats the purpose. Ask or observe if the code is real, if not, stop the show. The supplier's grade is zero. Tell them immediately and do not waste your team's time.

PowerPoint presentations can be informative, but they are NOT code and not taken at face value. It is the same as demo code and does not lead to the truth. Mark zero on your evaluation for all functions covered in this way. If all they have are Power Point presentations, cancel the meeting. It is a waste of time.

If required functionality is under development or listed as future enhancements, ignore them. A tested enhancement or added functionality may be weeks or years in the future. The truth is you do not know, and if you did, the data to match it to your needs will not be available. If they do not have it now, score a zero.

Parking Lot List

Few systems will offer all the needed functions. These issues must show up on the parking lot list. Match your activities plan to the parking lot list. Make sure nothing falls through the cracks. It is important to resolve all issues before signing the contract. In the heat of an implementation, getting key functions resolved and solutions implemented becomes difficult. The result is often a compromise forcing awkward and expensive work-a-rounds and/or higher development costs. In addition, it causes missed due dates and creates tension.

One purpose of a parking lot list is to isolate inadequate or unsupported functional requirements. Executive management needs to keep a sharp eye on this activity. Converting the list into ERP modification proposals generates expense and time-consuming investigations. Worse, the ERP supplier may not provide ongoing support to modifications, and you risk incurring additional expenses when installing upgrades or future modifications.

Site Visits

Save site visits until the finalists are determined. Arrange site visits to companies with business profiles similar to yours. Reference your enterprise shape and spider diagram. Match sites as closely as possible.

- Business type - vertical and manufacturing type
- Relational (product complexity)
- Process complexity
- Multi-facility
- Network complexity
- Spatial
- Transactional
- Real-time

Note that similar products are not criteria. Competitors are normally reluctant to share what could be sensitive information. An ERP supplier unable to find parallel clients within your vertical may not have experience with your business type.

Be careful. The people conducting the site visit may have a different agenda.

A company we visited was effectively using many of the features and functions of a package. The project manager was progressive. His support influenced our project team's selection of a specific package. After signing the contract and starting the implementation, the project manager contacted us. He offered to work as an independent contractor. We successfully installed the system without his help. The ERP proved to be a great fit for our client.

Make sure the walk meets the talk. Take notes and use the selection criteria defined for the evaluation. The goal of the team may be the same, but members gain different perspectives and make individual observations. Have team members immediately fill out evaluations.

Include the aforementioned forms and notes about the ERP system applicability to your organization, observations raising flags and other relevant information.

Selection

The team not only has the information required to make a decision but also is probably tired of the investigation. It is important for the team leader to keep everyone focused.

The team must evaluate the facts and reach a consensus on the winner and runner up. The ERP system must have the functionality to support all associates. If not, find a different package.

Select two vendors, because the process can still break down in negotiation. A split decision between office functionality and operations should favor operations. If the ERP system does not work for them, no one will be happy.

Share the decision with the steering committee. If they concur with the choice, notify the top two suppliers of their status.

Executive Visit to ERP Company

The executive visit to the supplier company is a critical step. The steering committee and the team need to work with the executive to prepare for the visit. The project team must provide an issue list, often the contents of the parking lot list. The executive team must get answers for each critical issue.

Use the opportunity to compare company values and establish relationships with the executive personnel. The visit will determine the partnership potential and the degree of transparently. The result needs to be a high-level commitment for both sides.

Discuss metrics and accountability. Make sure they understand that all contracts will get a legal review and there must be detail behind the proposal. Take a copy of the RFP or letter of deliverables. If they have not supplied a detail list of deliverables or adequate answers to the RFP, find out what the problem is. Make sure you discuss it openly and thoroughly, and most of all, do not reach a legal agreement without it.

If the ERP supplier has not provided financial information, ask now. If the supplier is not forthcoming, visit the runner-up to see if they are a viable supplier.

Homework

- Document issues
- Meet with the project team
- Understand all issues on the parking lot list and their proposed solution
- Consider taking a financial member of the project team
- Meet with the consultant
- Thoroughly understand the issues at question
- Review the billing structure
- Have finance review the contract before the trip

Site Visit

- Discuss timing and penalty for late install
- Discuss composition of the vendor project team and process for replacing incompatible personnel
- Make it clear what expenses will and will not be reimbursed
- Discuss other mutual opportunities, such as shared revenue for the development of an enhancement

- ☐ Discuss payment holdback percentage until the system is completed as promised

Final Decision

Following the visit, the executive group meets with the project team. They will exchange information and make a decision.

Notify the first place supplier, establish a date, and time to negotiate the contract. Ask again for any outstanding documents or deliverables.

Contract

The responsibility for contract negotiations belongs to executive management, not to the project team. Successful contracts are the result of practiced negotiators. Get a legal review. Executive management must review and approve all contracts, and approval by the Board of Directors is highly recommended.

The executive champion often conducts the negotiations. They should include other key personnel.

- ☐ Project leader
- ☐ Consultant
- ☐ Someone who understands contracts (e.g. – CFO)
- ☐ Someone who understands Information Technology (e.g.-CIO)

The person or team conducting the negotiations needs the following:

- ☐ Complete understanding of solution needs
- ☐ Technical knowledge or accompanied by someone with it
- ☐ Familiar with ERP negotiations (e.g. modifications, missed dates)
- ☐ Incorporate supplier proposals into the contract
- ☐ Make sure the deliverables and RFP process are incorporated
- ☐ Future state review to test inclusion of needed functionalities
- ☐ Make sure the contract undergoes a thorough legal review

The contract must cover all these points at a minimum:

- ☐ Software
- ☐ Maintenance
- ☐ Per user fees
- ☐ Upgrades
- ☐ Additional modules (lock in future)
- ☐ Consulting fees by classification
- ☐ How will the software company bill
- ☐ Hourly consulting rates
- ☐ Estimate of the total cost
- ☐ Expenses by category
- ☐ Application modifications
- ☐ Spell out training: who, when, end associates and technical personnel
- ☐ Train the trainer or train the company
- ☐ Training method – on site, via video conference
- ☐ Maintenance fees and when they start
- ☐ By whom and at what cost
- ☐ What are the cost saving's opportunities for co-development
- ☐ Compare costs for Big Bang vs. Phased implementation
- ☐ Make sure the conversion methodology is clear
- ☐ Negotiate percent hold back until the system functions as promised
- ☐ Ability to change incompatible supplier team members
- ☐ Hardware and other equipment supplied by software provider
- ☐ Time phased expenditure plan
- ☐ Spell out Disaster Recovery Plans
- ☐ Backup
- ☐ Restore
- ☐ Documentation
- ☐ Change management process
- ☐ Technical services

ERP Company Deliverables

The company buying the ERP needs to get an agreement of deliverables, including but not limited to cost, and the projected completion date.

- ☐ The contract has proposals meeting strategic requirements
- ☐ Specific solutions to the 20-30 key issues
- ☐ Solutions to the open issues including the parking lot list
- ☐ How many and what type of modifications are required, how much they will cost and when will they be done
- ☐ The persons assigned from the supplier
- ☐ Performance metrics
- ☐ Project Justification, cost/benefit analysis and ROI

If you do not like the way negotiations are preceding, terminate the process. If issues cannot be resolved at this level, before the sale is complete, they will be extremely difficult to solve after signing the contract and the project is in process.

Sign the Contract

- ☐ Legal review
- ☐ Executive approval
- ☐ Now it is time for action

Map Legacy Systems to New System

With the contract signed, technical personnel from the software suppliers will meet with your IT experts. Make sure everyone is qualified to perform this very important process. They must map the current system to the selected system in detail, field to field. Define what actions are required to convert from the legacy system to the new one. Review and resolve differences with prior agreements (earlier chapter).

The team of experts will define the data conversion methodology and identify the resources needed to achieve it. Some data conversion options are:

- Programmatic – must write and debug programs
- Data entry – must have trained entry personnel

Information technology personnel from both sides perform this analysis. It does not substitute for the boardroom review.

Detail Implementation Plan

Normally the project manager, lead consultant from the software company, and independent consultant lock themselves up and:

- Prepare the implementation plan
- Prepare project PERT
- Post copies to an intranet and visual tracking system
- Project matrix

Much of this plan exists in a preliminary form. This step requires filling in the details and time lines. The relationship between events is critical. A PERT or a Gant Chart will establish proper time sequences. The project manager is responsible for this activity.

Project plans must consider the rhythms of the business cycles. If, for example, September is the busiest month, and January is the slowest month, then January is a better "go live" date. There are counter cycles, sales cycles, and professional sales cycles, competing priorities, etc.

Plan implementations for the last weekend of the month cut over to accommodate end of month accounting. This provides the time to pull old paperwork and replace it with new.

Determine the need for a beginning physical inventory or comprehensive cycle count to initiate the system. This needs to be a joint financial and inventory management decision. Affinity Systems recommends taking a physical inventory, and normally auditors agree. When accounting problems occur, there must be a reference base of information.

- Timing issues
- Determine need for a physical inventory
- Cut over
- Financial
- Full team participation
- Make sure there is a contingency plan if the system fails
- Signoff by team

It is the project leader and ERP consultant's responsibility to get commitments from the team, prioritize, and apply finish dates to the action items.

- Early assignment of task responsibility to individuals
- The key task completion dates may realistically change
- Plan training to coincide with implementation
- It is the team responsibility to change dates
- The team should sign off on the plan
- Establish data conversion process:
    - Manual
    - Automated
- Develop a methodology for data purification and conversion
- Select cut over date and logic
- The task list - completion dates may realistically change:
    - Tasks to be completed
    - Expected duration
    - Planned completion date
    - Assigned responsibility
    - Consequences of being late (relational implications)
    - Signoff
- Progress measurements
- Stick to plan

Prepare the Organization

- [ ] The project team meets with the executive staff and reviews the plan, benefits and ROI
- [ ] Plan is go, no go or return to the drawing board

Project Kickoff Meeting

Bring all the members up to date on the project. Meet with the entire organization in one group or a series of meetings. Emphasize the importance of employee involvement and ask for their help and cooperation. At this meeting, it is normal for someone to ask if the project is going to result in layoffs or outsourcing of jobs. The executive staff must have an answer

- [ ] Communicate program: how it will work, what the process will be, what the expectations are and project metrics
- [ ] Emphasis the importance of the program to the future of the company - its ability be competitive and grow
- [ ] Announce who will be on the project team and their roles
- [ ] Explain how their jobs will be backfilled or handled
- [ ] Emphasis the project team will need support from all associates and top management.
- [ ] Establish communications and the project parameters
- [ ] Emphasis lack of tolerance for poor quality performance
- [ ] Reiterate consequences
- [ ] Explain tracking mechanism: Intranet, bulletin boards, or internal newsletter
- [ ] Spell out the training expectations and program
- [ ] Spell out communications loops
- [ ] Planned completion dates
- [ ] Grievance process

Step 7 Implementation

In our experience, individual implementation plans are variable but the overall steps are generic. We recommend using a viable project management approach. The following constitute authorization to move forward with the project. The enterprise has agreed on the following:

Document of Understanding

- ☐ Clear priority
- ☐ Product components to lifecycle – the business understands needed changes and actions required to achieve it.
- ☐ Personnel to support the implementation – team members at all levels have their assignments. Technical and end associates – there is sufficient support personnel to take care of the technical issues and there are persons on the team with knowledge of the processes.
- ☐ Internal people to support - team members understand their support roles.
- ☐ Preliminary costs documented and reflected in the budget.
- ☐ Current applications documented and understood.

Approval to Go

- ☐ Purpose of the new ERP
- ☐ Cost/benefit analysis
- ☐ Implementation schedule
- ☐ Selection rationale
- ☐ Team consensus
- ☐ Executive Champion approval
- ☐ Steering Committee approval
- ☐ Executive Staff approval
- ☐ Board of Director approval

Project Plan

- ☐ Big Bang or phased implementation
- ☐ Tasks to be completed
- ☐ Expected duration
- ☐ End dates
- ☐ Person responsible
- ☐ Establish intranet reporting methodology
- ☐ Define and Implement change control procedures
- ☐ Establish a process for a physical inventory or comprehensive cycle count

Business Simulation or Boardroom Pilot

This step, regardless of label, is critical in the process. In summary, the company sets aside several days for the ERP supplier and the associates to detail match the new ERP to the current system. The objective is to introduce the ERP team, teach the system to the associates, match functionalities, resolve mismatches, establish priorities and schedules, resolve conflicts between the systems and communicate the plan and expectations. Associates prepare scripts from actual documents and processes in advance of the meeting.

Highlight the unresolved issues on the parking lost list. This may be the last opportunity to resolve them without contention.

The entire process will be similar to the following process:

- ☐ Familiarize associates with the system
    - ☐ Features
    - ☐ Functions
    - ☐ Modules

- ☐ Environment review
    - ☐ User
    - ☐ Database
    - ☐ Tools

- ☐ Security
- ☐ Technology

☐ Establish the training process
- ☐ Relationship of training to implementation
- ☐ How training will be done to accommodate modifications
- ☐ Who will be trained
- ☐ How they will be trained -train the trainer or "everyone"
- ☐ Executive as well as associates

☐ Resolve issues such as:
- ☐ Multiple plants
- ☐ Timing
- ☐ How they are tied together
- ☐ Corporate and individual database architecture
- ☐ Equipment differences

☐ Systems codes of all types – setup
- ☐ This includes chart of accounts
- ☐ Identify contents
- ☐ Reach approval

☐ Load the systems codes and help determine if the interaction of the codes creates conflicts.

☐ Load the test scripts for the complete order / production / billing cycle and end of month financial closing.

☐ Analyze all outputs and compare the two systems. Document and resolve all deviations.

☐ Resolution of all parking lot issues discovered during the demo and subsequent discussions.

- ☐ Final definition of all work-a-rounds, process changes, modifications and middle ware.

- ☐ Review and resolve any conflicts with critical success factors.

Conversion Databases

- ☐ Establish appropriate data bases
    - ☐ A sandbox is a database where associates can play without concern for data or test integrity.
    - ☐ Testing – A database where associates can test their processes and no one can change the data without coordinating with others.
    - ☐ Go live – where corrected or converted files are stored.
    - ☐ Start a data conversion plan immediately.

Stick to Plan – Execution

- ☐ Stick to plan

- ☐ Implement production systems and information systems changes in parallel

- ☐ Coordinate process and software changes – special concern - modifications

- ☐ Make sure people are accountable for on time completion

- ☐ Update PERT charts and other visual documentation

- ☐ Find out what problems are preventing action

- ☐ Solve problems rapidly to prevent ripples of delay

- ☐ Check off completed events and tasks

- ☐ Implement change control

- ☐ Get user involvement on all data changes such as descriptions and codes

- ☐ Determine who has access to the supplier hotline

Daily Meeting

- ☐ Take minutes

- ☐ Document all issues

- ☐ Follow-up on open hotline issues

- ☐ Communicate findings, decisions and solutions to the team

- ☐ Do not get wrapped up in detail - call a specific meeting to address specific issues

- ☐ Stop all "thrashing" sessions immediately

Weekly Progress Meeting

Do not let the meeting become a problem resolution forum. Solve problems in a different meeting with the right people, not the whole team.

- ☐ Optional - rotate minutes among the project team
- ☐ Make sure the appropriate people attend
- ☐ Schedule individual reports and progress charts
- ☐ Visual progress charts
- ☐ Weekly status to team by the project manager
- ☐ Weekly status report to project champion
- ☐ Schedule a specific update on all of the data conversion efforts
- ☐ If data conversion starts to run late, elevate and fix the problem immediately

Monthly Progress Reports to the Appropriate Distribution List

- ☐ Executive Champion
- ☐ Consultants
- ☐ Steering Committee
- ☐ President/CEO
- ☐ Board of Directors

Policies, Procedures and Systems Documentation

The first requirement is normally setting up systems codes. It is important to get this done right. These are the premises upon which you are telling the system about your business and how you want to do business in the future. Each module (relate to a department or departments) has its own codes. They are highly interactive with the codes set up in other modules. Carefully document codes as well as what they do. It will provide understanding when results "just aren't right."

- ☐ Option to use an outside technical writer – may be expensive

- ☐ New processes will make the maps used to analyze the system obsolete

- ☐ Updating the process maps may be simpler if a business process mapping program was used at the beginning of the project

- ☐ Document units of measure and quantities per assembly

- ☐ Document commodity codes

- ☐ Document salesperson and territory codes

- ☐ Document company and multi-plant codes

- ☐ Document the model and part number schemes

- ☐ User's manual for all new processes and how to use the systems

- ☐ Flows

- ☐ Screen prints

- ☐ Problem resolution methodologies

- ☐ Document systems changes

User Manuals

- ☐ Build user manuals for all new processes showing how to use the system.
    - ☐ Flow charts
    - ☐ Process maps
    - ☐ Screen prints
    - ☐ Problem resolution methodologies
    - ☐ Document all systems changes

Use Temporary Help

- ☐ Free internal resources
- ☐ Speed up file building

Train

- ☐ Executives must make people available
- ☐ All training must be done with real data
- ☐ Training must be in sync with modules implemented
- ☐ End associates
- ☐ Technical personnel
- ☐ Create systems documentation and test the procedures
- ☐ Review and validate documentation – test by running process to document
- ☐ Technical support
- ☐ Hardware and software technical training must support the ERP system - if timed properly, it should not significantly delay the project, but it is required
- ☐ Do not move forward unless training is completed for a specific module

Test

- ☐ Specifically test all modifications

- ☐ Desired vs. probable result

- ☐ Unit test

- ☐ Tests by the end associates
    - ☐ Usability
    - ☐ Functionality
    - ☐ Test scripts prepared by associates
    - ☐ Expand testing to all associates in the department – module by module

- ☐ Take corrective actions immediately
- ☐ Do parallel testing to insure quality
- ☐ Where parallel not possible, do pilot
- ☐ Systems tests
  - ☐ Full systems
  - ☐ Functionality
  - ☐ Networks
  - ☐ Security
  - ☐ Backup and restore
  - ☐ Disaster recovery

Go Live

Create "Go-Live" checklists clearly spelling out responsibilities. Discuss contingency plans.

Bring the team together and coordinate the conversion. Provide detailed work schedules. Remind all consultants this is a working session and they need to be there. Anyone can check data and help to exchange paperwork, including consultants.

Conduct the physical inventory or cycle count (in all probability this will be in process before the weekend).

Check the reports, both online and hard copy, and new system to the old. Check detail line information as well as totals.

Sign off on systems acceptance. If someone refuses, find out the problem and fix it before going live. While people are cautious, they may have a good reason to delay the implementation. Listen to them, enlist them, and fix the problem, but make sure progress continues.

You will probably not convert every file programmatically. Make sure data entry personnel are available.

Immediate Problem Resolution

Problem resolution is a responsibility of the project leader and consultants. Members of the conversion team will help fix problems on the go live weekend. Consultants need to be there.

Make sure there is help-line support available. Project leadership must determine exactly how to use the hotline and who can use it. Hotline calls must be prompt and answered. The user community has the need and right to expect fast answers and solutions. Management expects each one of them to be able to do their job. They are highly justified to insist on good working tools from the vendor project team.

Everyone must focus on fixing the problems.

Record All Reported Problems

Immediately after going live, test all modifications.

The team reviews the critical processes and paperwork (may be electronic images). These include inventory records, orders, invoices, accounts payable, shop paperwork, and picking lists.

The financial system requires exceptional attention. Taking a pre-implementation physical allows the validation of balances and facilitates spot-checking and correcting inventory balances. The sub ledgers and general ledger must be accurate. Review all problems and correct immediately, otherwise, they may snowball into the end of month financial statements, causing them to be late or inaccurate. Temporary workarounds are often required but make sure they are temporary. Incorporate the resolution into the Lean program and fix them.

If required, replace all shop floor paperwork. Installing a paperless system requires matching shop paper to online images. In either case, this can be a major task.

The system will still have bugs. The entire user community can help find and fix them.

Whoops

There are instances in the ERP world where the first reaction in the face of implementation problems is to go back to the old system. In the majority of cases, this is an overreaction. However, it is normal. This is where the executive champion and the project team leader must remain calm, logical, and provide the appropriate direction to the team.

While the post implementation stage is frequently stressful, the business can operate with some system deficiencies as long as they do not affect critical processes. That is the criteria against which to gauge moving ahead or going back. Going back will cause as many problems as fixing the differences and moving ahead. Each company faced with this choice will have to make their own decision. If all the process steps were correctly completed, and the team is ready for some anticipated firefighting duties, they will probably be able to overcome any startup problems.

Step 8 Measure Post Operational State

ERP systems are complex and even with complete procedures, it is difficult to test all conditions and combinations. Post implementation issues occur at different points in time. For this reason, anticipate the probability of post implementation problems, which take many forms and range from simple to fix to showstoppers.

- Hardware and ERP issues
- Inaccurate procedures
- Operational problems
- Process changes
- Reports will not have the data expected.

Problems are frequently in the seams, where information passes from one module to another. Middleware or other integration methodologies can increase the complexity of trouble shooting. Frequent errors occur in data mapping, resulting in information showing incorrectly, or using the wrong fields in the calculation. The use of proper testing and sign off procedures reduces errors. Post implementation problems are precisely the reason for doing weekend implementations. Start any activities in advance, if they do not affect the business.

Communication-All the Time

One of the problems encountered is the failure to communicate how jobs will change. Associates need to understand why they are doing procedures differently. For example, their duties may be increased but the overall effect will make it more efficient for downstream operations. People need to understand this result. They may have been doing the same thing for a number of years. When coming to work on Monday morning, their world will have changed. On this day, they will suddenly have to do it a different way. They may have been trained but suffer from a lost feeling while working with a new system.

Those of us engaged in project management are aware of how much a change scares people and how insecure it makes them. Management and supervision must be prepared to spend some soft time with associates reinforcing the new procedures, work rules, and methods. Additional training may be required. Provide it in good humor.

Management needs to listen to and involve the team. They can help resolve problems or explain conflicting situations. The user community will go out of their way to make the system a success when management positively interacts. Ignore the user community at peril. They are after all, the customers. In time, surveys may replace the walks but management may rediscover the value of daily communications as they implement other programs, such as Lean Six Sigma.

If the system fails to meet expectations all project leadership, internal and external, must explain why they have failed, and provide options to improve the situation. This is the moment for final accountability.

Follow-Up

The system was justified based on certain expectations and anticipated return on investment. Whenever ROI is justified using:

- Inventory turns - measure inventory turnover
- Headcount reduction- measure headcount
- Cash cycle reduction - measure the cash cycle

These measurements occur with predetermined frequency and consistency. Review the results with the management staff and the Board of Directors if required. Post them on the bulletin board and on-line project web site.

Immediately implement an auditing procedure for inventory and financial transactions.

Start user surveys. It is the responsibility of executive champion, team leader, and consultant to walk through the operation at least daily and talk to the people doing the work. They will take some justified criticism but it is unfair and cowardly to hide in the office and hope that problems will magically disappear.

Conduct post implementation lessons learned sessions with all the team members, consultants, and executive sponsor. Dissect how the problems were resolved. Discuss remaining problems, their status, and solutions. Have the consultants document unresolved issues and brief the project team. It signals the end of a Big Bang ERP project, and moving to the next step for phased rollouts.

Personnel Evaluation

Take the time for employee performance evaluations. Who were the stars? Who has demonstrated potential? Who are the candidates for development? You owe it to the team to perform the evaluation.

Celebration

An ERP project is long, arduous and involves the extraordinary effort of many people. The members of the project team deserve special recognition in some form. This may be a dinner with the executive staff. New leather coats. A weekend Bahamas cruise or any of a number of other rewards. Another type of celebration is to cater a lunch or have a picnic as a thank you to all employees. A better idea is to do something special for your team plus the lunch. The methods are varied and dependent on the culture of the business. The important thing is to celebrate the completion in a positive way. It may also be one way to start a culture change in the business as it uses new work tools to beat the competition.

The celebration step is easy to forget and normally is. The enterprise should reap huge returns using the new system. It is only fair to share a little with the people who made it happen. In addition, the next step in this process is to implement a continuous improvement program of some form. The executives of the enterprise will be asking and expecting many team members to take leadership roles in this effort, increasing pressure on operations.

Summary

- Measure performance
- Compare results to expectations
- Make adjustments where necessary
- Metrics - the system is providing the required functionality as planned
- Achieving ROI is the next step
- Share the rewards with the project team and organization

Step 9 Continuous Improvements - Perfect the System

It is time to "show me the money." When the core project is completed, the timing may be right for a project continuum. The objective is to perfect the system by changing and squeezing the waste out of all business processes.

There are reasons for this approach.

The organization has already undergone some process improvement training. If it has been a full-blown business transformation program, training has been comprehensive, placing the enterprise in an excellent position to move forward.

Teams have successfully completed a complex project. The team members for a VMP may be different from those required for the ERP system, but in most organizations, some of the ERP members will play an active role in the continuous improvement program.

The organization has learned how to function without the full-time involvement of many key team members. This does not mean exploiting members who sacrificed additional hours and made commitments to the ERP project. People will perform at a high level for a short-range project, but do not expect the same time commitment with a new program. Develop compensation or reward systems for long-term VMP.

For many companies, the decision will be to take a different path than VMP. This may be a new program such as supply-chain, CRM, a WMS program, or some other change process. While there will be pain in the transition, it is important to ride the momentum and reap the rewards.

Summary

Perfect the system.

- Process improvement is nearly always required to meet the ROI.
- Title – Lean Six Sigma not important, only the RESULTS count
- Concepts – process improvement is another topic, but the basic concepts are:
    - Eliminate non-value adding activities
    - Eliminate waste
    - Reduce variability
    - Compress time (increase velocity)
    - Standardize

Enjoy the process and celebrate the success, then further refine the information and physical realities.

About the Author

Wayne Staley has been actively involved with ERP since the early days of the concept, as a programmer, systems analyst, IT Director, and independent business consultant.

Educated in computer technology, quality, business, and production systems, he has managed Corporate Information Services, Materials, Logistics, and Manufacturing.

His shop floor experience includes Manager of Shop Operations of a complex fabrication facility, with foundry, aluminum casting, metal punching, machining, and assembly operations. Wayne worked on integrated SCM programs with China based suppliers, and collaboration and product development programs with Dow Chemical.

Wayne established Affinity Systems LLC, a system consulting company, in 1997. He has managed numerous strategy, Enterprise Resource Planning (ERP), and process improvement projects in manufacturing, government, distribution, agribusiness, vertically integrated forest products, and convention management. He developed training materials for ERP, SCM, strategy, change, process Improvement, and decision-making. Affinity Systems launched CompetitiveAmerica.us, a website advocating for American industry, in 1999.

Wayne started Phase Four Graphics LLC (phasefourgraphics.com), a graphic arts company, in 2010.

His other books are:

Pathway to Adaptability – Executive Lean and 8 Steps to the Adaptive Enterprise - 2008

Crunch Time for Health care - 2011

Pathway to Adaptability

Wayne L Staley

"If you don't know where you're going, any path will take you there."

The Cheshire cat

Alice's Wonderland is a labyrinth filled with strange places, unusual ideas, unexpected occupants, and unpredictable events. One danger is running ever faster but staying in the same place, a clear sign of lost direction.

This description applies to the real business world but even more volatile and unforgiving forces' sort it all out – the marketplace. It demands the correct products, appropriately priced and available now. Speed is King!

Pathway to Adaptability is for corporate leaders, executives, managers, and administrators who govern businesses of all types.

In Pathway to Adaptability, you will travel on an eight-step pathway through the corporate alignment process. The book provides assessments to track your progress.

Enterprises must become very smart, building real-time intelligence into every activity. Without accurate information foundations, and process improvement, adaptability is not achievable and significant opportunities will be lost.

"This book has invaluable information on LEAN Six Sigma Methodology that is used in my company, and has been used as a reference point in many of our LEAN Focus Groups across the country. I highly recommend Wayne Staley's book." Amazon review by Black Belt

Get Pathway to Adaptability at - http://www.competitiveamerica.us
Amazon.com - The book is available in Kindle (Electronic book) format.

Crunch Time for Health Care

Wayne L Staley and Jon Bingol

People are the Competitive Advantage

Here is why you need to read this book.

Time is running out for health care as we know it - Dramatic changes in the health care system will cause paradigm shifts in patient care. While the intent is to improve quality, the cost of medical care is still unchecked and profitability is suffering.

Time is Life - Medical care must embrace patient-centered process improvement such as reducing the "door to balloon" time. An example is moving the 12 lead EKG from the emergency room to the ambulance, allowing the patient to go directly to the cath lab.

Current and future patients need this information to help them make informed medical decisions in the new world of healthcare.

Time is Money - H-Lean is a concept designed around health care. Every person in the industry will be involved in or affected by the dramatic changes. This book will help you become more knowledgeable, allowing you to participate through positive ACTION.

Get Crunch Time for Health Care at - http://www.competitiveamerica.us
Amazon.com - The book is available in Kindle (Electronic book) format.

Bibliography

The Production Information Control System
                                        IBM

MRPII Unlocking America's Productivity Potential
                                        Oliver W. Wight

Business Simulation   CMS manufacturing Systems

Tying the Shop Floor to the ERP System   Plex Systems

10 Famous ERP Disasters, Dustups, and Disappointments
                                        Thomas Wailgum, CIO

Successful ERP Implementations the First Time
                                        R. Michael Donovan

Top 15 ERP Software Vendors Revealed 2010
                                        Business-Software.com

ERP Software-Implementation Best Practices
                                        Pollyanne S. Frantz
                                        Arthur R. Southerland
                                        James T. Johnson

Enterprise Resource Planning – Factors Affecting Success and Failure
                                        Patricia Barton

The Essential Guide for Selecting Todays Business Software
                                        SoftResources
                                        John Adams
                                        Richard Dance
                                        Joe Kersey
                                        Trisha Tubba

Top 15 ERP Software Vendors Revealed-2010 Edition
                                        Business-Software.com

Selecting an ERP Solution: A Guide   INFOR

11 Criteria for Selecting the Best ERP System Replacement
                                        EPICOR

The Next Generation of ERP Software   David A. Turbide-EPICOR

Rapid Implementation: The New Age of Oracle
                                        Mindy Blodgett

ERP/EDI Integration Methodologies – In-house vs. Hosted	John Simmons - www.dicentral.com
Best Practices in Extending ERP	Aberdeen Group
Executive Guide to Business and Software Requirements	Keith Ellis, IAG Consulting
Midmarket/Enterprise ERP Solutions Comparison Guide	FOCUS
ERP Systems Market Guide	FOCUS
Essential Features of Manufacturing ERP Software	Scott Priestley, FOCUS
Lateral Thinking for Management	Edward de Bono
The 2010 Meltdown	Edward E. Gordon
Leadership and the New Science	Margaret J. Wheatley
Thriving on Chaos	Tom Peters
Complex Organizations	Amitai Etzioni
The Change Agent	Lee Grossman
Consilience: The Unity of Knowledge	Edward O. Wilson
Performance Consulting – Moving Beyond Training	Dana Gaines Robinson, James C. Robinson
Complexity – The Emerging Science at the Edge of Order and Chaos	M. Mitchell Waldrop
Leadership and the New Science: Learning about Organization from an Orderly Universe	Margaret J. Wheatley
Successful Management by Objectives	Karl Albrecht
Liberation Management	Tom Peters
The Machine That Changed the World	James Womack, Daniel Jones, Daniel Roos
The 13 Secrets of Power Performance	Roger Dawson
Value Migration	Adrian J. Slywotzky
The Mind of the Strategist	Kenichi Ohmae
The Rise and Fall of Strategic Planning	Henry Mintzberg

The Fifth Discipline: The Art and Practice of the Learning Organization	Peter Senge
The 7 Habits of Highly Effective People	Stephen R. Covey
The New Rules	John P. Cotter
Leading Change	John P. Cotter
Crossing the Chasm	Geoffrey A. Moore
Top Management Strategy What it is and How to Make It Work	Benjamin B. Tregoe, John W. Zimmerman
The Theory of Inventive Problem Solving	www.mazur.net/triz/
40 Principles-TRIZ Keys to Technical Innovation	Genrich Atschuller
One Minute Manager	Kenneth Blanchard, PhD, Spencer Johnson, MD
To Err is Human: Building a Safer Health System	Institute of Medicine
What the CEO Wants You to Know	Ram Charan
High Velocity Leadership	Brian K. Muirhead, William L. Simon
Lean Thinking	James P. Womack, Daniel T. Jones
The Frontiers of Management	Peter Drucker
The Handbook of Strategic Expertise	Catherine Hayden
Quality is Free	Philip B. Crosby
Kanban – Just In Time at Toyota	Edited by Japan Management Association
The Japanese Art of War	Thomas Cleary
It's Not Luck	Eliyahu M. Goldratt
Bionomics: Economy as Ecosystem	Michael Rothschild
Business at the Speed of Thought	Bill Gates
Theory of Constraints	Eliyahu M. Goldratt
The Goal	Eliyahu M. Goldratt, Jeff Cox
How to Manage Change Effectively	Donald L. Kirkpatrick
Technology, Management and Society	Peter F. Drucker

Performance Consulting –Moving Beyond Training	Dana Gaines Robinson
	James C. Robinson
Lightning Strategies for Innovation	Willard L. Zangwill
CRM at The Speed of Light	Paul Greenberg
The Reengineering Revolution	Michael Hammer
Beyond Reengineering	Michael Hammer
World Class Manufacturing-The Lessons of Simplicity Applied	
	Richard J. Schonberger
Computer Applications in Manufacturing	
	Thomas G. Gunn
Best Practices – Building Your Business With Customer Focused Solution	
	Robert Hiebeler
	Thomas B. Kelly
	Charles Ketterman
Solving Business Problems by Simulation	
	Jan Szymankiewicz
	James McDonald
	Keith Turner
Customer Centered Growth-Five Strategies for Building Competitive Advantage	Richard Whiteley
	Diane Hessan
Inside Teams – How 20 World-Class Organizations are Winning Through Teamwork	Richard S. Wellins
	William C. Byham
	George R. Dixon
Supply Chain Development for the Lean Enterprise	
	Robin Cooper
	Regine Slagmulder
The Concept of Corporate Strategy	Kenneth R. Andrews
Complexity and the Experience of Leading Organizations	
	Edited By Douglas Griffin
	Ralph Stacey
The Art of Innovation	Tom Kelly
	Jonathan Littman
Principle Centered Leadership	Steven R. Covey
Predicting the Future of Business	Wayne Rash

Future Tech: Where Will ERP Be in 2 Years?	inside-erp.com
Your Strategic Guide to Converged Infrastructure	Bob Violino
Breakthrough Thinking – The Seven Principles of Creative Problem Solving	Gerald Nader, PhD Shozo Hibini, PhD John Farrell
Great Leaders Grow: Becoming A Leader for Life	Kenneth Blanchard Mark MIller
Systematic Innovation: An Introduction to Triz	John Terninko Alla Zusman Boris Zlotin
Toolbox	Wwww.toolbox.com
APICS (The Association for Operations Management)	www.apics.org
AberdeenGroup	www.aberdeen.com
WWW.Technology Evaluation. Com	
Private Cloud ERP in a Hybrid Cloud	Oracle Corp.
SaaS versus on-premise ERP	Ziff Davis B2B
A SaaS Primer	PLEX
The Real SaaS Manifesto: Defining "Real SaaS" and how it can benefit your business	Workday, Inc.
Best Practices for Managing Just-in-Time (JIT) Production	Richard Bird Jerry Durant Michele Tomasicchio Lonnie Wilson
Changing the Way Business Intelligence Is Managed	SAP
Business Growing Pains? How to Tell When You Need a Modern ERP Solution	Sage North America
Mobility in Consumer Products	*Simon* Ellis
Best of Breed vs. Integrated Systems	Online Consultant Software
A Smarter Path to ERP Selection	Compare Business Products

The 2011 Focus Experts' Guide to Enterprise Resource Planning	
	Michael Krigsman
	Michael Fauscette
	Eric Kimberling
	Phil Simon
	Brian Sommer
Ten Critical Questions to Ask a Manufacturing ERP Vendor	
	PLEX Online
Focus Experts' Briefing: ERP in the Age of Mobility	
	Dana Craig
	Sophie Dumas
	Jimar Garcia
	Jonathan Gross
	Nick Parker
	Vee Srinivas
	Ferman Thornton
Mastering the Management System	Robert S. Kaplan
	David P. Norton
Ten Warning Signs Your ERP System Is Killing Your Business	
	PLEX Online
Software-as-a-Service ERP Versus On-Premise ERP Through the Lens of Total Cost of Ownership	Simon Ellis
ERP Implementation Best Practices: Manufacturers and the SaaS Delivery Model	PLEX Online
Capturing Project Cost in Project ERP	Carrie Ghai
Magic Quadrants and MarketScopes: How Gartner Evaluates Vendors Within a Market	www.gartner.com
Software Research Tools	softwareresearchtools.com
The Top Ten ERP Predictions for 2011	Panorama Consulting Group
Epicor ERP Software Solutions	Epicor
General ERP Comparison Guide	Ziff Davis
Selecting an ERP solution: A guide	Infor
SaaS versus on-premise ERP	Johnathan Gross, LL.B,M.B.A.
A Next-Generation Analytics Ecosystem for Big Data	BIresearch
Exposing the Myth of Top-tier ERP solutions: bigger is not better, just more expensive	Exact Software

Detailed Criteria for Evaluating Analytic Platforms	ParAccell
5 Advantages to Using Industry specific software	VISCO
IBM Sterling Supply Chain Visibility	IBM Corporation
Magic Quadrants and Market Scopes: How Gartner Evaluates Vendors Within a Market	Gartner.com
The Power of Focus	Jack Canfield
	Mark Victor Hansen
	Les Hewitt

Cross Reference Index

A Proven Selection Process, 119
ABC inventory analysis, 221
Ability to Work with the Company Employees, 131
Accounting Practices, 103
Allocation, 76, 80, 221
Analysis, 29, 179, 182, 219, 236, 245
Analytics, 6, 7, 8, 274
Analyze Responses to the RFP's, 235
Analyze the data, 178
Analyzing Potential ERP Suppliers, 225
Application Service Provider
ASP, 23, 25
Appoint the Executive Champion, 208
Appoint the Executive Steering Committee, 208
Approval to Go, 249
Areas to be included in the study, 177
Assessment of Current ERP System Functionality, 175
Asset Management Systems, 224
Automation, 3, 11, 223
Available to promise, 172, 221
Bar Coding, 223
Barcodes, 98
Basic records file organization, 221
Best practices or assumed strategies, 161
Big Data, 7, 274
Bill of Material
BOM, 29, 42, 43, 99
Billing Hours, 131
Branch Locations, Mergers and Acquisitions, 103
Bribes and Kickbacks, 126
Budgets, 223
Build a Conceptual Plan, 182
Business Intelligence
BI, 17, 21, 166, 177, 224, 273
Business Rationalization, 159
Business Shape, 73
Business Shape Charts, 73

Business Simulation or Boardroom Pilot, 250
Call Current Customers, 236
Capacity Planning, 222
Celebration, 262
Cellular Manufacturing, 188
Charging by the Pound, 129
Commission processing, 221
Commitments, 136
Communication-all the time, 260
Companies Not Using an ERP or MRP System, 14
Companies with Obsolete Systems, 15
Complex Tracking Requirements, 97
complexity, 11, 17, 19, 20, 22, 51, 55, 66, 67, 68, 69, 70, 72, 73, 99, 117, 126, 217, 225, 240, 260
Complexity profile, 68
Compliance Issues, 97
Component requirements gross to net, 221
Computing power and data transmission speeds, 3
Conceptual Systems Design, 182
Configuration inquiry / matrix, 221
Consultants, 122, 129, 131, 132, 133, 134, 167, 254, 258
Content Management Systems, 224
Contract, 243, 245
Conversion Databases, 252
Core Competency, 96
Corporate Direction, 115
Creation of factory paper, 222
Credit, 129, 169
Culture, 123
Currency, 102, 224
Customer Order Processing, 220
Customer Relationship Management
CRM, 6, 91, 92, 177, 223
Customer service, 173
Cut the List, 236
Cycle, 36, 75, 94, 183, 221
Daily Meeting, 253

Dashboards, 150
Data Collection and Reporting, 65
Data Integrity, 118
Data, Files, Fields, and Codes, 54
Database, 3, 49, 50, 233, 250
Deceptive, 127
Decision to proceed, 219
Decisions, 204
Define and establish the change process, 218
Demand, 57, 58, 61, 71, 192, 193
Demo – Potential Combat Zone, 237
Descriptions, 53
Detail implementation plan, 246
Dispatching sequence, 222
Document Management Systems, 224
Document of Understanding, 249
Drill down capabilities, 221
DRP, 57
Easy customer and ship-to process, 221
E-Commerce, 4
EDI, 60, 94, 176, 230, 270
End Associates, 214
Engineering Change, 40
Engineering Data Control, 221
Engineering drawings, 221
Enterprise Manufacturing Intelligence EMI, 224
Enterprise Performance Management EPM, 224
Environmental Scanning, 157, 181
ERP Company Deliverables, 234, 245
ERP Selection Method, 155
ERP System
ERP, Enterprise Resource Planning, 18, 19, 20, 56, 82, 175, 193, 269, 274
Establish a Data Conversion Program, 217
Establish a general philosophy on program modifications, 218
Establish a Matching Process, 116
Establish and Communicate the Project Philosophy, 168
Establish the Teams, 213
Evaluation and measurement, 220
Evolutionary, 142

Executive Commitment, 207
Executive Leadership, 115
Executive Management, iv, 51, 121, 216
Executive Overview, 119
Executive Priorities, 121
Executive Role, 206, 207
Executive Statement, 161
Executive Visit to ERP Company, 241
Extended ERP, 7, 223
Features and Functions, 39, 231
Field Service, 223
Final Decision, 243
Financial Planning and Budgeting, 223
Finished production requirements – gross to net, 221
Following are some of the areas of focus, 172
Following Are Some Safeguards, 132
Follow-Up, 261
Forecast, 58, 88, 220
Formulas, 66
Forward pick replenishment, 223
Free Consulting Services, 122
Full where used capabilities, 221
Functionality Check List, 220
Globalization, 67
global, 53, 70
Governance, 224
Group Technology
GT, 39
Homegrown Systems, 15
Horizontal, 96
Immediate Problem Resolution, 258
Independent / Dependent structure, 43
Inform the Organization, 170
Information Systems Assessment, 175
Initial team training, 216
Integration, 5, 72, 95, 101, 102, 104, 176, 197, 198, 199, 202, 270
Interactive, 169
Interface with production equipment, 221
Internal Leadership, 166
Interview, 14, 161, 171
Inventory Control, 221
Inventory maintenance and update, 221

Inventory management, 174, 177
Inventory Records, 61
Kanban, 39, 63, 66, 83, 84, 85, 86, 87, 99, 184, 187, 188, 189, 190, 192, 198, 271
Key Performance Indicators
KPI, 149, 168
Labor planning and reporting, 222
Language, 102, 223
Lead-time Offsets, 35, 45
Lean, 266, 271, 272
Legacy systems, 34
Legal and Compliance, 103
Load leveling, 222
Load summary by work center, 222
Location/lot tracking, 221
Lot sizing, 222
Lying, 128
Machine utilization, 222
Make Plans So Business Continues to Operate, 218
Make/Buy, 45
Management of FOB timing, 223
Manufacturing and Distribution, 15
Manufacturing Execution Systems, 6, 40, 90, 224
Manufacturing System, 186
Map Legacy Systems to New System, 245
Map of the Future State, 183
Mapping Future to Current States, 181
Master and Inner Pack Configurations, 99
Master Files, 50, 173
Master Scheduling, 57
Material movement, 222
MES, 40, 91, 97, 174, 193, 204, 224
Methods, 171
Metrics, 149, 150, 179, 263
Mobile technology, 5, 49, 224
Model selection, 220
Modular designs, 30, 34
Monthly Progress Reports to the Appropriate Distribution, 254
Multi-facility, 67, 70, 240
Multi-location for domestic and international, 221
Multi-Plant processing, 224

Multiple charts of accounts, 224
Multiple picking methods, 223
Net change, 222
Network, 67, 72, 198, 233, 240
Not Me Coach, 137
Offset requirements, 222
Once in and Never Out, 132
On-line credit checking, 221
Operation Scheduling, 222
Order estimator, 222
Order policy, 221
Order processing, 20, 59
Order start date calculations, 222
Organize the Project, 168
Outside Consultant, 209
Palletizing Guidelines, 100
Parking Lot List, 239
Part Number, 52
Pegged requirements, 222
People are the Competitive Advantage, 112, 268
Personnel evaluation, 262
Phased rollout vs. Big Bang, 217
Physical inventory, 221
Planned order load, 222
Plan-O-Gram, 101
Policies, Procedures and Systems Documentation, 254
Preliminary Budget -Estimated, 202
Prepare the Organization, 248
Principles of Lean Six Sigma, 142
Priority, 116, 117, 222
Priority rules, 222
Problem Employees, 136
Process, vii, viii, 7, 8, 9, 42, 67, 70, 73, 75, 76, 109, 117, 118, 141, 146, 151, 152, 155, 163, 170, 171, 174, 208, 224, 229, 240, 247, 255, 260, 265, 266
Process Complexity, 70
Process Improvement, viii, 8, 141, 265, 266
Process Mapping, 118
Process outputs, 163
Product, 29, 31, 33, 34, 40, 53, 67, 69, 71, 76, 78, 179, 196, 197, 215, 221, 223, 233, 249

Product Categories, 53
Product Data Management
PDM, 223
Product Design Responsibility, 34
Product Lifecycle Management
PLM, 223
Product structure, 221, 233
Product trace ability, 221
production, 196
Production Activity Control, 17, 63
Production and Engineering Systems, 40
Project Kickoff Meeting, 248
Project Management, 119, 224
Project Plan, 168, 195, 197, 250
Project Review, 204
Projected work center load report, 222
Purchase evaluation, 222
Purchase order follow-up, 222
Purchasing, 20, 53, 177, 222
Putting the project plan into place, 216
Quality Management Systems, 224
Radio Frequency Identification
RFID, 98
Rapid Sample Production, 35
Real time, 10, 50, 67, 78, 93
Record All Reported Problems, 258
Report to the Executive Staff and Board of Directors, 219
Reporting, 64, 65, 215
Request for Proposal
RFP, 231
Requirements, 17, 46, 48, 57, 61, 75, 76, 78, 165, 221, 270
Requirements Planning Calculations, 46
Requisition and PO preparation, 222
Responsibilities, 167, 212
Return on Investment
ROI, 202
Revision tracking, 221
Revolutionary, 141
RFID, 64, 65, 94, 97, 98, 99, 101, 173, 198, 203, 223, 231
Risk Compliance, 224
Rough cut capacity planning, 222
Routing, 40

Sales analysis, 221
Sales and Operations Planning
S&OP, 57
Sales Forecasting, 220
Sales History, 89
Salesman's Commission, 54
Select the Project Manager, 211
Selection, 119, 155, 220, 232, 241, 249, 273
Sequential (traditional), 169
Server Platform, 199
Shop Floor Control
SFC, 17, 222
Simulations, 223
Site Visits, 240
Software Companies, 126
Software Options, 21
Software sophistication, 16
Spatial, 67, 71, 240
Special features, 222
Special packaging, 223
Speed, i, viii, 3, 11, 50, 179, 256, 267, 271, 272
Statement of the System's Objectives, 182
Stick to Plan – Execution, 252
Stock status control, 221
Strategic planning – Intensive Planning Session, 160
Strategic RFP, 230
Supply Chain collaboration
SCC, 223
Supply Chain Management
SCM, 7, 95, 96, 223
Sustainability, 224
Take a Total Systems Approach, 152
Team, 23, 118, 137, 146, 169, 206, 213, 215, 216, 219, 249
Technical Persons, 213
Telephone interviews, 231
Temporary Help, 256
Test, 110, 144, 145, 146, 147, 177, 256
The Consequences, 113
The Consultant as Facilitator, 130
The Consultant as the Project Manager, 130
The decision, 7, 210, 215, 217
The System is Broken, 180

279

Timing, 50, 102, 217, 247, 251
To do MRP/ERP requires accurate inputs, 66
Tool control, 222
Tool planning, 223
Toyota, 271
Train
Training, 118, 170, 244, 256
Training, 108, 118, 120, 202, 212, 216, 244, 256, 270, 272
Transactional, 67, 72, 240
Translatable Strategic Definitions, 164
Transportation Management, 223
Trashing Ignorance, 137
Understand the Business Shape, 117
Unit of Measure

UM, 53
User Community, 134
User Manuals, 255
Vendor evaluation and selection, 222
Vendors, 214, 232, 269, 274, 275
Visual controls, 223
Warehouse management System
WHM, WHMS, 223
Web Based Orders, 60
Weekly Progress Meeting, 254
Whoops, 259
Work center capacity planning, 222
Work issues, 210
Work-in-process feedback, 222